RATANA
THE PROPHET

KEITH NEWMAN

Published by Oratia Books, Oratia Media Ltd, 783 West Coast Road, Oratia, Auckland 0604, New Zealand (www.oratia.co.nz).

Copyright © 2024 Keith Newman
Copyright © 2024 Oratia Books (published work)

The copyright holders assert their moral rights in the work.

This book is copyright. Except for the purposes of fair reviewing, no part of this publication may be reproduced or transmitted in any form or by any means, whether electronic, digital or mechanical, including photocopying, recording, any digital or computerised format, or any information storage and retrieval system, including by any means via the Internet, without permission in writing from the publisher. Infringers of copyright render themselves liable to prosecution.

ISBN 978-1-99-004258-4

Parts of this book were first published in *Ratana Revisited: An Unfinished Legacy* (Reed, 2006)
First published by Penguin Group (NZ) 2009
This edition 2024

Printed in China

CONTENTS

PREFACE	THREADS IN THE TAPESTRY	5
ONE	PREPARING THE WAY	12
TWO	THE BIG FISH STORY	30
THREE	LIGHT IN THE DARKNESS	41
FOUR	HEALING ESCALATES	53
FIVE	DOCTRINES OF DIVISION	68
SIX	ROYAL REJECTION	84
SEVEN	DENOMINATIONS CLOSE RANK	104
EIGHT	AMERICAN EXPEDITION	115
NINE	GOOD NEWS FROM AFAR	126
TEN	THE PHYSICAL WORKS	135
ELEVEN	A LABOURED ALLIANCE	149
TWELVE	LIGHT FROM THE EAST	165
THIRTEEN	A PREMATURE AFFAIR	172
FOURTEEN	SIGN OF THE BROKEN WATCH	184
FIFTEEN	THE PARLIAMENT OF IHOA	193
SIXTEEN	PASSING OF THE PROPHET	205
SEVENTEEN	DRAWN AND QUARTERED	213
EIGHTEEN	BEYOND THE CLOUDS	231
	BIBLIOGRAPHY	254
	INDEX	260

PREFACE

THREADS IN THE TAPESTRY

I will never die, for I am a seed broadcast from heaven. I stand on Mount Hikurangi, in the land of light and enlightenment, although I am small in numbers and do not command great physical powers, I will tread many waters of the world.

—Riwha Titokowaru, Ngāti Ruanui leader, 1860s

Soon, very soon in the future you will no longer speak, but instead a very different person [generation] will reveal to you all the fruits of these prophecies. Not only will it be revealed exclusively to you the morehu only, no, but to the whole country.

—T. W. Ratana, 1929

It has been my privilege to weave together the many threaded legacy of Māori prophet, healer and visionary Tahupotiki Wiremu Ratana, which continues to speak from the past into the present and the times ahead.

Ratana was a creator and collector of stories — a kaitiaki (caretaker) of historical records, biblical understanding, cultural wisdom and indeed prophecies — that came to him directly or from those who went before. To the best of my understanding this book is a factual and respectful 'interpretive account' of the life of T. W. Ratana and the political, spiritual and social impact of the movement he founded.

In 2024 Aotearoa New Zealand, struggling with post-COVID and post-Cyclone Gabrielle recovery and compliance with the United Nations Declaration of the Rights of Indigenous People (UNDRIP), is working through complex issues of identity including what shape 'co-governance' will take as it permeates public and private life. The reader might be surprised to learn of Ratana's significant role in rescuing the Treaty of Waitangi from obscurity and neglect, and how in 1924 a Ratana-Kingitanga petition lodged with the League of Nations in Geneva was influential in the drafting of UN guidelines for restoring rights to indigenous peoples. Perhaps this timely revised edition of *Ratana the Prophet* will further cement Ratana's important role in championing unity and the restoration of all things Māori as Aotearoa New Zealand navigates the transformative journey toward the 200th anniversary of the Treaty signing.

This book is largely derivative of the comprehensive *Ratana Revisited* (Reed, 2006), which is brimming with footnotes, sources and references. That rare tome can now most likely be found only at the local library. Neither book claims to be an official or approved Ratana history. Although I initially spoke to people at the highest levels within the church and movement, I resisted requests for the manuscript to be vetted by the church hierarchy back in the early 2000s. I continue to stand on the original advice and warning of then Ratana legal adviser Wayne Johnson to 'do a scholarly job and get all your sources right, because it's on your head'.

I am frequently asked how it is a sixth-generation Pākehā of English-Irish descent came to write about Ratana the Māori prophet. A Māori writer associated with specific iwi (or tribal connections) could easily be accused of bias as Ratana is a pan-tribal movement; and if anyone from Ratana Pā or from the Ratana Church had attempted the task they would never have gained official approval, largely because the members of the Kōmiti Hāhi Matua or Hui Whakapūmau, the church governing bodies, have difficulty agreeing on an official line themselves.

It might be said the book chose me. I kept meeting people connected with the movement who wanted to know more about their own heritage. I tried to get as close to the original sources as possible, starting with news clippings, historical records, books, pamphlets and unpublished manuscripts in the public domain. Personal interviews and oral history from key individuals were often given only when trust had been gained. This resulted in access to previously undisclosed material, much of it translated into English for the first time, enabling me to weave the final threads around the edges to tie it all together.

Nation-changing mission

While I had much help from key individuals and leaders in the Ratana movement, some remained strongly opposed. One humbling outcome from the 2006 book was that several such individuals, seeing my intentions were honourable, admitted they had over-reacted and had purchased copies for their families. Both books were considered taonga (treasures) by those glad to have their own history back in their hands. The reviews by Māori academics in particular were mostly favourable. Sales, however, were a slow burn and although there was steady demand eventually both titles were out of print; even my own personally acquired remaindered stock was exhausted by 2018 as awareness grew and demand increased.

The church and movement marked its centennial on 8 November 2018 (Te Waru), celebrating the divine encounter (some object to the term 'vision') in 1918 that propelled Ratana on his nation-changing mission. It was surreal to be invited to speak on that occasion and to discover at the last minute that my closest supporters, my elderly father Ron Newman and my mum Marjory, were in the audience. They were later given a guided tour through the temple by local kaumātua. I couldn't have asked for more. Many of those who contributed and supported both Ratana books are no longer with us, including my dad who died in 2019.

The death of Rehimana Harerangi Meihana (Harry Mason), the seventh tumuaki (leader) of the Ratana Church and movement, signalled the end of an era. He had been a gentle leader and despite being on the paepae for important occasions, he took a less conspicuous role in his final years due to an ongoing illness. Harerangi, grandson of Ratana, passed away aged 88 on 11 May 2022 after 23 years as tumuaki.

Harerangi had been a supporter of both books, as was Whetu Tirikatene-Sullivan (1932–2011), whose shared memories, meticulous note taking and ongoing encouragement were of major assistance. Whetu served ten terms as a Labour minister, succeeding her father, Ratana's close friend and first political candidate Eruera Tirikatene, who tabled the Ratana-Kingitanga Treaty of Waitangi petition (40,000 signatures) in 1932. Jim McLeod Henderson (1925–2013), the original Pākehā scribe of the Ratana story,

Ratana tumuaki Harerangi Meihana in 2006 with an early copy of *Ratana Revisited*. (Keith Newman)

quizzed me thoroughly about my intentions before giving his blessing to use excerpts from his book. And the charming and authentic photographer and commentator Ans Westra (1936–2023), famed for her depictions of Māori life and a regular at Ratana Pā over many years, will be sorely missed by many.

Since 1932 there has been a continuous and often generational presence of Labour MPs with a Ratana affiliation. After Whetu Tirikatene-Sullivan left office in 1996, Tariana Turia (Ngāti Apa, Ngā Rauru, Tūwharetoa) was elected (she crossed the floor to become Māori Party co-leader in 2004). Eruera Tirikatene's grandson Rino Tirikatene (Ngāi Tahu, Ngāti Hine) was elected to Te Tai Tonga (the South Coast, Te Waipounamu) in 2011. In 2014 Adrian Rurawhe (Ngāti Apa), a great-grandson of T. W. Ratana, was elected MP for Te Tai Hauāuru (the West Coast), and in 2022 he became Speaker of the House of Representatives. Both men lost their geographical roles in October 2023 with a change of government, but retained list membership in the Labour Party. Soraya Peke-Mason (Ngāti Rangi, Uenuku, Tamaupoki, Ngāti Wairiki, Ngāti Apa, Ngāti Haua) was defeated as Rangitikei MP in 2023 and remains a list MP. She is the wife of Andre Meihana.

Determined archivists

My initial 20 years of research were triggered by a 1986 trip to Ratana Pā aboard the Morehu Express, where I was accompanying band members who would perform at the weekend celebrations. That's when I first recall meeting the persistent carrier of the flame, āpotoro wairua Kereama Pene wandering from carriage to carriage with a large pile of reference documents and books. He was founder of Uri Whakatupuranga (New Generation), along with Ruia Aperahama and Arahi and Puawai Hagger, who were gathering photographs and records, conducting interviews and translating material. While much material had been lost, including film and audio footage destroyed in two fires at Ratana Pā, they were convinced important memorabilia still existed. In meeting with ageing Ratana Church members and families of those who had been close to the founder, they discovered there was indeed a treasure trove of material never before revealed publicly.

After watching my progress over those intervening years, members of the archive team finally agreed to supply material to ensure this book and its predecessor delivered the best possible public record of Ratana and the movement he founded. Their persistence has opened doors that few have been able to walk through until now.

Special thanks to Ruia for Māori translations, deep and meaningful conversations, and guidance; Kereama and wife Mariah for encouragement from 1986 onward; and Arahi and Puawai for their passion and determination. This book could not claim to be so comprehensive without the co-operation and friendship of this intrepid team, and their patron, the late Naka Taiaroa, who supported them in rescuing the records of Ratana's legacy.

Background basics

The earliest records referenced in this book were based on eyewitness accounts, minutes of meetings, records kept by personal secretaries and editors, and meticulously maintained diaries of Ratana and his son Tokouru. Secretary Pita Te Turuki Moko recorded several personal interviews with T. W. Ratana. The first external publications were *Ratana the Healer* (1921) by Salvation Army officer Lieutenant-Colonel Carmichael and Hector Bolitho's *Ratana: The Maori Miracle Man* (under the pen name Rongoa Pai) in 1921. The movement's own *Te Whetu Marama o Te Kotahitanga* newspaper, launched in time for Ratana's world tour in 1924, was an invaluable source of information.

From late in 1921, however, Ratana became fed up with the way the media were treating him with often scathing articles and he began to withdraw from the public eye, prioritising dealings with his own people over contact with Pākehā, particularly journalists. Following his death the movement he founded became increasingly secretive. Today Ratana family members or the Ratana office retain tight control over Ratana's personal diaries, world tour diaries, the unpublished three-volume work *Te Rongo Pai Hou a T. W. Ratana (The Good News of T. W. Ratana)* compiled by Matiu Tane, a former Ratana secretary and editor of *Te Whetu Marama* (1931–38), and the 'blue diary', a collaboration between Pita Moko and T. W. Ratana with illustrations by Pikitea Te Rata. Even senior people within the movement were not given access.

In 1955, before the Polynesian Society published the first edition of Jim McLeod Henderson's *Ratana: The Man, the Church, the Political Movement* (1963), typewritten copies of his thesis could be found in some libraries. Henderson had close contact with the highly respected Methodist Reverend A. J. Seamer, who had been a close friend of Ratana. He also had support from Ratana's sister Puhi o Aotea Ratahi, who was tumuaki, or guardian of the faith, at the time of his research in the late 1940s.

Interest from publishers A. H. & A. W. Reed saw Henderson go back and recheck his sources for a re-release in 1972. His task was unenviable and even in the rewrite he knew he wouldn't please everyone. In that second edition there is the expectation that *Te Rongo Pai Hou* would soon make it to print. Like many of the other important publications and documents of the church it remained largely untranslated. Reasons given are that it doesn't represent the official church position, resources are not available, lingering disputes over the meaning of certain 'prophecies' and sayings, and the fear that having it in English would somehow diminish its authority. (Portions of this work were, however, acquired and translated for *Ratana Revisited* and *Ratana the Prophet*.)

In the early 1960s further efforts were made to have material published in English resulting in the Ratana newsletter *Te Whetu Marama* appearing in both languages. Selected text and quotes gleaned from the earliest *Whetu Marama* and *Te Rongo Pai Hou* by Whaimatua Anaru (Sam Andrews), along with interviews and eyewitness accounts from fellow researcher Rapine (Robbie) Aperahama, were also published in the movement's newspaper. Andrews compiled those recollections, along with information from workshops or wānanga run during the 1960s, into four spiral-bound books known as *Nga Akoranga*. These were published for internal use in 1982 under the watch of Ratana's daughter Te Reo Hura (Maata). *Nga Akoranga* was revised and republished in 1997 with a foreword written by Raniera Ratana, who succeeded her as tumuaki. This material was invaluable for *Ratana the Prophet*.

Photographer Ans Westra charmed some of the elders with her sincerity and skill and began chronicling life at Ratana Pā at the dawn of the sixties. Her photographs first appeared in 'T. W. Ratana and the Ratana Church', in the March 1963 edition of Māori Affairs Department newspaper *Te Ao Hou*. Her photograph of the Ratana Temple also adorned Henderson's 1972 book. Ans provided a number of her warm and enlightening images for this book. Historic photographs from Hall Raine, Frank J. Denton from Tesla Studios, and Sam Dale also appear. Many images were supplied by Uri Whakatupuranga Trust or Ratana Community Archive Trust, the breakaway group determined to collect and preserve Ratana history as custodian of material donated by mōrehu (faithful survivors) from around the country.

I gratefully acknowledge the thorough and detailed research into Māori prophets and spirituality by writers Judith Binney, Bronwyn Elsmore and Angela Ballara. Ralph Ngatata Love's Victoria University thesis 'Policies of Frustration' (1977) was of enormous value with its insights into the Ratana-Labour alliance. His principal sources were key people within the Ratana movement, Labour politicians, and the records and papers of Eruera Tirikatene. Librarians at the Methodist Church Archives in Auckland, the Alexander Heritage & Research Library, Whanganui, the Titirangi Library, Te Papa Tongarewa Museum of New Zealand and Alexander Turnbull Library in Wellington were extremely helpful.

Arohanui to Mihi Rurawhe (1939–2014) and her whānau, the Paikea whānau, and Bella Hura and Reo Munn, the daughters of Te Reo Hura or Maata, for hospitality and their willingness to share memories. Thanks to Jemaima O'Brien — constant companion to her grandmother Te Reo in her later years, and a 'shout out' to Tiki, Wiremu and their amazing wheelchair-bound but spirited siblings. Thanks also to Derek Dixon for introducing me to the family.

Appreciation to church historian Peter Lineham for background and guidance in establishing context, the late Reverend Alan Thrift for early discussions and documents, and much respect to the late Wyn Fountain for being a mentor and sounding board. A mihi to Rangitāne elders and long-time friends Wiremu and Trieste Te Awe Awe, to the late singer and friend Mahia Blackmore (RIP) from Bulls, Tony Littlejohn and Mina Paikea, 'heartwarriors' from the north, Billy T. K. Snr, Tainui Pene and the wider Pene whanau, Australian mōrehu Marama Eruera Best and Bev Broughton for their help and encouragement, and to the dozens of mōrehu including Christine Waitai-Rapana, Grace Taiaroa, Heni McGroder, Desiree Docherty, Dave Eden, Rod Williams, Kua Ranea Aperahama and others who shared their insights, memories and support.

Special thanks to my wife Paula for continuing to believe in me despite feeling like a writer's widow at times, and for permission to use her artwork, which appears on the cover and the interior. And to my children Olivia and Miles, their partners and my six grandchildren. As seventh and eighth-generation New Zealanders this is their history too.

A big thumbs-up to publisher Peter Dowling and editorial director Carolyn Lagahetau at Oratia Books who believed my 2009 book *Ratana the Prophet* deserved a reprint. After receiving numerous rejection slips, it was Peter, then publishing manager at Reed, who took a chance on *Ratana Revisited* in 2005, so it seems appropriate that he should take the lead in reprinting this edition of its more compact companion.

While I stand on the shoulders of all who have gone before, the true tūrangawaewae, the foundation or place on which I stand, is the life and teachings of Ihu Karaiti and years of Bible study, which were essential to understanding the true heart of Ratana.

The 'golden threads' of synergy — and perhaps Ratana's prophecies of spiritual and economic prosperity for Māori once the Treaty was affirmed — continue to evoke something more than the cynical eye can see. In my considered view, the threads of Ratana's legacy, including his unshakeable faith in core spiritual truths, his call for unity and determined pursuit of justice for dispossessed Māori, along with his amazing healing powers and prophetic insights, weave a fabric that goes way beyond a specifically New Zealand history.

Ratana: The Prophet belongs to all those who are hungry for reconciliation between tribes and nations and to 'the generation' that Ratana believed would pick up his spiritual and political mantle and lead the way through the open gate or doorway to enlightenment and prosperity.

Keith Newman
January 2024

ONE

PREPARING THE WAY

Tera ka ara ake he kaari he maara me ona putiputi ki te wahapu o Whangaehu, e puta ai ona kakara ki nga topito e wha o te motu.
    A garden of many flowers shall come forth from out of the mouth of the Whangaehu River, and its fragrance will be dispersed throughout the four winds of the country.

—Te Kooti Rikirangi

I, Ihoa, have heard the cry of the people, this is the reason why I have come to you, the Maori people, to be my footstool upon the earth. Go forth and unite the Maori people under me, Ihoa, heal them in all their infirmities, in the name of the Father, the Son, the Holy Spirit and the Faithful Angels.

—T. W. Ratana, 1918

Ko te Paipera Tapu ki taku ringa matau, ko te Tiriti o Waitangi ki taku ringa maui.
    The Bible in my right hand and the Treaty of Waitangi in my left hand.

—T. W. Ratana, 1921

A prophetic lineage

A life-changing encounter in 1918 inspired an ordinary man to accept an extraordinary challenge. In championing a deep cultural shift among the decimated Māori people of New Zealand, Tahupotiki Wiremu Ratana helped rechart the course of a nation.

The series of uncanny, almost inexplicable events that began to unfold on a family farm in the rural outbacks, between two world wars, continues to impact the political, social and spiritual fabric of the country over a century later. The words spoken and actions taken during that period were so influential they reached across the great oceans of the world and touched many peoples and nations.

As the saying goes, a prophet often remains unknown in his own land, and so it was for T. W. Ratana, whose premonitions of colliding world affairs were spine-chillingly accurate, while at home in his native New Zealand he was often dismissed as a cultist or a dreamer. While the names Ngata, Pomare and Buck roll off the tongues of historians and commentators in considering the heroes of Māori history, their less-educated but equally influential peer Ratana, has too frequently been put to one side like an ill fitting piece of the wider puzzle. And he is an ill fit, particularly for academics used to squeezing history into sociological frameworks with rational explanations for everything. To truly understand Ratana we must put aside our preconceptions and be open to the possibilities outside political, social or spiritual boxes.

Ratana's legacy to the world is embedded in the design of the buildings at Ratana Pā, the sayings and symbols he left behind and the tens of thousands of followers who remain loyal to this day. However, the full story of his life, his mission and the movement he founded were progressively shut down following his death in 1939. From that point access to the writings, diaries, unfinished books, and material recorded by eyewitnesses who had lived and worked with him, was either locked away by various committees and families or scattered across the country as key people shifted back to their tribal territories.

There remains a fear even today that personal histories from the annals of Māoridom will lose their power if they are translated from the native tongue into English, or passed on to young people who have more enthusiasm than wisdom. This dilemma is faced by all societies, where elders who have been custodians of important family or historical knowledge have taken their legacy with them to the grave.

Perhaps it is because the next generation has moved away to the cities or not taken the time to listen; or those koro and kuia (elders) waited too long to find the right people to mentor. Unfortunately, many, fearing their mana or authority will be undermined, continue to hold on to their documents and stories. As a result the lines of communication — once kept true by a strong oral tradition so each generation is connected to the land, the people and a broader history — have been fractured.

While there is token recognition of Ratana's far-reaching political legacy, the most recent books on the Treaty of Waitangi or the modern day Māori renaissance hardly mention him. Even less has been said about his influential healing ministry and his extraordinary prophecies. After 20 years of personal research and close collaboration with the small but dedicated Uri Whakatupuranga (New Generation) Archive Trust, the story of T. W. Ratana, his uncanny foreknowledge of local and world events, his model for social transformation and the journey of how the Treaty of Waitangi was placed back on the political agenda, can now be told in a way that has not previously been possible.

The literal heritage of T. W. Ratana can be traced down through the ancient Māori prophets and the kotahitanga (unity) political movement to a point in history where it became patently obvious that circumstances, a 'divine calling' or a combination of both arranged an appointment with destiny.

Biblical influences

From 1827, a handful of missionaries, still largely gridlocked in the Far North, began establishing mission schools teaching the foundations of the Christian faith to the children of chiefs and slaves, and distributing the first Bible stories.

The Lord's Prayer, the first three chapters of Genesis, excerpts from Exodus, hymn and prayer books and various tracts were hastily translated into Māori, printed in Sydney and shipped off to pre-colonial Aotearoa. Wesleyan and Anglican missionaries worked together on New Testament translations but no real progress was made until the arrival of printer William Colenso and a printing press in the Bay of Islands, which from 1835 began cranking out individual Gospel books and ultimately 5000 copies of the full New Testament in te reo Māori.

As the missionaries won the trust of the people, often mediating between warring tribes, the demand for Christian material soon exceeded the ability to supply. While the result was the wholesale freeing of slaves and a rapid close to the age of cannibalism, the gospel also underwent significant modification as it was applied to Māori thinking. By 1836 a critical point was reached, where what is commonly termed 'a revival' was underway, transforming the Māori way of life, in many parts of the country.

Both missionaries and Māori could see similarities with the Hebrew customs and traditions in the Old Testament. They could identify with the tribal structure, their relationship with the land, marriage rites, the importance of whakapapa (genealogy), the strong significance given to colours, symbols, numbers and prophetic guidance, their sense of loss through being made slaves in their own country and the view that religion and politics were inseparable.

In fact the Old Testament stories so inspired Māori that New Zealand (Aotearoa) became known among some tribes as Kanana (Canaan) and the people as Tiu, or Jews. Their quest became the attainment of a new state of existence as symbolised by the Promised Land, or the Christian equivalent, Hiruharama Hou, the New Jerusalem. Samuel Marsden, who had preached the first sermon on these shores in 1814, had encouraged such belief with his own theorising: 'I am inclined to think that they have sprung from some dispersed Jews, at some period or other, from their religious superstitions and customs, and have by some means got into the island from Asia.'

Māori had little difficulty aligning themselves with Jehovah, or Yahweh, the God of Israel, who the more astute tohunga (those skilled in the spiritual arts) and chiefs quickly identified as their supreme deity Io – the parentless, the eternal God of light – spoken of in hushed tones in their whare wānanga or mystery schools. They could relate to the Old Testament and the constant warring to protect tribal land. They could accept the stories of the patriarchs Abraham, Isaac and Jacob (Israel), the prophets Isaiah, Ezekiel and Daniel and kings David and Solomon and their dreams, visions, trials and encounters with angels.

The colourful stories, parables and spiritual insights of the Old Testament were familiar to the Māori. The biblical heroes were undoubtedly great warriors, powerful men who had influence and favour with their God and the people. However, the idea that God would have a son, and then allow him to be put to death, presented a great dilemma. They struggled with the teachings that the Son of God was manifest in the flesh, preaching love, forgiveness, grace, mercy and salvation. They doubted the virgin birth, and because Christ had not proven himself on the battlefield, but suffered a cruel death on the cross, he seemed a much lesser being than their own gods. Certainly, the resurrection proved a great stumbling block. There were too few missionaries to provide the interpretation or explain the context required for a deeper understanding of many of the biblical stories, so Māori gleaned from their own traditions and cultural perspective.

After the great chiefs signed away their independence through the Treaty of Waitangi, and their treaty partners were either unwilling or unable to keep their promise to protect Māori from the colonists who now sought land at any cost, there was an even deeper empathy with the Israelites. It was easier to identify with this scattered people, enslaved by a succession of foreign nations, from which Jehovah sought to gather a faithful remnant. Like the twelve tribes of Israel, Māori also sought a modern-day Moses or kaiwhakaora (saviour, Messiah or anointed liberator) as they rapidly became a nation under siege, an underclass in their own land.

Despite the great sacrifices made in coming to this new land, and efforts by the majority of them to ensure Māori interests were protected, missionaries were increasingly seen as agents of the government. Amid political and denominational pressures everyone it seems was forced to take sides, further confusing the gospel message of love and reconciliation. To see Christians killing Christians on both sides of a battle for land while claiming God was on their side was hard enough, but to see government troops burning down Māori churches with the sacred Bible and prayer books inside was the ultimate violation.

Māori prophets and tohunga, borrowing heavily from the Bible, often spoke of great visions or encounters with angels, which had a strong appeal to a dispossessed people, hungry to regain a sense of spiritual identity. There was talk across tribal boundaries of one who would inspire kotahitanga and mana motuhake (self-determination); one who would arise from among the people carrying two books, the Treaty of Waitangi and the Bible (Paipera Tapu). It was said he would put things right for the Māori and lead them into the Promised Land.

The people may have recalled the words of Te Ruki Kawiti, the great warrior born in 1770 who had defied the Crown's plans to control New Zealand, and been one of the last to sign the treaty.

> My illustrious warriors and people, I fought with God last night, but I survived. Therefore I call upon you to trample anger and fighting under your feet. . . . Hold fast to your faith, for the day will come when you will be ruled over by your Pakeha friends. Be patient, wait until the sandfly nips the page of the document [the Treaty of Waitangi], the Sacred Covenant, then and only then shall you rise and question and oppose. Lest you break the Sacred Word of your ancestors, their Covenant . . . look to the distant horizon of the sea.

The words of the northern prophet Aperahama Taonui in 1863 also echoed down through the decades. 'And you, Ngapuhi, who won't listen, well the person who will live in this house with all its customs and habits shall be a spider. The day is coming when you will see a man carrying his two books, the Bible and the Treaty of Waitangi. Listen to him.' The South Island prophet Hipa Te Maiharoa, chief of the Waitaha people, living at Arowhenua near Temuka, prophesied before his death in the late 1870s that 'A very little child will come forth under Taranaki mountain; he will finish my works for Jehovah.' He had also stated: 'The one who will save you all will come forth in the Taranaki area; he will bring with him that for which you have waited so long, for he will be carrying with him two books.'

Te Kooti Rikirangi had mused at Wairoa about the arrival of one who Māori had been waiting for:

> If that young man were to stand on this marae, or when he sets foot within the boundaries of Wairoa, then you will see a rainbow descend upon the marae, then you will hear the voice of Ihoa. Then you will know that he is the young man you have been waiting for according to the prophecies . . . When this young man arises in this very land he will turn this waka upright to sit on an even keel; he will put his treasures upon it and he will paddle it to a place

already decided by him. The man's highway will be faith and his refuge will be Ihoa o nga Mano.

Resurrection of a race

The Māori population appeared to be in a death spiral, decreasing from an estimated 120,000 in 1769 to 70,000–90,000 by the time the Treaty of Waitangi had been signed. The devastating impact of muskets meant that Māori were wiping out one another at a phenomenal rate. At least 20,000 had died in the Musket Wars up until the late 1830s and around 2000 in the Land Wars of the 1860s. The population halved again, to 42,000 by 1896, when life expectancy was 24 years for women and 28 years for men.

The 'fatal decline' was attributed to ongoing land wars and the impact of new infectious diseases, including influenza, measles, whooping cough and dysentery, for which Māori had no resistance. MP Dr Isaac Featherston had stated in 1856: 'The Maoris are dying out, and nothing can save them. Our plain duty, as good compassionate colonists, is to smooth down their dying pillow.' His comments were reiterated in 1884 by Sir Walter Buller who believed only a remnant would be left within the next 25 years.

The non-Māori population had doubled between 1861 and 1864 to 171,000 and within a further decade had reached 255,000. Māori continued to acclimatise as best they could. The total population of the Dominion on 31 December 1908 was just over a million with Māori making a mild recovery to just over 50,000. Deep discontent among tangata whenua (people of the land) was magnified from 1910 when the government resumed extensive land purchasing, and again when the government passed a law forcing all Māori to have a vaccination certificate before they could travel, after the 1913 smallpox epidemic further devastated their communities.

Although the New Zealand Government exempted Māori from conscription during the First World War (1914–18), Māori men were still encouraged to leave their villages and fight for their country. Without their men some communities had barely enough to survive with many living in substandard conditions resulting in a high infant mortality rate and a growing incidence of disease. Many who did not join the military moved to cities and towns to work in essential industries to help the war effort.

Those warrior soldiers who had joined the military and served with distinction found themselves returning from the battlefields to a more insidious kind of warfare. While their non-Māori counterparts were rewarded with parcels of land for their efforts on behalf of the empire, Māori were rarely compensated. In fact they discovered their lands were still being acquired, often for little or no return. Ans Westra in the Māori periodical *Te Ao Hou*, musing on the times of transition, described the social conditions.

> In North Auckland, the Bay of Plenty, the Waikato and in the South Island, frequently landless, backward, withdrawn from educational influences and often very bitter, the people awaited the coming of a new messianic leader. Apirana Ngata, Maui Pomare, Peter Buck and many others had done much to help but at this time they were still fighting a very hard battle. Tribal antagonisms were still strong, and in many districts the great mass of people, the morehu, remained stubbornly aloof from developmental schemes, educational and otherwise. Nor was help always available. Superstition was widespread and tohunga were making capital out of the illnesses of the people. The First World War unsettled them further . . .

In times of uncertainty and confusion when a society is faced with sudden change a leader often arises to act as a mouthpiece, voicing their concerns. As religion is an expression of people's deepest emotions, such leaders, aware of the breakdown of old customs and ways, are inspired to preach a new version of the old religion to help the people adjust and reclaim their sense of identity and place.

Māori, increasingly divested of their land through the misuse of a treaty that now seemed broken and beyond repair, often retreated further into the backblocks, away from the shame of being overtaken by those who were now thriving in their place. Many turned again to the tohunga for answers, becoming deeply embroiled in the old superstitions that the early wave of Christianity had sought to displace. However, the prophecies passed down through the generations of one who would arise among the people to restore their lands and their spiritual heritage, kept hope burning in their hearts.

The encouragement kept coming. Don't give in to despair; a change is ahead, and with it a visionary who will help rally the Māori spirit. Akuhata (Hata) Kiwi, an elder from Mangakahia Valley near Whangārei, speaking during the First World War, said: 'After this war this pillar shall come, a man; when this young man comes, he shall be the young man who will turn the people to the true faith, he shall not be lost, for his voice shall be like that of a bird.' He further stated: 'After this war, Ihoa's blessing and saving of the Maori people will come to be known.' In another prophecy he proclaimed: 'This young man will come before I have passed through death's veil. There will be no prophets, or knowledgeable teachers after him, never. If and when this young man comes, he will bring with him peace and the faith, and he will be instrumental in getting back for you your remaining lands.'

The warrior-prophet Te Kooti had undergone something of a transition from the Old Testament-style 'eye for an eye' literal battle for liberation, into a gentler New Testament-based faith. He had travelled extensively from the mid- to-late 1800s not only looking for refuge from the government troops but for

The warrior-prophet Te Kooti, in making the transition from Old Testament to a New Testament-style Christian faith, prophesied of one who would set the Māori canoe upright and lead the people into unity under Ihoa o ngā Mano. After searching for where this person might arise he identified the Whangaehu Valley, in the heart of Ngāti Apa territory.
Oil painting by Thomas Ryan, 1891, New Zealand Graphic, *April 1893.*

the promised child he had seen in his visions. At the time, the Kīngitanga (King movement) had created a separate parliament, the prophets Te Whiti and Tohu in the Taranaki were deeply divided, and Te Kere Ngataierua of Rangitikei was strongly opposed to Te Kooti's plan to move into his territory. All these leaders had claimed to be 'a mouthpiece of God'.

Te Kooti's vision was increasingly focused on uniting Māoridom under one God. At Petane near Napier on 23 July 1891, he stated:

> The days remain when man will bow down in the presence of the Creator and climb onto the canoe to paddle as one . . . Then also Te Whiti will bow down to the one faith. After that another day will be called there. I will not call it but he himself (the Creator) will . . . Then we will all know that this is the day of the prophecies concerning the teaching and the Churches on which [we] will come together, to be one in our directions and our canoe.

He said that the different factions within Māoridom and Christianity must reject their separate authorities and search for the correct way. He supported the Anglicans and Catholics, saying all others were false. The power and spirit of the one God alone could unite the tribes. 'I am a carrier of the love of man and the gospel.'

In July 1892 he reminded his followers of an earlier prophecy he had made in the Waikato in 1880, concerning a beautiful tree which grew in the Whangaehu Valley (between Mangamahu and Te Kauangaroa) where the river runs down from Mount Ruapehu to the sea. The tree 'spoke' with a soft appealing voice, and all who heard it flocked to it. It had twelve branches and six leaves to each branch. The only thing he could think to compare it with was 'a well-kept Pakeha garden, full of different kinds of flowers'. Then he said: 'Do you remember me telling you about that beautiful tree I saw in the vision in the Whangaehu Valley? Well I saw a better vision here.' He said it was a 'beautiful cloud above' and after looking at it for a bit 'a voice came from the cloud and it said, "This is my Son in whom I am much pleased. Listen to him".'

Te Kooti had been a man on the run, pursued by government troops and urged to give up his campaign for Māori independence and submit to the Crown. He was formally pardoned by the government on 12 February 1883, when living at Ōtewā, near Ōtorohanga. From there he made a series of journeys, visiting his followers and making peace with his enemies. Te Kooti had previously found the local tribes and the predominately Catholic community hostile to him but at Kauangaroa, north-east of Whangaehu, on 24–25 January 1893 he was profoundly affected by the hospitality he received from Ngāti Apa chief Eruera Te Kahu (Edward Sutherland) in Kimihana, the house that had been built for him.

At the mouth of the Whanganui River, Te Kooti spoke of a garden coming forth from that place, but it wasn't until he met with Te Kahupukoro, a Ngāti Apa elder, that he said the 'promised one' would come from beneath his 'armpit', suggesting the child he was waiting for was from Whangaehu and Ngāti Apa. 'Tera ka ara ake he kaari he maara me ona putiputi ki te wahapu o Whangaehu, e puta ai ona kakara ki nga topito e wha o te motu . . . And a garden of many flowers shall come forth from out of the mouth of the Whangaehu River, and its fragrance will be dispersed throughout the four winds of the country.'

Just before he died in April 1893, Te Kooti elaborated on the long-standing prophecy about certain stars signifying the rising of the next great Māori leader. 'From Kati Kati to Cape Runaway there will be one child. If he arrives within six years there will be great tribulation. If his advent does not take place in that time, in 26 years he will rise from the west and will unite the people.' Rua Kenana claimed to be the one prophesied to arise within six years and was even proclaimed to be Mihaia (Messiah), or 'younger brother of Christ', by many of his own Tūhoe people and some followers of Te Kooti's Ringatū faith. However, Te Kooti had seen a star rising from the east and then two more striving against each other and shining very brightly.

Rangitikei chief Te Kere Ngataierua and the Wairarapa prophet Paora Te Potangaroa had both prophesied the coming of a new movement to unite the Māori people. Even though Te Kere had opposed Te Kooti, he was still considered a tohunga of peace and healing in the Whanganui, Taranaki and Wairarapa regions. Before his death he erected a wooden cross from the branches of the tapu (sacred or set apart) hunakeha tree on Te Tikanga, a distinctly carved house beside the Rangitikei River. The house was located in

Ngāti Raukawa territory close to the borders of Rangitāne and Ngāti Apa, the people who share the *Kurahaupō* canoe. Te Kere said the person on whom the cross fell would continue his prophetic tradition.

Māramatanga origins

When the cross toppled it struck Atareta Mere Rikiriki Kawana Ropiha, a descendant of Maata, a noted 1840s healer from Oroua on the Manawatū River. She was born in 1854, the daughter of Mere Rikiriki of Ngāti Te Rangitepaia and Kawana Ropiha of Ngāti Apa, with strong connections to Rangitāne iwi (tribe).

Mere was whāngaied into the Ngahina family and raised as the daughter of her uncle, chief Ngahina Pakaru Ratana, who lived at Parewanui, a mile from the northern banks of the Rangitikei River, in the densely populated heartland of the Ngāti Apa people. He recognised her spiritual strengths early on, believing she had been visited by the Holy Spirit.

In adulthood Mere Rikiriki, described as a 'tubby little woman' with a light moko (facial tattoo) and freckles who wore her hair in two long plaits, lived in her own home between two meeting houses at Parewanui marae, where she flew a huge flag with the words 'Ko Rongopai He Mea Paihere Na Te Rangimarie' (Peace and goodwill to all men). The old people recall she fasted a lot and had a special room in her house where she prayed and meditated among the photographs of her tūpuna (ancestors).

She had spent time with the prophets Te Whiti o Rongomai and Tohu Kakahi at Parihaka. When they asked her what her foundations were she allegedly said, 'Matthew, Mark, Luke and John.' She was held in high regard and King Tawhiao, who sent one of his followers to investigate her in the 1890s, gave her a prized flag with the words 'E Te Iwi, Kia Ora' (Blessings to the people). The flag featured a white crucifix and a brown boar on a blue background.

Mere Rikiriki had no children of her own but there were always children around her. She adopted several, including Rikiriki Tamati Ropiha, a crippled girl who could neither walk nor talk. She carried her 'daughter' everywhere on her back. If there was a tohunga or someone antagonistic towards her mother the girl would become agitated and point out who was the cause of the unrest.

On 27 July 1910 Mere Rikiriki baptised herself seven times (some say 40) in the Rangitikei River in a special ritual calling upon the Holy Spirit. She then established Te Hāhi o te Wairua Tapu (the Church of the Holy Spirit), which embraced members of the Ringatū faith and other Māori churches. Her spiritual home became the Parewanui church building Wheriko (Jericho), built by the missionary Reverend Richard Taylor in 1862. Her movement was based on Christian scriptures and principles, with a strong emphasis on the role of the Holy Spirit, the unity of Māori under one God and the importance of the Treaty of Waitangi.

She had extensive knowledge of the Bible and her preaching would become particularly forceful when she was moved by the Spirit; in her services she would bless each person and sometimes conduct ceremonies to remove tapu. Father Peehi Waretini said she used to sit on an 'old kerosene box' to do her healing. People needing help would stand before her and she would speak to them, sometimes attributing their misfortunes to bad conduct and giving them a precise time when they would be healed. If they were not she would often say 'a seed' remained and if they admitted it, they would be healed. The words she used were Christian and always in Māori. She had a room full of crutches and aids no longer needed by those she had healed. She always denied having any personal power and would say 'Pray to God, not to me, for I am only an instrument.'

She chose four apostles or 'corner posts' from local families representing different tribes, indicating her commitment to Māori unity: Ringapoto (short hand or quick action), Tikaraina (the straight line), Whakarongo (listen to show and inform) and Kawaitika (correct lineage). She would send out a team of little children to visit and pray for the sick and had two faithful women companions who acted as 'bodyguards and servants'. People came in wagons, carts, cars and on foot along the beaches from Taranaki, or crossed the Rangitikei River, to listen to her and seek healing.

It was through Mere Rikiriki that the term māramatanga, in reference to the Kingdom of Light or enlightenment, first came to prominence. Hundreds from different tribal areas gathered on her marae over the years to seek her advice or healing, and relationships that were to have a major impact on the nation developed across a range of religious, political and tribal boundaries.

She had prophesied:

> O people hasten to me, I am a woman, and being so, I minister unto you as a woman would to her own child. For beware! The time is near when a young man will rise in my place; when he comes there will be weeping and gnashing of teeth; when he comes the true and the false will never survive together, neither with righteous and the unrighteous, nor doctrines that are of God and the doctrines of man and the Devil.

There were allegedly three families in line to receive the prophetic blessing. However, Mere Rikiriki was impressed by the intuition of Ratana Ngahina, who believed his grandson Tahupotiki Wiremu Ratana was destined for much higher things than labouring on the farm and adding to the profits of the local tavern. Events confirming her choice would occur just 26 years after Te Kooti's very specific prophecy.

Tracing Ratana's roots

According to Charles Larkin (Tareha Te Awe Awe), the Ratana whakapapa can be traced back to Ruatea, the captain of the *Kurahaupō* canoe, and it includes two ancestors who signed the Treaty of Waitangi. According to Reweti Te Whena, a president of the Kīngitanga Parliament in the 1920s, Ratana descends from Whitikau, who was one of the first to be nominated for the position of king during Potatau's time. Another of Ratana's tūpuna, Hone Tamati o Raupo, was also nominated.

> Ratana's tribal origins are Ngati Apa, Nga Rauru, Nga Wairiki and Ngati Hine with connections to Ngati Ruanui, Taranaki and Ngati Raukawa. In official documents however his immediate family associated largely with Ngati Apa. Te Pakaru Ratana Ngahina, was a respected rangatira (chief), a member of the Anglican church and a strong government supporter.

His ancestors had owned the land between the Turakina and Manawatū rivers, which was sold to the Crown in 1866. Ratana Ngahina remained at Parewanui until after his marriage to Erina Waitere when they settled on 430 acres of her land known as Orakeinui, on the Waipu Block, about 15 kilometres south of

Erina Waitere, who owned the Orakeinui block where Ratana Pā is located, was married to Ngāti Apa chief, Ratana Ngahina. She poses here for a formal portrait in the late 1800s. *ATL 1-2-012409-G, Tourist and Publicity Collection (PAColl-3063), Alexander Turnbull Library, Wellington.*

Above left: Urukohai or Wiremu Kowhai, the father of T. W. Ratana. *Above right:* Te Ihipera Koria, T. W. Ratana's birth mother. *Uri Whakatupuranga (Ratana Archives).*

Wanganui. He purchased additional land adjacent to this at Awahou, where he developed a profitable sheep and cattle station and grew wheat.

With a neighbour he petitioned the New Zealand Government to help cover the cost of a loading station on the railway line that ran near his property. One of his sons, Urukohai or Wiremu Kowhai, an Anglican, married Te Ihipera Koria from Patea who had gained her faith through pioneering Methodist missionary Reverend T. G. Hammond. They settled at Te Kawau on the west bank of the Rangitikei River near Bulls for a time and made generous contributions toward building several churches in the district.

On 25 January 1873, Te Ihipera, who already had a number of children, gave birth to Tahupotiki Wiremu, who was whāngaied a week later and raised by Ria Hamuera (Ria Te-Ra-i-Kokiritia-Ai or Ria Samuels), one of the older women, or kuia, in the family. From the age of eight Wiremu began attending Kai Iwi School, north of Wanganui. It was a struggle for him to graduate to standard one but he persisted and four years later, after growing 'wearisome', left the education system. He worked at Awahuri, on the state highway between Wanganui and Palmerston North, selling melons and peaches from a cart. From the age of fourteen he spent time at a local flax mill and then began learning about stock, dairying and wheat farming, cropping and fencing, and also helped his foster mother train racehorses.

At the age of eighteen he returned to live with his grandfather Ratana Ngahina (Te Ratana) at the Orakeinui homestead and helped out on the family

Ria Hamuera (Samuel), who whāngaied (fostered) Wiremu Ratana when he was a week old, had been blessed by King Tawhiao, who placed his hat upon her head in a sign of anointing. *Samuel Carnell, S. Carnell Collection, ATL 1-4-022212-G, Alexander Turnbull Library, Wellington.*

farm and other farms in the district. He often stayed with his aunty Mere Rikiriki at Parewanui which he considered to be 'the true homestead'.

In 1893 at the age of 20, Wiremu Ratana married Te Urumanao Ngapaki, also known as Ngauta Urumanao Baker, a part-European who was raised at Patea and of the Methodist faith. She was born on 25 October 1873, the daughter of chief Ngapaki, and was of Ngā Rauru and Ngāti Hine descent. The couple were wed in the Methodist church at Parewanui and initially lived in the old family homestead there. In 1894 Wiremu and Te Urumanao had a son, Haami Tokouru and later three daughters, Maata Tawhirimatea in 1904, Rawinia in 1906 and Piki Te Ora in 1908. The surname Ratana was not in common use in the earlier days. At the Waipu Block, the location of Ratana Pā today, the family were known as Ngahina and down in the Turakina Valley they were known as Wiremu. In the school records Tokouru and Maata were initially known by the family name Wiremu.

Wiremu, or Bill Ratana as he was more commonly known, was allegedly a wild and moody youth who rode horses furiously. When he was so inclined, he could work alongside the best of his peers and excelled as a champion ploughman and wheat stacker. He drank heavily and often acted as the local

When T. W. Ratana was 20 years old he married Te Urumanao Ngapaki Baker, daughter of chief Ngapaki. She was raised at Patea and of the Methodist faith.
Tesla Studios Collection, ATL 016602, Alexander Turnbull Library, Wellington.

bookie. Competing for his attention however was the knowledge that all was not right with the world, or among the Māori people. Despite his lack of formal education, he was fluent in both English and Māori and learned much by listening to Anglican and Methodist missionaries, and absorbing knowledge and understanding from the many wise thinkers and orators around his family circle as they debated political, social and spiritual matters. Like his father and grandfather before him he had a strong interest in Christianity, but cared little for denominations.

He often attended church services held by Mere Rikiriki, who was well versed in faith-healing techniques and the use of Māori herbal remedies but opposed to tohungaism. She saw in her relative the potential to extend the work she had begun through the formation of the Church of the Holy Spirit. Wiremu Ratana had been married for four years when his grandfather Ngahina decided he should attend theological school, and encouraged him to study the Bible in preparation. He applied himself to the task with vigour, but found his eyesight failing him as he stayed up late at night engrossed in the stories of Jehovah's dealings with the tribes of Israel and the exploits and miracles of the Messiah, Jesus Christ. In frustration he began to slip back into more secular pursuits.

At a prayer meeting at Parewanui at Christmas 1910 Mere Rikiriki said the spirit of prophecy had entered her:

Oh people of the land, hasten unto me, the woman. I have peace. In a while it shall be upon a man who will take action directly and strongly (with a great

The Ratana family. Back row, from left: Maata, Matiu, Te Urumanao (Te Whaea) and Rawinia. Front row, from left: Te Omeka, Piki Te Ora and Te Arepa. Originally published in the *Auckland Weekly News*, 4 May 1922, with the caption, 'The family of Ratana, the Maori who has gained fame as a Christian faith-healer'. Z. A. Morton, ATL N-P 1052-31, Alexander Turnbull Library, Wellington.

mission) without favouritism (he will be more than a man in his attributes). He Ringa Poto, He Ringa Kaha.

That year, twin sons were born to Wiremu and Te Urumanao Ratana at their Orakeinui family home. Ratana Ngahina insisted the Holy Spirit had instructed him to name them Arepa and Omeka. Wiremu was uncomfortable that these sacred names were being imposed on his children. It wasn't until after his grandfather had passed away in 1911, and his father a year later, that he followed through with the baptism of the boys. At the age of 39, Ratana and his wife went to Parewanui where Mere Rikiriki officially gave them the names Te Arepa Te Timatanga (the beginning) and Omeka Te Whakamutunga (the end or conclusion).

They were confirmed in the Anglican Church by Iwiora Tamaiparea, a clergyman married to Ratana's sister Puhi o Aotea. When it was time for the family to return home, Aunty Mere had some parting words: 'Wi [Wiremu], return to your home and take with you the God of your ancestors, the God of Abraham, the God of Isaac, the God of Jacob, so that the light shall shine among you and your wife and children.'

Chief Ratana Ngahina, T. W. Ratana's grandfather (centre), was pro-government, but was also a member of the Confederation of United Tribes of New Zealand and the Kotahitanga Māori Parliament.
Uri Whakatupuranga (Ratana Archives).

Challenges and changes

Indeed, the light was about to shine on the life of Wiremu Ratana, but not in the way that he could have expected. He was to come face to face with a series of tests and challenges that would turn his life upside down. Soon after the baptism, Te Arepa became so ill the family didn't know where to turn. They went back to see their aunty, who made them wait for a day and a night before she would see them. Even then she refused to touch the child. 'I am speaking the truth when I tell you all that this child is far above me, his name is directly from the Son himself'.

Then they travelled with one of the church elders to Patea, where there was a large gathering of people. Te Poi Awarua, who was married to another of Ratana's sisters, Te Raupo, echoed Mere Rikiriki's words: 'I am not able to be above the child, he is far higher than I, for his name is from the Lord himself.' Te Raupo pressed her husband to act, so he turned towards the sick boy and prayed he would be made well. Everyone was amazed when Te Arepa (also known as Tommy) was instantly healed. However, there was a terrible price. As soon as the healing was complete Te Poi lost his eyesight, and his gift of healing faded. Within a year the family was in for another shock: Omeka, the other twin, died suddenly.

When the call came for New Zealand soldiers to fight in the First World War, Ratana sent his oldest son Tokouru as part of the Hokowhitu a Tu Maori Pioneers contingent. During his four years' service he fought in Gallipoli and France, where he was badly gassed. During this time Wiremu Ratana's interest in religion grew, and he once more began making regular visits to Mere Rikiriki. She believed he shared the same prophetic lineage as herself and saw in him the spark that had fired leaders of the past, including kings Te Wherowhero and Tawhiao, Taranaki peacemakers Te Whiti and Tohu, Titokowaru, Te Kooti Rikirangi and Paora Te Potangaroa, warriors who converted to a form of Christianity and took on the status of prophet.

Ratana returned to studying the Bible and read many medical books; he expanded his understanding of Māori herbal remedies and began to look into the importance of the Treaty of Waitangi. His aunt told him to believe in the Trinity and pray, predicting a sign would come to him.

Another regular visitor to Mere Rikiriki at Parewanui was Tupu Taingakawa Te Waharoa, a leader in the King movement, who had attempted to create a separate Māori parliament. He was the grandson of Tarapipipi Taingakawa Tamehana Te Waharoa, who was involved in crowning the first Māori king, Potatau. He had accompanied Tawhiao, the second Māori king, to England in 1884, and was a close associate of King Te Rata who had been crowned in November 1912. Following his visit to the prophetess in 1913, Taingakawa committed his life to God, unity among the Māori people and raising the profile of the Treaty of Waitangi.

> In 1913 when I heard of the voice of Mere Rikiriki which was speaking forth at Parewanui, I went there to see and learn about her maramatanga and her plans for the people. Two things were accomplished . . . first Te Kahupukoro and I pledged our allegiance to God; secondly we pledged ourselves to support the call for our people to unite, or to form a kotahitanga, so that something could be done concerning the Treaty of Waitangi.

Taingakawa was so determined to succeed in this new direction that he and his children joined King Te Rata on his pilgrimage to England in 1914 'to see what we could do about the land and social and economic problems that we bore at that time'. However, the Great War had begun and the party, like those who had sought redress from the British Government previously, were told to go home and put their grievances to the New Zealand Government.

In 1912 Ratana's wife Te Urumanao had given birth to another son, Matiu, and on 29 July 1915, a fifth son, Joe Mick, was born. Sensing this child represented an important next step in the prophecies of Mere Rikiriki, Ratana gave him the spiritual name Omeka in honour of the twin he had lost earlier.

TWO

THE BIG FISH STORY

When a prophet of the Lord is among you, I reveal myself to him in visions, I speak to him in dreams.

—Numbers 12:6 (NIV Bible)

I, Ihoa, have heard the cry of the people, this is the reason why I have come to you, the Maori people, to be my footstool upon the earth. Go forth and unite the Maori people under me, Ihoa, heal them in all their infirmities, in the name of the Father, the Son, the Holy Spirit and the Faithful Angels.

—T. W. Ratana's vision, 1918

A visionary encounter

On 17 March 1918, Ratana and his wife and children were fishing at the mouth of the Whangaehu River, a sheltered inlet tucked between the Whanganui and the Rangitikei rivers, when a swell forming out to sea caught his eye. Several mountainous waves crashed to the shore, and then one seemed to 'stand on end' with a 'large fish' surfing in behind it.

As the next wave broke a whale was left stranded on the sand and soon became still. The family were amazed. Then, as they looked up, another wave with a whale in tow dumped its passenger on the foreshore. This second whale thrashed about for a long time, and some accounts say that it bled profusely before dying. However an oral account told to Kereama Pene by Ratana's daughter Maata, who was present at the time, says her father got close enough to carve his initials on it and speak to the struggling mammal.

The old Ratana homestead, known as Orakeinui, in the Waipu block, fifteen kilometres south of Wanganui, fell into disrepair after Ratana's death in 1939. The whale vertebrae are seen mounted on the gateposts. *Uri Whakatupuranga (Ratana Archives).*

My father was overcome by the Spirit . . . and spoke to the spirit of the whale, saying he had the power of life and that Satan's power was at an end. At this point the tail began to move and life was restored and a large wave like the first one carried it out. As the whale left, Ratana said, 'Take my name to the four corners of the world, the time will come when you are called back to the Takutai Moana o Whangaehu, it will be then that my works will be completed.'

Suddenly, there were smaller fish everywhere, flapping around on the sand. The Ratana family dropped their fishing equipment and began excitedly gathering the gifts of kaimoana (seafood) scattered liberally along the shoreline. As word got out, a crowd of onlookers from Whangaehu and Turakina townships began arriving. Ratana harnessed a team of eight of the best horses from the farm to haul the remaining whale to higher ground. The whale oil filled eight large kegs and twenty kerosene tins. This would provide lighting and heating at the farm for many months. Lanterns were created from milk tins with cloth wicks. The blubber and meat would be part of the diet for guests who, on hearing of the curious goings-on at the Ratana farm, would arrive in their droves over the following months.

Ratana took the beached whales as a symbol that he, like Christ's disciples, was called to be 'a fisher of men'. He thought the whales were like those that

The Orakeinui Ratana family homestead, where T. W. Ratana had his vision in 1918, was restored in later years. *Uri Whakatupuranga (Ratana Archives)*.

guided the canoes of the Māori ancestors in their migration from the ancient homeland of Hawaiki, and a sign that the shores of Aotearoa New Zealand would no longer be under the control and influence of Satan, but would be in the palm of Jehovah's hand.

Then, twelve days after the miraculous fishing trip, Ratana and his wife were at home on the farm when three-year-old Omeka was led into the house by his older brother Arepa, crying out in pain. Blood was oozing from his knee and it was thought a sharp object had broken off inside. His parents tried to comfort him and find where the object, possibly a needle, might be lodged. Reviewing the recent events, Ratana exclaimed to Te Urumanao, 'One comforting factor at least is that we can depend on Ihoa', and he began praying in the name of the Father, the Son, the Holy Ghost and the Holy Angels.

> This was the first time I had ever uttered the words Matua, Tama, Wairua Tapu me nga Anahera Pono. Before this I never gave it a thought to pray. Night after night, day after day, this child just continued to groan and cry. He did not cease. Finally, we decided to take him to a doctor in Wanganui. As we were preparing to go with our son I said to my wife, 'As we go with our son, Ihoa and his heavenly host shall be before us.'

In Wanganui the doctor examining Te Omeka's knee couldn't locate the cause of his pain; all he could do was bandage the wound. Soon after arriving home a peace fell on the family. For two days there was improvement, so Ratana went to catch up with his drinking buddies at the Turakina and Whangaehu pubs. As soon as he left home the pain in Te Omeka's leg returned. A call was placed to the hotel but Ratana took his time. When he did arrive home, despite having consumed a considerable amount of alcohol, he prayed and pleaded with Jehovah into the small hours of the morning.

On waking the next day, Te Omeka's condition had settled and, as the day wore on, Ratana was again off to the 'local' to take phone bets on the local horse races on behalf of patrons. The moment he left home, the boy once more began to writhe in pain. After a long drinking session Ratana arrived home to find his son rolling around on the floor. Another trip to the doctor only resulted in advice to come back in several days. Ratana was furious. By then the boy might be dead, he exclaimed.

Divine intervention

Back at the farm the pattern continued. Te Omeka's condition deteriorated, and the pain only seemed to ease after prayers. It became apparent that Ratana's drinking sessions might have to end if his son was to come to a full healing. 'I felt as if I was in a stupor. There and then I said, since we have brought our son back home he shall not be taken to the doctor again. Leave him here where the spiritual doctors shall make him well.' Then on Friday 8 November 1918, between 2 and 3 p.m., three days before the end of the First World War, Ratana received a phone call from friends warning him that his son would most likely die unless he was returned to the hospital.

Ratana went outside onto the veranda to gather his thoughts. He was standing there with the sun beating down when he felt a strange sensation, as if he was being 'engulfed and consumed by fire . . . ko taku ahua pena tonu me te mea e wera ana i te ahi'. The burning sensation lasted for about an hour. He became increasingly restless and, unable to sit or stand still for any length of time, began to pace in and out of the house. Then as he stood on the veranda, leaning on one of the pillars, gazing out to the west coast, he saw a cloud formation moving in from the sea. It rose above the sand hills, shifted on to Waipu Lake, and headed towards the farm. Realising it would descend on the very place he stood, Ratana became afraid. 'There and then I thought this must be the end of the world. The station was left behind and I realised it was coming directly towards me, ever near. Then a flash and my eyes began blinking.'

The cloud was dark on the outside, but the centre was pure white and at the back was a bright glowing colour like a flame. When it was directly over him it 'broke open', and he was overwhelmed by its presence. It was then that he saw highways, roads and pathways from all over the world leading to his house. As if in a trance, he walked into the kitchen, jumped onto the table and exclaimed: 'Peace be unto you all, for I am the Holy Spirit that speaks unto you

T. W. Ratana, shortly after he began his healing ministry in 1918, aged 45.
Tesla Studios, J. McLeod Henderson Collection.

all. Straighten yourselves. Repent.' Ratana then said to his wife, 'The spiritual doctors are here now to heal our son.'

After stepping outside again for a time he returned to the kitchen where his wife Te Urumanao was sitting with a Mrs Pito and a Pākehā friend, Charles Cornford, along with Ratana's children Rawinia, Piki, Maata and Te Omeka. They were startled by Ratana's appearance. His eyes were bloodshot and he was frothing at the mouth. He loudly proclaimed to his wife that Te Omeka would not die, saying the Father, Son and Holy Ghost were in the house and would protect him. Maata ran to get the family Bible and handed it to her father. He said the message was in the Bible, and then threw it on the mantelpiece, causing an old clock, which had belonged to his grandfather Ngahina, to fall and break on the stone hearth. In response to their concerns, he said that the time had come for the clock to finish its work. He added, everything that was in the clock was in his heart.

The story, as later told to Ratana's secretary (Pita Moko), has him taking hold of the clock and breaking it into pieces, crying out, 'If you wish that this clock shall ring at 5 o'clock then it shall be.' He then kicked it with his foot, and it rang on the fifth hour.

> After that, I threw the pieces of the clock into our stove where the fire was burning, and giving out a lot of heat. Our Pakeha immediately came forward to try and take the pieces out, because he had a loving regard for this clock that belonged to my grandfather, and because of the way he saw me treating it. When the pieces of the clock were heaped up on the floor, it rang again on the 5th hour.

After this intense encounter, Ratana continued to act strangely, often appearing to be in a daze, talking to himself and then answering his own questions. He disconnected the phone and the power and packed up everything in the house that didn't belong to him. He was not only facing his inner conflicts at having inherited a family home and belongings that were not his, but something else was driving him. By 10 November everything had been moved out of the house, all the furniture, the food and ornaments. All that was left was a large pile of clothes on the bare floor in one room.

Then he gave his immediate family water and made them walk with him through the night across the rugged land near the property. On their return Ratana, with his son Arepa, lifted the front step to the homestead where they found a taiaha (long staff with a tongue-shaped blade) and an old teapot, which he claimed was part of a curse placed there in an attempt to destroy his grandfather. The next day, Ratana's wife and children moved in with a neighbouring family while he continued his cleansing process, dragging and carrying ploughs and discs and other farming equipment out from the sheds. He then sent word to his mother and family to leave the township of Patea as a voice had told him that a disaster was about to strike if they remained. His mother and his nephew, Ngawakataurua Pehimana, followed his advice. The family members who stayed died within days, including most of those who owned the clothing Ratana had piled on the floor of the now barren family home.

October and November 1918 was a testing time for Ratana and his family, and for Māori in general. The government had been warned about an outbreak of influenza aboard the SS *Niagara* returning from the First World War. Regardless, the ship with Prime Minister William Massey and his deputy Joseph Ward on board was given permission to dock in Auckland. Sick crew and soldiers were also allowed to disembark. Subsequent evidence suggests they were only infected with ordinary influenza. Meanwhile the 'Spanish flu' spread like a plague in two virulent waves, leaving about 6700 people dead in its wake. The mate urutā, or epidemic, claimed almost 1000 Māori lives. Ratana had a slight attack, but his family suffered severely — only his two sisters remained among the 21 grandchildren of Ratana Ngahina. This left Wiremu Ratana as the sole male heir to the family farm.

He remained quiet for some time, exhausted but somehow invigorated, conscious that a great work had begun. He spent long periods in meditation or working in the garden around his home. At other times he would become restless again, saying he had a new māramatanga (enlightenment) for the people, claiming he was being spoken to by the Holy Spirit and by the angels Kapariera (Gabriel) and Mikaera (Michael). He felt that he was undergoing an important period of teaching.

Over the succeeding weeks he had a number of fresh encounters, including a pivotal message that was to further shape his mission.

> I am the Holy Spirit, I have visited the scene of the war which has recently raged in Europe. In my travels I have found that the whole world has forgotten me. I have looked all over for some place to establish myself, and to ensure that God will again be truly known and accepted in the hearts of men. That is why I have come to you, the Maori people. I have investigated your behaviour, and found that you have sinned also. You have sinned in that you have bowed to tohungaism and other Maori gods. However, despite these misdemeanours, I see that you have not forgotten the Lord Jehovah, the Father and Creator of Heaven and Earth. He has this day heard your call and made his choice.

A time of testing

Ratana was shocked by the deaths of his close relatives, the wider toll taken by the influenza epidemic, the ongoing struggles of the Māori people and the loss of around 18,000 New Zealand lives and another 41,000 wounded (a 58 per cent casualty rate) in the Great War. The curious events manifesting in his own life and the ongoing sickness of his son also weighed heavily on him.

Some of those now gathering at the farm started to believe he had lost his mind. Te Urumanao, his wife of 25 years, kept constant vigil with Te Omeka, and was increasingly concerned at her husband's behaviour and the fact he was failing to provide for his family. She challenged him: 'If this is the Holy Spirit that is making you work, I shall be patient; if it is another spirit, I shall not agree that you remain here.' Then she had her own encounter. A voice speaking through Ratana asked: 'Are you willing to support and be loyal to me and my work?' She replied: 'If you are the Holy Spirit which we know and worship, then I will be loyal to you but if you are a false spirit, I shall denounce you.'

The Wairua Tapu impressed on her that she would receive confirmation on 11 November 1918, when the Great War would end. Seeing her great compassion for her husband and her faith in Jehovah the voice continued:

> I am satisfied as to your faith and strength, and I see that you will be a woman among all women. I have therefore decided that from this day forth you shall be known as Te Whaea o Te Katoa or 'Mother of All' . . . I shall make this place a great Pa, a beautiful Pa, where the customs and habits of the islands shall be brought, and indeed those of the world also.

Ratana's trials, likened to the 40 days of fasting and temptation experienced by Christ ahead of his earthly ministry, continued. In his whakamātautauranga – time of testing – he was forced to look closely at his true nature and to repent of all his sins. According to his daughter Maata, Ratana was tested by the Holy Spirit for two weeks and went without food or sleep for a further two weeks while he was taught about man's weaknesses, the remedies, and about creation and life. She said he was tempted to curse God but was found obedient and strong enough in mind and spirit to teach the divine will to the people.

According to accounts in the *Whetu Marama*, Ratana felt he was being tormented and in this state of mind found himself trying to jump over barbed wire fences and gorse and blackberry bushes to prove he was equal to the tasks that lay ahead of him. He failed many times and was cut and bleeding when he returned home. He believed the tests were to overcome doubt, strengthen his faith in Ihoa and remind him that he must fear nothing except God.

He was learning more than how to become an athlete; he was working out his own frustrations and becoming stronger and wiser mentally and spiritually. During this time, his son Arepa was often with him carrying a lantern. 'He never faltered or was discouraged, he just kept on going, right through to the next day.'

Ratana later told his secretary, Pita Te Turuki Tamara Moko (Peter Moko), that he was approached several times by the angel Gabriel, initially stating his credentials as head or president of the angels or messengers from the Throne of God to man, announcing the angels would be his helpers. He was told he would 'be made to die', but should not be afraid.

> The Holy Spirit stood before me, 'Wiremu, lie down, you shall be made to die presently.' I laid down and my mind was overwhelmed. From here, I saw my heart and all the biological parts of the body of man, very similar to the wires joined to the telegraph poles. The base reasons or causes of illnesses and the cure of medicines, the heart that cures and makes everything well, what causes pain and lessons about trees and flowers were given. When the Holy Spirit was satisfied, my mind was once again my own. I awoke and I was alive again.

He said he was also led to the tobacco plantation and asked a question: 'Do you see the small seed inside the flower of the tobacco plant?' On replying that he did, he was informed this was the meaning of the words written in the scriptures: even if your faith is as small as the mustard seed, if you say to the mountains to move they shall move. Often he could not remember the things he had said, and his wife had to remind him or refresh his memory about what he needed to do. They discussed his experiences and insights and, as his behaviour settled, family members and those who had begun to gather at the farm were increasingly convinced he was not mad but divinely inspired.

Meanwhile there was the ongoing concern about Omeka's ordeal. A newly introduced technology, the X-ray, was used to try and locate the offending object in his leg. A needle was observed, but an operation failed to find it. More X-rays were taken but the needle had moved and blood poisoning had set in.

The tiny Ratana railway station built by Ratana's grandfather had never been so busy, with carriages full of the curious stopping off at the Ratana farm for healing and to witness the birth of the new movement. *Uri Whakatupuranga (Ratana Archives)*.

Doctors didn't have the right drugs or antibiotics to treat him and eventually gave up all hope.

Despite advice from the doctors, Ratana insisted on bringing his boy – by now reduced to 'skin and bone' and pitifully weak – back to the farm. He was put to bed, but this time his father remained constantly at his side. Ratana and Te Urumanao fasted and prayed for three days, and they received word from the Holy Spirit that the illness was allowed, so that first miracle of healing in the name of the Father, the Son, the Holy Spirit and the Faithful Angels would be known.

Te Omeka's strength gradually returned until he was sitting up and wanting to get out of bed. He found it difficult to walk at first, so his father fashioned a tiny crutch and he began hobbling around the farm. No one knows what happened to the needle; some accounts say it miraculously 'came out of Omeka's thigh' but one thing was certain, the seven-month ordeal was over.

Big picture vision

At this point Ratana was told by the Holy Spirit that the Pā would be known not only nationally but internationally, and that he would travel to marae across the country and the great oceans. He would come into contact with distinguished people and enter the great cities of the world, including 'the great city Geneva where sit the 12 kings who pass judgement for the world', a reference to a prophecy by Te Whiti and Tohu: 'Those young men who went to war will also travel with you to preach the "new gospel" upon the land where war took place.'

Above left: Te Kooti's East Coast Ringatū bell, passed from Mere Rikiriki and the Ngāti Apa people to Ratana, and the smaller bell once owned by Taranaki prophet Titokawaru from the West Coast, symbolic of future unity among the people. Ratana used the larger bell to summon the people when he wished to address them. Both remain at Ratana Pā. Kereama Pene. *Above right:* Backbone sections of the Arepa or 'Bible whale' are still in storage at Ratana Pā. *Kereama Pene.*

It is alleged the angel Gabriel told Ratana that he had passed his tests with 'patience, courage and strength', but one final text would determine whether he would be a holy man or an ordinary man. Ratana's reply was: 'Whatever you so desire, O Lord.' The response was:

> So be it, you shall remain an ordinary man. Tohungaism, prophets and intellectuals will not rise in your presence. You shall destroy all things evil, that they may never overcome you . . . go forth and remain humble.
>
> I, Ihoa, have heard the cry of the people, this is the reason why I have come to you, the Maori people, to be my footstool upon the earth. Go forth and unite the Maori people under me, Ihoa, heal them in all their infirmities, in the name of the Father, the Son, the Holy Spirit and the Faithful Angels – those of the Maori people who will follow you shall be called morehu, from this day forth, you shall be called Te Mangai [mouthpiece].

At a tangi (funeral) for all those who had lost family members in the influenza epidemic, the Whanganui chief Te Kahupukoro, who had several years earlier visited Mere Rikiriki with Tupu Taingakawa and committed his life to God, came with his bedridden daughter. Ratana talked to her about the divine power and, once he had confirmed the girl believed in the Father, Son and Holy Spirit, clicked his fingers and told her to rise. She recovered to lead a normal life. A nine-year-old boy had undergone several unsuccessful operations, and was about to undergo another when Ratana said: 'The boy will be operated on but not by doctors. It will be by the hand of God.' He was cured.

From that time Ratana did little else but attend to the illnesses of his people. Another early example was that of an old man from Te Kūiti who was well known in the settlement. He went to visit Ratana with crutches and returned without his walking stick, able to walk briskly down the street. As word about Ratana's healing ministry got around, pilgrims from all over the country began making their way to the Ratana farm, which quickly underwent a transformation, becoming known as Te Pā o ngā Ariki (the sanctuary for the chiefs of all tribes).

When Ratana wanted to call the growing audience together for prayer, or to gain their attention, he would have someone ring Te Kooti's Ringatū bell, which hung from a tower at the side of the family homestead. The bell had been left with Mere Rikiriki and the Ngāti Apa people from Kauangaroa Marae on the eastern bank of the Whangaehu River and then gifted to Ratana.

The *Wanganui Chronicle*, *Wanganui Herald* and United Press Association (to become the New Zealand Press Association in 1942) soon made Ratana a household name, reporting the testimonies of those who claimed to be healed, and any scrap of news relating to the goings-on at the Ratana farm. By early 1919 the trickle had turned to a flood. Many brought tents, while others created crude lean-to shacks so they could be a part of the miraculous events.

To maintain some order and ensure people's needs were met, Ratana set up an office and, as the cost of meetings increased, gifts of food and money were sought from other Māori settlements and tribal areas. The inflow of people meant extra buses were run from nearby Marton and Wanganui, taxi drivers were doing a roaring trade and passenger trains regularly offloaded dozens of people at the tiny Ratana station. The Railway Department placed a special flag near Ratana's camp so that Māori could find the 'miracle man'.

THREE

LIGHT IN THE DARKNESS

He pou tohu noa iho ahau i te huarahi o te pono. I am but a finger pointing the way to the true way of life . . . Be at peace . . . Set yourselves straight. Repent . . . Each of us has the power to communicate with God in seeking relief from pain . . . but that seed can be lost through neglect.
—T. W. Ratana, Christmas 1920

The cures effected during that time are too many for record. Every hour, every minute almost, some unfortunate native would waylay Ratana and pray for health. There was always the same quiet question: 'Do you believe in God?' Then, the inevitable result, a sick man cured and able to join with the others to voice the wonder of the man of miracles.
—Rongoa Pai, *Ratana: The Maori Miracle Man*, 1921

Challenging the old gods

A critical part of T. W. Ratana's mandate was to raise Māori consciousness so that superstition and fears encouraged by the dark side of tohungaism would be dispelled under the true light of Ihoa, and Māori could adopt a mindset more suited to the massive changes and challenges that lay ahead.

Traditionally, the tohunga was a priest with knowledge or experience of communing with the spirit world, allegedly the ancestors or atua Māori (old gods). Much of their 'power' came from their ability to inflame the imagination, and thereby coerce or manipulate people. They might claim to conjure kēhua (ghosts), and influence people and events, often reinforcing customs with potential for violence, such as utu (reciprocity). If disobeyed they might leave a curse (mākutu) on individuals, articles or locations. Under this psychological spell, people feared to act or undertake even the most basic activities without first consulting the local tohunga.

While it has been said that many ancient Māori tohunga exercised some of the most powerful witchcraft in the world, not all had entrapment and manipulation in mind. Tohunga piki te ora, for example, were the equivalent of healers or wise advisers, and there were also those who simply exercised great skill as historians, carvers or custodians of culture and tribal wisdom. In later years, however, less scrupulous tohunga, likened to witchdoctors or charlatans, were peddling unlikely cures for illnesses, and threatening people if they didn't comply or pay the stated amount.

The passing of the Tohunga Suppression Act (1907) meant people could no longer openly depend on the tohunga to handle relations with the spirit world, and many were simply driven underground. The people continued to revere tohunga, and many who were ill refused to consult qualified doctors, resulting in unnecessary deaths and infectious diseases spreading unchecked.

T. W. Ratana's mission to turn Māori from the ways of tohungaism often brought him into direct conflict with those who practised the dark arts, and some even sought to openly challenge him to see whose power was greatest.

SIGN OF THE CAMELLIA

Flowers and shrubs played an important part in Ratana's wider symbolism. He often referred to his followers as his 'garden of flowers', echoing the prophecy of Te Kooti. On the gate and alongside the short path leading to the veranda of Orakeinui, the family homestead where Ratana received his vision, were bones from the whale that had beached at Whangaehu, signalling the beginning of his mission. Also along that pathway were several geranium bushes and two camellia trees planted by his grandfather, which would have an important part to play.

In 1919 Ratana went to Wellington with his wife and family, taking a geranium cutting from one of those bushes which he planted in the grounds of the original Parliament buildings, saying, 'I plant you here today and sometime in the future I will return and pluck the flower.' Over the ensuing years he revisited the bush. The timing of the planting and its ultimate blossoming were seen to mark milestones along the way to achieving his goal of restoring the Treaty of Waitangi to a place of prominence and improving Māori representation in Parliament.

In 1920, while speaking from his veranda, Ratana stopped mid-sentence and urged everyone to fall to the ground and be still. Then, when he felt it was safe, he resumed his story. Apparently a well-known tohunga had arrived by train and sent an evil spirit to attack Ratana. In the midst of his message he received news there was a seriously ill man at the Ratana railway station. The man was carried to the veranda, accompanied by a group of tohunga, who refused to allow Ratana to treat him.

One stepped forward and issued a challenge by pointing to one of the camellia bushes: 'Ratana we have come to show you that our gods are stronger and more powerful then yours', and with that the tree he was pointing at withered up. Ratana approached the old man, and said:

> So it was you who sent that spiritual axe to kill me. I sent it back to you, and now you are ill and will shortly die. I say to all who have come to destroy me, it is not I you seek to kill but that which is in me, the Wairua Tapu, and this Spirit cannot be killed. The power I have comes from above, the power you have comes from below.

Then, as if pricked in his conscience, he backtracked, saying his work was not about death but bringing life, and then quoted the words of Christ: 'I have come to bring life and bring life more abundantly' (John 10:10). He pointed to the dead camellia tree and it started to move. In a short time the leaves and branches had formed again but that was not all; on the tree, to the amazement of the people watching, different types of fruit began to sprout.

On seeing this, each tohunga accepted that Ratana's power came from the true God. They repented, and asked to join his movement. Even the old tohunga who had 'an epileptic fit' recovered and later became a follower. Several went on to become apostles and lead their people into the new māramatanga.

Prepared with prayer

Before a healing session Ratana would spend long periods in prayer. While many who came to him were lame, blind or paralysed, there were also those who suffered from mental illness, or mate Māori, as a result of their poverty, their fears and superstitions, and their loss of land and identity. It was only through confession of wrongs, rejection of tohungaism and accepting the Father, Son and Holy Spirit that healing came. Jim McLeod Henderson says Ratana understood how the Māori mind worked.

> By skilful questioning he brought out confession of belief in atua or perhaps the influence of a tohunga. Then, puffing a cloud of pipe smoke, he took possession of fetish objects in order to show the power of faith in Jehovah over the evil

As word got out about the events unfolding at the Ratana family farm there was a growing need to keep the pot boiling, put down hāngi pits and gather wood for the ovens to feed the multitudes. *Frank J. Lenton and Mark Luder Lampi, Tesla Studios Collection, ATL G-16935 1/1, Alexander Turnbull Library, Wellington.*

spirits lurking in them. Usually the next question asked of the patient was: 'Kei te whakapono koe ki te Matua te Tama te Wairua Tapu? Do you believe in the Trinity?' Then turning to the crowd gathered about him he would point his pipe at the sky and say: 'Kei te pono koutou? Do you all believe?' 'Ae!' they said, whereupon the Mangai pulled out his gold watch and gave the patient five minutes in which to arise and walk.

Rather than claim instant healing, Ratana often told the crippled to give up their walking sticks, crutches or wheelchairs over several days. Every patient, when healed, was asked to sign a black book which contained a kawenata (covenant) that believers had renounced all Māori superstitions and tribal affinities and committed to belief in the Trinity.

Ratana was soon besieged with letters from all around the country and the world. A Mrs Jackson, wife of the postmaster at Edendale, Invercargill, had 'a tubercular spine and went through periods of terrible agony'. Doctors told her she should simply lie in bed. In July 1920 Mrs Jackson wrote to Ratana, telling him of her absolute faith in God. He said he would pray for her, but she must also pray for strength. He sent her Matthew 6, verse 24, as a text: 'No man can serve two masters; for either he will hate the one and love the other, or else he will hold to the one and despise the other. He cannot serve God and mammon.'

> Some days later, having followed Ratana's advice, I made an attempt to get up, and had to be carried back to bed feeling very exhausted. On the following day, Thursday, I had turned over in bed intending to try to sleep, when the thought came to me that in obeying the doctor's instructions to keep in bed, I was really putting him before God, so I got up, and stood, and walked without difficulty or feeling of weakness. Further, all pain left me immediately, and I have been free of it for the first time in 10 years. I walked about the house with difficulty, and when my husband was telephoned that I was up and about, he would not believe it. Today, I am feeling quite well, and am secure in the knowledge that at last I am well on the way to permanent recovery. There is not the suggestion of pain, and I must confess that, although I was in bed for so long, there is no weakness in any of my limbs.
>
> My doctor states that the trouble is dormant and that nothing short of a miracle could have worked the change, and it is a miracle. There are times when I feel that there is a strength helping me that is not my own. Undoubtedly my cure is due to the Great Physician. The work that Ratana is doing is such that no one who benefits should be afraid to admit it, for there may be many who could be helped by him.

That report was verified by her husband and married sister. Several months after the healing, Hector Bolitho (Rongoa Pai) – who wrote many articles for the *New Zealand Observer* and was a respected royal biographer – reported in his booklet *Ratana: The Maori Miracle Man*, that Mrs Jackson was 'improving every day . . . now enjoying good health, the reward of her faith in the Great Power'.

After visiting Ratana Pā, a large party from Hawke's Bay returned home with tales of healing, and in November 1920 across the other side of the island in the King Country, Māori who were fired up by stories of miracles and wonders, made their own journey. Bolitho wrote:

> They did not claim him as a tohunga as he received no payment . . . Ratana receives no fee at all. Te Kuiti was greatly excited by the Maori exodus. A thousand Maoris soon spread a story, and the tales of Ratana's power were the only topic of conversation in the King Country town. Tohungaism previously obtaining a great hold on the natives, died a sudden death . . . The Maoris saw that Ratana's belief in Christianity was the inspiration of his healing power and this practical evidence convinced them that their old pagan faith in tohungaism was useless. So they ignored their old practices and built a church.

Above left: The non-denominational church Piki Te Ora (Seek the Light), largely funded by Ratana himself, was officially opened during Christmas 1920. *Uri Whakatupuranga (Ratana Archives). Above right:* Methodist Reverend A. J. Seamer believed the time was right for a Māori Christian movement and gave his full support to Ratana over many years. *Methodist Archive.*

On 6 December 1920, Ratana was asked about the few cases where his cures were not effective or where there were relapses. He replied that it was due to lack of faith.

> The natives whose cures had failed had been talking with the unbelieving Pakeha and from that had doubted the power of God. They doubted and went back to the old Maori beliefs in tohungaism and makutu. When Maoris did that, there was no hope. I am trying to make them believe in God and the Holy Ghost.

The Reverend A. J. Seamer, superintendent of the Methodist Māori Mission, had a compassionate heart for the Māori people. He spoke the native language fluently and was considered by many to be the last European missionary worthy of a chiefly position among them. He was a close friend of Māori leaders in Northland, Waikato, Taranaki and the South Island, and had been a personal friend of Te Whiti. He had a sense that the time was right for a significant Māori movement to arise and unite the people under Christian principles. When he first heard of the miracles at Ratana Pā he took a strong interest, soon becoming a close friend of Ratana, describing him as the most practical faith healer he had known:

> He had a number of anatomy charts and medical books, and often referred to Pope's *Health for the Maori*. I never heard him give anything but sound advice on health, and he often sent people to doctors when there was organic trouble.

During a healing session when Ratana was seated on the veranda with a queue of patients, a European visitor called out: 'Is it true that you advise people not to use medicines?' Ratana smiled and pulled out of his waistcoat pocket a small jar of ointment. He then rolled up his sleeve displaying a rash on his skin. 'I'm using this . . . it's very good stuff.'

In May of 1920 Ratana received another 'divine' visitation urging him to go to every Māori settlement that invited him. He had begun to describe the nation as embracing Aotearoa for the North Island, Waipounamu for the South Island and Whare Kauri (the Chatham Islands) rather than the traditional inclusion of Stewart Island. The significance of the Chatham Islands, 800 kilometres due east of Christchurch – apart from being the first populated landfall to see the sun each day – related directly to Ratana's great sadness that some of his own kinsmen from Taranaki had been involved in the near genocide of the peaceful Moriori tribe in 1836. Te Kooti, who had prophesied the rise of Ratana, had also been imprisoned on the Chathams until he escaped to the mainland, and after a vengeful rampage, eventually softened and began preaching a more Christian-based revelation.

In preparation for his 1921 national tour, Ratana had appointed āpotoro wairua (spiritual apostles) to take the gospel to the people and gain signatures on his first public kawenata. This was 'a clear and sacred statement' embodying the Ture Wairua (spiritual law) and the Ture Tangata (physical law), a framework of direction and purpose for the future. The signatories pledged:
1. To unite under Ihoa o ngā Mano (Jehovah of the Thousands), as the power and authority over all things and protector and refuge for those willing to trust him.
2. To ask forgiveness for the wrongs that had been done.
3. To worship no other than Ihoa and to join T. W. Ratana in spreading the Good News of Ihoa's power, glory and great love.
4. To work to atone for the wrongs of their ancestors.
5. To cast away the evils of corruption, tohungaism, devil worship and witchcraft.
6. To work to tear down and cast away all the tribal barriers and jealousies and live together as one family of mōrehu.
7. To work together for the glory of Ihoa only and for the good of the people without thought or desire for personal gain.

The word is out
When the newspapers reported that a hui was planned for Christmas, extended families from across the country began heading to the Ratana farm for what was allegedly to become the largest gathering of Māori people since the signing of the the Treaty of Waitangi.

The significance of Whare Kauri (the Chatham Islands) in Ratana's description of the country, was not only to honour the Moriori people who had been decimated in 1836 by those with affiliations to his own tribal area in Taranaki, but to commemorate the first place to see the sun each day, and the location where Te Kooti had been imprisoned. Ratana formed a close friendship with the last full-blooded Moriori, Tommy Solomon (Tame Horomona Rehe), who he ordained as an apostle in the church. The Chatham Island Māori signed Ratana's covenant for unity and had their own land grievances added to documentation and petitions that Ratana took to England in 1924. *PAColl-5469-048, Alexander Turnbull Library, Wellington.*

Four large marquees, 130 smaller tents, a large meeting house and Ratana's own house were used to accommodate the visitors, with hundreds more sleeping out in the open. It took four days to transport 20,000 gallons of water by tanker from Turakina. A generator provided electricity. In the hāngi they cooked eight bullocks, 20 sheep, 20 pigs and 50 tons of potatoes. Other supplies included 350 large loaves of bread, six tons of sugar, dozens of boxes of butter, 1500 dried sharks, 1500 fresh and smoked eels, sacks of mussels and pipi, 30 bags of muttonbird, 1400 tins of biscuits and hundreds of tins of jam and fruit.

Over 3000 people had assembled to spend Christmas Day at the Ratana farm and to participate in the opening of the new non-denominational church Piki Te Ora (Seek the Light) that had been built mostly with Ratana's own funds. The church opened on the Saturday before Christmas, with the service presided over by Ratana's cousin, Methodist minister the Reverend Robert Tahupotiki Haddon, and attended by members of every Christian denomination. A Roman Catholic priest celebrated mass, and Protestants held their own service.

As well as the numerous crippled, ailing and curious who flocked to Ratana Pā, leaders from throughout Māoridom were determined to check out the miracles and motivation of this man who was creating such a stir across the nation. Key individuals from the Ringatū Church and King movement remained suspicious. Ringatū leaders, in particular, did not want to embrace anything contrary to the legacy of their founder Te Kooti, and they struggled with some of Ratana's teachings.

King movement leader Tupu Taingakawa, the uncle of King Te Rata and grandson of Tawhiao, had heard about the events at Ratana Pā on his return from England where he had failed to get a hearing to raise concerns about the Treaty of Waitangi. He arrived at the Pā on 24 December, and on Christmas Day addressed Ratana on the veranda of the family homestead: 'Young man, I have come before you not because I am sick or troubled personally but to bring before you the sicknesses and troubles that have come to bear upon the treasures left us by our ancestors, in particular our lands and our people.'

Ratana responded:

> Oh Tupu, may you be given strength and enlightenment but don't keep that maramatanga shut up in a box. Place it on a lampstand, otherwise it will not shine all over the land; make it flash like lightning so that it will be seen all over the world. The first thing you must do is unite the people under Ihoa o nga Mano, otherwise what you and Te Rata seek will never come to pass. Let Ihoa show you and Te Rata the way. If you do what I tell you your task will be accomplished within six months. If you are not successful within 12 months then you will know that the people have made it so.

A paraphrase of that conversation is more simply stated in some sources as: 'Kei te pai! Whakakotahi ki te Matua i te tuatahi ana tatou ki te whakakotahi ki te whenua. Good! First let us unite in the Father, and then we shall unite in the land.'

On Christmas afternoon Ratana held a four-hour service, telling the people they must believe in the Holy Trinity and cleanliness of the body, and reject Māori superstitions. 'I have opened the door but you yourselves must go in. He poutohutohu i ahau i huarahi pono. I am but a finger pointing the way to the true way of life.' He continued, 'Be at peace . . . Set yourselves straight. Repent . . . Each of us has the power to communicate with God in seeking relief from pain . . . but that seed can be lost through neglect.' He told the assembled people that pagan Māori beliefs were the cause of mental, spiritual and physical illnesses. About a hundred healings were reported in the newspapers.

While the King movement did not align itself with Ratana, Tupu and several other prominent members became deeply involved in the Ratana movement. Soon after the Christmas gathering, their pan-tribal Maori Council, or Kauhanganui, met to unanimously support the call by Ratana for all the tribes to abandon tohungaism for the true God. They passed a motion 'to ask Parliament to legislate so that the preaching of the doctrine of tohungaism might be a punishable offence'. This decision by the powerful council, led by Taingakawa, gave Ratana even greater mana among his own people and the number of visitors to the Pā continued to escalate.

While Māoridom was certainly taking notice of what was going on, attempts to get anyone in the government to take an interest in, or assist with, the grow-

Tupu Taingakawa Te Waharoa, the Māori kingmaker who converted to Christianity under Mere Rikiriki and joined Ratana early in his mission. *Morrin Museum, Morrinsville.*

ing movement appeared futile. Even the Māori members of Parliament and the Native Department seemed intent on snubbing Ratana. For example, an application for special trains to Ratana Pā and reduced fares for the sick was dismissed with a letter from the Native Affairs Department to the Native Minister, the Honourable J. G. Coates, suggesting any assistance to Ratana 'may be construed as a countenancing by the Department of the tohungaism of Ratana'. This correspondence clearly ignored Ratana's stated aim: to eliminate tohungaism.

Blind eyes opened

Rangi Solomon from Banks Peninsula in the South Island was holidaying with his cousins, the Broughton-Paratene family, at Mohaka in Hawke's Bay when they decided to take a sightless woman to the miracle man. Solomon went along for the ride and witnessed the woman, who had been blind from birth, gaining her vision.

He was so impressed he immediately contacted his father, Abel Abraham Solomon (Horomona) at Port Levy, to seek help for his mother Miria, who suffered from an 'incurable' illness. On the ferry trip across Cook Strait she dreamt a man spoke to her, saying, 'My girl, your faith shall cure you.' Alighting from the train at Ratana station she pointed to a man in the crowd and said, 'That's Ratana, the man in my dreams.' She was restored to health, and from that day a deep relationship developed, with Ratana becoming like her son and she his disciple.

That experience was to have a dramatic impact on her entire family. She

Miria Solomon (centre) with four of the five whānau members she helped to raise. Mihara Huiarei Tainui (Bess), mokopuna (grandchild) of Chief Taare Tikao and his wife Hana Solomon (back centre), and her three Tirikatene mokopuna, Nukuroa, Whetu and Te Rino. The fifth (not shown) was Wharetutu, her son Rangi's eldest child. Miria Solomon, healed from an 'incurable illness' by Ratana, moved from the South Island with her husband Abraham and family to live at Ratana Pā where she ran Miria's dining room, baking bread and making pies for the people.
Tirikatene-Sullivan Collection.

remained at the Ratana family farm and established the first shop and dining room, which would cater to the hundreds camped there and the thousands who came to see the great healer. During Easter 1921 her son-in-law Eruera Tirikatene and his family visited Ratana Pā. He was impressed with the spirit of the people and the loyalty they showed towards their leader.

Wild horses were roaming across the land and, on hearing of the visitor's skills as a former rodeo rider, a nephew of Ratana asked him to catch one of the animals and break it in. Tirikatene agreed and, while casually talking to the nephew, remarked on the quality of the land and its suitability for wheat and other crops. Word got back to Ratana, who was already concerned at the increasing needs of the large number of people he was now effectively having to support.

Ratana asked Tirikatene if he would prepare the rough land, covered with gorse and blackberry, so they could plant wheat and other crops to feed the people and provide work and income for them. He said: 'I see a big thing on you.' Tirikatene, with his traditional Māori upbringing, took this 'thing' to be a mākutu or an evil omen and decided to leave Ratana Pā immediately. Ratana, however, took him aside and showed him a place near his own house which he marked out with his foot, saying, 'Build here.' It took encouragement from his mother-in-law, and Ratana himself, to clear up the misunderstanding that the big thing Ratana saw was in fact a more important role.

Tirikatene, a certified oil, gas, electric, fuel and marine engineer, was asked to stay and develop the land. His skills, together with his extensive farming experience, would make him an invaluable member of the team developing the new settlement. Soon, a close bond developed, and Ratana convinced him that his life's mission was to serve the people as a leader in his movement.

FOUR

HEALING ESCALATES

All at once the miracle happened. Life and strength flowed into me . . . I put my feet out of bed and praying for strength I stood up and walked with perfect ease and freedom. I was not even giddy. I knew instantly that I was indeed cured . . . It happened exactly 19 hours after I received Ratana's letter.

—Joseph Kemp, *How I was Healed: A New Zealand Miracle: a biographical sketch of Miss Fannie Lammas*, 1923

Everywhere Maoris could be found earnestly studying the Word of God. Hundreds of Maori men who had been hopeless slaves to alcohol were suddenly transformed and liberated from their bondage. The moral stimulus of those early days of the Ratana movement was more wonderful even than some of the marvellous physical healing which undoubtedly took place.

—John Rawson Elder, *The History of the Presbyterian Church of New Zealand 1840–1940*, c. 1940

Taking the gospel literally

Ratana was tall and slightly built with a thin face, a moustache and piercing black eyes. His voice was quiet and cultured, and his English and Māori faultless. He smoked a pipe, often wore a dark grey felt hat and long coat and, as he grew older, walked with a slight stoop. While he was accessible, particularly to the children at the Pā, in public he had managed to create an air of mystery about himself.

He was particularly private and secretive among Europeans. He could disappear in a crowd, so the media or anyone who didn't know him would have great trouble identifying him. He was generally considered a humble man, and

T. W. Ratana, aged about 47.
Uri Whakatupuranga (Ratana Archives).

spoke simply and quietly to each person he ministered to, never engaging in dramatic gestures or ritual during his faith-healing sessions.

He typically shied away from anything that would focus on his personality rather than his mission, although he was far more forthcoming among his peers, some of whom considered him arrogant. The more educated Māori often expressed their suspicion of him; others thought he was a new breed of tohunga and said so. That he smoked a pipe and often walked among his own people chatting frivolously was sometimes considered rude, and it was these trivial points that were raised in the media and by critics who sought to minimise his influence.

Ratana's teaching and healing were typically done at night in the meeting house at Ratana Pā. To get through all the demands on his time his days were highly structured. After half an hour of prayer he would have breakfast at 8 a.m. Believing people were eating about twice as much as necessary, he mostly went without a midday meal and would work from 8.30 a.m. until 5 p.m. During this time he would constantly engage with those who sought help, and sign the letters prepared by his secretaries in response to the many written requests for healing. He would have an evening meal at 5 p.m., and from 7 p.m. engage in prayer before retiring unless there were other pressing matters to deal with.

Ratana's work was not only about the miraculous. It was also about the practical. He saw the plight of his people and their need for simple guidelines to improve living standards. He wanted them to have a clear moral and social

Jack Rennie, the first Ratana policeman, whose job was to keep order when the crowds flocked to Ratana Pā. He was the forerunner of the Ratana security team, the kātipa.
Uri Whakatupuranga (Ratana Archives).

base for their faith, to take better care of their children and avoid excessive smoking and drinking.

Funeral services (tangi) that often took men away from paid work for weeks on end were not helping the community. Nor was the unhygienic situation where mourners paid their respects by kissing decaying bodies that should have been buried days earlier. Several clergymen and lay readers from the Methodist, Anglican and Presbyterian churches helped him draw up the guidelines:

- Obedience to Ratana's message.
- Acceptance of absolute faith in the Christian God.
- The renouncing of all Māori superstitions.
- Baptism of all.
- That marriage be more sincerely honoured.
- That greater care should be taken of children who should be wisely fed and tended.
- That people pray for power to resist intoxicating liquor.
- That cigarette smoking among children and women nursing infants be discontinued.
- That family prayers be held in every home.
- That the duration of tangi be shortened.
- That people should retain membership of churches founded on Christian faith.
- That even if Ratana himself should fail, he has now shown them the right way.

The Anglican Church was impressed with Ratana and his work, and passed a resolution pronouncing a blessing on him and expressing its 'deep thankfulness at the success that has attended his efforts for the physical, moral and spiritual welfare of our Native race'. John Rawson Elder, in the *History of the Presbyterian Church of New Zealand*, described the excitement generated by the Ratana movement as a spiritual revival.

> Since the early spread of the Gospel in New Zealand there has been no other spiritual awakening of Maoridom to compare with this. Many Maoris whose religion had been purely formal were seized with intense religious conviction, and everywhere Maoris could be found earnestly studying the Word of God. Hundreds of Maori men who had been hopeless slaves to alcohol were suddenly transformed and liberated from their bondage. The moral stimulus of those early days of the Ratana movement was more wonderful even than some of the marvellous physical healing which undoubtedly took place.

On the gospel trail

Within a year of establishing his first covenant, Ratana had given up farming and taken on full-time ministry, gathering around him a core group of volunteers, including many who had fought in the Great War.

He needed loyal people in secretarial, administrative, catering and public-relations roles to ensure everything ran more smoothly at the Pā and on the healing and fact-finding tours, and to respond more rapidly to the thousands of letters requesting healing.

His 1921 national tour saw Ratana and his growing entourage setting up colourful marquees at each stop where thousands attended rallies and many were converted, if not to the Christian faith, then certainly to his vision for Māori unity. They carried with them a large, white flag with a star and crescent moon over a Union Jack and the words 'God the Father, God the Son, the Holy Ghost and the Holy Angels' in English and in Māori. The stories of his healing power continued to be reported, often long after he had passed through an area.

Ratana saw the pride in tribalism both as a barrier to Māori unity and as the cause of ongoing disputes, which had resulted in wars and acts of utu (revenge) for events that may have occurred years or even generations previously. In some locations more than half the Māori population agreed to relinquish their old superstitions, belief in many gods and strict adherence to tribalism. Formerly hostile tribes began setting aside their grievances for the common goal of peaceful co-existence under one God. Even their bitterness against the Pākehā began to dissolve.

On one brief journey through the Waikato, Ratana and his retinue of 300 –

> Ratana
> 14/1/21
>
> All things are possible with god He has promised to do with his hands that which He has promised with his mouth. Appeal to your Lord Jesus Christ with a real heart belief that He and He alone heal you of your ailment. Pray to Him in the name of the Father Son Holy Ghost & the Holy Angels, with a sincere truthful & reverent prayers so therefore repent that ye may recieve His grant as I will also pray to Him to grant your request. Sanction His name & sing His Praise for ever & ever Amen
>
> your faithfully
> TW Ratana

As well as personally attending to those who sought healing, Ratana responded to thousands of letters, with many cures reported by those who acted on his advice through the mail.
Uri Whakatupuranga (Ratana Archives).

including about thirteen 'Ratana policemen' (kātipa) whose job it was to keep the peace and keep Pākehā at a distance – arrived at Morrinsville on 23 March 1921. He was welcomed like royalty by 2400 Māori. Ratana stepped forward and gave what was described as a 'quietly impressive' 90-minute speech urging the people to 'higher living and higher thinking'. He spent two days in retreat and prayer while thousands of curious waited outside. Then came the moment everyone had been waiting for, the time for healing when 150 Māori, including the crippled and those aged and bent with rheumatism, lined up before Ratana to tell of their willingness to believe and their need of healing.

Among them was a 70-year-old man, who had been crippled for fifteen years, who slowly made his way up to Ratana on a pair of crutches. Ratana worked with him for half an hour, then took away his crutches, saying, 'Follow me.' There was a gasp of astonishment as he not only followed Ratana without assistance, but in his excitement soon 'danced and hopped about in childish glee to have experienced such a recovery'. A man with a paralysed arm was able to move it freely within minutes; another, brought to Ratana on a stretcher, after a few quiet sentences, rose and walked behind him.

Journalist Hector Bolitho witnessed the events, and said that Ratana did not claim the works were entirely his own. 'His greater work is with the inner man and he gives each of these unfortunate sufferers a potion for his soul as well as

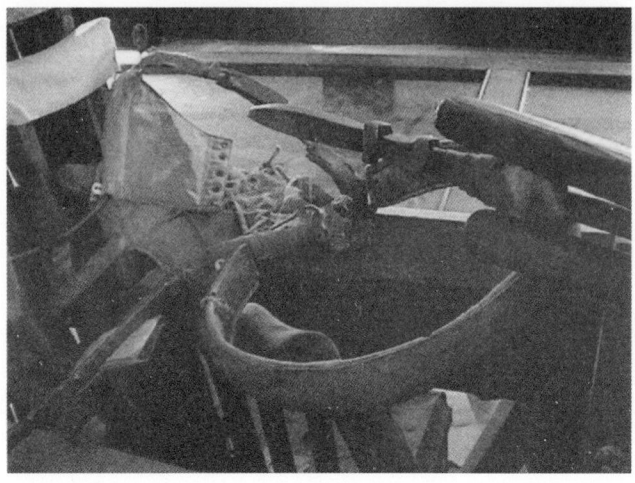

The body frame Fannie Lammas was required to wear whenever she got up from her bed during her nineteen years of 'living death' until she was completely healed in 1921 after receiving a faith-building letter from T. W. Ratana. *Uri Whakatupuranga (Ratana Archives)*.

his body. Ratana in every case exhorts the Christian beliefs and tells his people to ignore the old pagan beliefs.'

Restored after nineteen years

The most publicised healing was that of Fannie Lammas, a member of the Baptist Church in Nelson, who had been virtually paralysed for nineteen years and needed to be strapped into a steel frame whenever she had the energy to get out of bed. Doctors and specialists had given up hope, but were proven wrong when she was completely healed after receiving a letter from Ratana in February 1921.

'It is said the day of miracles is ended. Well in me you have a living proof that such is not the case,' said Lammas in a challenge to sceptics, non-believers and those who criticised the work of Ratana. In the *Nelson Evening Mail* of 7 January 1922, in an article headlined 'A Miraculous Cure, Bedridden Cripple Walks', her story was confirmed by her doctor, the last of 30 medical advisors who had treated her.

The newspaper reported her first long trip in nine years. She had visited Wellington, Wanganui and Te Aroha and was staying at an Auckland hotel 'where she walks up three flights of stairs to reach her room'. At the request of Ratana, Miss Lammas spent a day at Ratana Pā where she met the man responsible for her cure.

> She was given a cordial reception by the Maoris and had a most interesting interview with Ratana himself, who regards her case as one of the most notable with which he has been connected. When told that many people are still skeptical about the value of Ratana's work, and demanded absolute proof of his cures, Miss Lammas replied: 'I shall only be too willing to talk to any clergyman

Sceptics who wanted to dismiss what was happening at the Ratana farm as hysteria were soon challenged by the growing pile of crutches and walking sticks left behind by those who had been restored to health. *Uri Whakatupuranga (Ratana Archives).*

or doctor or anyone else who seeks proof. But for Ratana I should now have either been dead or enduring what was little better than a living death, the only form of existence I had known for 19 years'.

In another account, recorded months earlier by Hector Bolitho in *Ratana: The Maori Miracle Man*, Lammas explained the circumstances of her healing.

> I have been ill since I was a little girl. I had a badly dilated heart to begin with, and then my chest and spine became useless. For 19 years I used a steel frame to move about in. I had always to wear this when I was out of bed. Even my head was propped up in iron and my shoes were screwed in to the end of the frame. Prior to having the steel frame I had to lie on my back for a number of years.

Her situation had been complicated by serious illness. 'A masseuse who treated my back for nearly a year pronounced my case to be hopeless. There had been no end of consultations, and on the very day that I wrote to Ratana, my doctor held a consultation with another medical man, and the result was that my case was again declared to be helpless.' Just before that, some friends who had been to 'Ratana's camp' were greatly impressed by the evidence of his cures. On discussing this with her doctor, he responded, 'We have tried everything human, now try the super-human. It will be a real miracle if you are cured'.

Lammas wrote to Ratana immediately, giving him a short account of her case and a week later received a reply.

> Ratana demanded absolute faith in Jesus Christ, and said that I must pray fervently and untiringly, asking it in the name of the Trinity. He added that he would also pray for me. On the day that I received Ratana's letter I prayed nearly

all day, but nothing at all happened. As a matter of fact I felt weaker than before [but] continued praying nevertheless. Early next morning when I was praying again, my back suddenly received power. To my great delight I was able to sit up in bed, and then to stand and walk without aid, the first time for years. For the previous 12 months I had not been out of bed.

I walked around my bed a half dozen times that day. I sat up for a little while both morning and afternoon, and to my great surprise I required no support and felt no pain. I felt marvelously better straight away.

A few weeks after the receipt of Ratana's letter Miss Lammas was able to walk down the street:

I carry only a stick, but I do not require this at all for the support of my body. It is really for my ankles, which are subject to a weakness that is not connected with my late serious bodily ailment. I can now hold up my head wonderfully well. Before I wrote to Ratana, I had for eight years to wear complex glasses for astigmatism of my eyes. I mentioned this in my letter and I have not needed to put on the glasses since the day on which I recovered the power to walk.

In June she wrote a letter to Bolitho confirming her healing:

I am pleased to tell you that I have made wonderful progress since you saw me, in spite of the cold weather, which always made me so much worse. I grow stronger daily and am increasing in weight entirely to the doctor's satisfaction. He thinks my recovery just marvelous. I can eat practically anything now, and sleep like a top, two things previously impossible. Only three months ago I was so seriously ill I was waiting to die. Now, I am a new being having neither pain nor support. It is almost like being raised from the dead . . . Truly the day of miracles is not past. The first time I went to church there was great rejoicing and the whole congregation arose and sang the Doxology.

In *How I was Healed: A New Zealand Miracle*, a biographical sketch of Fannie Lammas, Reverend Joseph Kemp records that, after her healing, she spent six months travelling, visiting Baptist churches including the Tabernacle in Auckland, and speaking of God's power to heal. In the booklet, which went through four editions, the Very Reverend Dean of Nelson, Dr G. E. Weeks, says he visited Lammas every week for almost four years and found her in an extremely weak condition either unable to get up or at least confined to an invalid's chair. In March 1921, after a month away, he found a very marked improvement and heard from her the story of her remarkable recovery, which she attributed entirely to answered prayer.

After explaining the futility of her condition, her letter to Ratana and his response, Lammas described her healing:

> All at once the miracle happened. Life and strength flowed into me . . . I put my feet out of bed and praying for strength I stood up and walked with perfect ease and freedom. I was not even giddy. I knew instantly that I was indeed cured; just as Jesus Christ made the people whole when he was on earth, so did he make me whole . . . I looked at my watch to record the time of such an amazing deed. It was exactly 5.30 on February 24th, 1921 . . . It happened exactly 19 hours after I received Ratana's letter. I immediately thanked and praised God for his wonderful goodness to me. Then walking to the door I called to my parents that I was cured. They got up and hurried in just beaming with joy and gratitude. I will never forget their dear shining faces as long as I live . . .

Another healing attributed to Ratana's ministry was that of Miss C. Winter, a member of the Nelson Church of Christ, reported in a local church newsletter:

> We have before us now a letter from Miss Christina Winter of Nelson Church who says: 'At the beginning of March, I followed his [Ratana's] instructions and prayed for health and my cure has been marvellous. I am walking long distances without support of any kind, having quite discarded the steel surgical splint I have had for the last 14 years and practically given up my invalid chair. I have never been in such good health in my life, for my lameness dates from early infancy, and besides this, there was a nervous malady that was hereditary and life-long.'

Rahui sees the light

In May 1921 Ratana and an entourage of about 30 motor vehicles headed through the Manawatū Gorge between the Ruahine and Tararua ranges, towards the East Coast and ultimately farther north. In Hawke's Bay, Ratana cured a man who had been severely crippled for 28 years, who then walked into town and purchased his first pair of shoes. It is claimed thousands were healed on this stage of the journey.

Ratana spent a week in Whakatāne at the end of May and visited the small towns of Waimana, Ruatoki and Paroa, 'healing and adding to his reputation as a miracle worker', before travelling on to Rotorua where he spoke to, and allegedly healed, thousands more Māori. He ended his East Coast tour in Tauranga, staying at the Waitoa native settlement just out of the main centre. While he refused to see Europeans, he continued to answer letters.

On 4 June, Ratana and a number of his followers boarded the passenger ship *Ngapuhi* at the Port of Tauranga, bound for Auckland. The ship was met on

As he toured around the country on his healing mission, T. W. Ratana listened closely to the concerns of the people. He and his party carried a huge white flag that called for unity under one God and featured the Union Jack, indicating he was willing to work with the Crown and the government to have the Treaty of Waitangi honoured.
R. R. Woodcock Collection. ATL-F-89569 1-2, Alexander Turnbull Library, Wellington.

arrival by reporters and photographers, but Ratana refused to be interviewed or photographed, or to hold a meeting in the Auckland Town Hall, opting instead to visit Māori in their own communities. The newspapers featured many letters from those wanting to know more about the man and his cures.

The day after his arrival, Ratana went to the Waipapa Maori Hostel in Mechanics Bay where he met with the usual crowd of sick and crippled, along with people from Ōrakei, the only native township to survive the growth of Auckland city. At Ōrakei Marae that evening, according to eyewitnesses, there were many cures of the sick and lame. He then visited settlements in and around the region. At the town of Rewiti, near Helensville, he was met by about 250 locals, who had prepared a great feast in his honour, and set aside a church building for his followers.

From there, at the invitation of Henare Toka of Batley Marae, Ratana and 45 others caught a train to Ranganui and a launch to Otamatea, along the upper reaches of the Kaipara Harbour, to meet with 350 Ngāti Whātua people. Among those who welcomed Ratana and his entourage was Rahui, a much-respected woman in her eighties, who had inherited from her father, the great chief Te Kiri, the land rights for Pākiri, Ōmaha, Great Barrier Island, Little Barrier Island and other offshore islands.

She had lived at Pākiri until the death of her first husband in the late 1850s, when she married a chief, Te Heru Tenetahi, and a decade later moved to Little Barrier Island, establishing a trading business with the mainland. They were later involved in a legal battle with the Crown over ownership of the islands and, even after being evicted, refused to pick up the compensation money as a matter of principle.

Bolitho recounts that on one occasion, when crossing from the mainland to Little Barrier, their boat capsized in a storm and they had to swim through the raging sea for the island:

> The chief, a strong man, called out to her that he would have to give it up, but she called: Haere atu, haere atu (Go on, go on). With his wife's help he eventually reached land . . .
>
> Rahui is very old. She is one of the aged Maoris who remember New Zealand before the triumph of the white man. She knew Auckland when there was no city here and when her dark lord and his fellows hunted for their food and fought for their independence against their tribal enemies and then against the white invader. So she was an interesting subject to test Ratana's powers. Blind and almost helpless with the marks of age upon her, she was carried before Ratana. He spoke to her and then lit a match. Ratana held the light before the blind woman's eyes and said: 'Can you see?' She responded, 'Ah! I can see something like a star.' 'How is that?' he asked as he moved the match further off. 'Yes,' she said, 'that is all right.'

It was a dramatic moment. Rahui, who had been blind for five years, was excited and her people went wild with enthusiasm, cheering loudly with many falling on their faces as the old woman walked out of the building unaided. Bolitho says the healing of Rahui was vouched for 'by two Maoris well known in Auckland', Otene Paul (Otene Paora), a Ngāti Whātua elder, and his brother from Ōrakei, who carried the old woman up to Ratana.

After Otamatea, Ratana and his entourage went to Dargaville and the Kaihu settlement. Four hundred people were waiting there, and the preaching and healing continued. The next stop was Toetoe marae, Otaika, on the outskirts of Whangārei, and then on to Kaikohe, where hundreds of Māori who marvelled at Ratana's message and healing powers began adopting the name mōrehu.

Crossing the Strait

The events of 1921 continued like clockwork, in part because of the organisational skills of Ratana's team, who were either travelling with him or were back at the Pā, planning ahead in response to the huge interest from around the country. There was a growing enthusiasm for his teaching that urged Māori, regardless of tribal affiliation, to break away from the ancient superstitions, adopt practical codes relating to health and morality, and consider themselves as one people under Ihoa o ngā Mano.

There was a brief return to Ratana Pā before the South Island (Te Waipounamu) leg began in July 1921. Like other Māori prophets before him, Ratana sought to remove the ancient powers of tapu (the sacred), including curses on the land. He would pay respect to those prophets who had foretold a new era for Māori, and turn the people towards the teachings of Christ. Ratana took a core group with him, including his wife Te Whaea, his sons Arepa and Omeka, his daughter Piki Te Ora, his secretary Pita Moko, and a party of about 20 South Island followers who had come to live at Ratana Pā.

They caught the Lyttelton ferry. A *Christchurch Press* reporter was amused that Lord Jellicoe, the Governor-General, disembarked unnoticed because the full attention of the crowd was on Ratana.

Among the group was ardent young follower Rangi Wawahia Solomon, who had kept his southern relatives informed about the events he had seen at Ratana Pā and informed Ratana about tapu areas which were affecting locals. It didn't matter which denomination people belonged to, it was faith in the Christian God that mattered. Anglicans, Methodists and Catholics flocked to see Ratana at his meetings and signed his covenant. Ratana encouraged them all to remain in their churches.

At the Rapaki Hall they were welcomed by kaumātua (elder) Te One Taare Tikao, the influential Ngāi Tahu leader, last of the powerful South Island tohunga, and a former member of the second Māori Parliament at Kohimarama. He had been gripped with rheumatism for many years, and at the evening service it was he who first went forward for healing. He was restored and travelled with Ratana, opening the way for widespread acceptance of his mission among southern Māori. From this time, Ratana began referring to the South Island as Omeka, honouring his young son and symbolising his physical works, which would be more evident in the next stage of his mission.

The party were given a full Māori welcome at the Arowhenua Hall (Te Hapa a Niu Tireni or the Broken Promises of the New Zealand Government) and visited the marae of the prophet Te Maiharoa, where many of the South Island chiefs had signed the Treaty of Waitangi and continued to meet in succeeding years to discuss issues arising from it. Te Maiharoa was a tohunga piki te ora specialising in healing, given to making prophecies that uplifted people rather than inspiring fear. He had studied the Bible and chosen twelve young South Island leaders to whom he would pass on his knowledge. He had prophesied that a leader would arise when only two of these āpotoro remained. Those who remained at this time were Te One Tirikatene and Kerikeri (Fred) Gregory, both of whose sons were later to enter Parliament.

It was at Arowhenua that Te Maiharoa had made his famous prophecy in the late 1870s: 'Listen to me, my Maori people, the one who will save you all will come forth in the Taranaki area; he will bring with him that which you have waited for so long, for he will be carrying with him two books.' Ratana had intended to dedicate the Arowhenua Archway – which led into an empty field – to the memory of South Island Māori lost in the Great War, Māori who had died before 1840, and to the spiritual names given his sons Arepa and Omeka. While the base had been built, the work hadn't been completed and there was a dispute with local authorities. On the evening of his arrival at Arowhenua Marae, one of the kaumātua saw a shooting star and, recalling the prophecy of Te Maiharoa, pointed at Ratana, saying: 'That's the man'.

At Port Chalmers on the Otago Harbour, utmost secrecy was maintained as memorial services were held for the people who had been taken prisoner from Parihaka and used to build roads, with many dying in captivity. On 29 July Ratana travelled to Ōrari and Ōnuku Marae at Akaroa, another location where local chiefs had signed the Treaty of Waitangi. All the while he was quietly gathering signatures from the local people who pledged their commitment to his cause of uniting under Jehovah, and agreed to have him deal with their land grievances.

The party returned to Ratana Pā for three weeks before heading south again on 20 August to complete the work. They went to Marlborough, travelling to Wairau Pā where 'a large number of crippled and diseased Maori were waiting for his arrival'. In Picton, Nelson and Motueka various services were held and cures reported.

Word also reached them of a number of reported healings from letters to which Ratana had responded. It is alleged that between January and August 1921 he received 51,000 letters from around the world – an average of 275 a day. Large sums of money were often sent as incentive to heal Europeans, but he asked his secretaries to return the cash and refused to bank the cheques, which remained pinned to a large calico sheet in his office to prove he took no bribes.

Critics out in force

Ratana's healing mission was obviously causing some discomfort for mainstream churches and traditional Māori leaders, judging by the sceptical letters and commentary starting to appear in the media. Some who attended his meetings said they had seen no cures. Reports of miracles were often secondhand, or described to journalists by Ratana's secretary, Pita Moko, a former boxing champion, reputed to be the godson of Te Kooti. It is said many of his followers were refusing to visit doctors, and even the famous cure by letter of Fannie Lammas was alleged by some critics to have been 'through auto-suggestion'. Ratana did not publicly defend his healing methods until 1925, when he insisted he had never instructed anyone to avoid medical help or stop taking their medicine.

Ratana's spokesperson, secretary, world-tour organiser and unsuccessful political candidate, Pita Moko. After over a decade of service Moko had a falling out with his leader, calling Ratana a hypocrite when he took a second wife. *Uri Whakatupuranga (Ratana Archives)*.

What I said plainly to them time after time was that, if the Divine Light of the Trinity and Their Faithful Angels is in them, and trusted by them, they shall receive the providence of God; but if the light disappears from them (through their own weakness) by all means go to a doctor remembering the while, the presence of the Holy Trinity and Their Faithful Angels, because not by man are cures effected, but by the will and power of God.

Accounts of the events at Ratana Pā and the healing rallies around the country were increasingly sensationalised or ridiculed in the media. Some respected Māori academics tried to dismiss Ratana as a modern-day tohunga, despite his obvious efforts to turn the people away from such influences. There was opposition to his call for a pan-tribal Māori movement representing the people at all levels of government. Among those who defended Ratana in print were superintendent of the Anglican Māori mission, the Reverend W. G. Williams, as well as Arthur F. Williams, who claimed that Ratana preached a simple biblical faith, and that his revivalism and work against tohungaism were invaluable.

Although Ratana had received more than 70,000 letters from New Zealand and other countries, he was concerned at the frequent antagonistic public criticism of his activities. From late 1921 he would no longer treat Europeans personally or allow journalists to photograph or interview him. They would have to settle for Pita Moko. However, a public notice in many newspapers only served to make people more curious:

RATANA
This is to notify our Pakeha friends of the Dominion of New Zealand and of the other Isles that you are absolutely barred from approaching our Brother, T. W. Ratana at present until the Maoris have been treated – The Union of the Maori Race.

Meanwhile the 39 acres belonging to the Ratana family was rapidly morphing into a permanent settlement for around 300 people. It had its own dirt roads and shops, and while buildings continued to be transported from other villages, the bulk of residents lived in basic shacks. There was no plumbing or drainage, and the only water supply was through a hand pump sunk down into a large well. The new community began to evolve its own culture. Football, kapa haka, poi and dancing teams were organised; choirs, cultural groups and bands regularly rehearsed and played at functions and fundraising events, and soon they had their own distinctive uniforms.

A building programme had been underway to improve the basic facilities in preparation for the onslaught of guests expected to attend the 1921 Christmas celebrations. There were now four large meeting houses, and a double-gabled cooking and dining facility known as Ki Kopu. During the evenings, dances and fundraising events were staged there. Piki Te Kaha at night was a sleeping facility for visitors; by day it was a venue where young people were taught taiaha, patu and Māori martial arts along with the 'positive side' of Māori culture. Te Aroha was also used as a sleeping facility, a band practice room and a schoolroom for the children. Political meetings and discussions on the welfare of the Māori people were held in the building known as Rangimarie (heavenly peace). Te Whare Marama was used as a hospital to care for the sick and elderly, with up to 40 beds attended by trained nurses or āwhina (sisters of mercy).

Ratana declared the 80 children living at the pā must be educated properly, so they began using a hall as a whare kura (schoolhouse) with benches, blackboards and a copy of *The Children's Encyclopaedia* for teaching. Instruction was in Māori, with successive headmasters arranging a syllabus of Christian doctrine, arithmetic, dictation, reading, English, writing, history, composition and poetry, and Māori spelling, pronunciation and grammar.

FIVE

DOCTRINES OF DIVISION

Seventh Day Adventists on Saturday were followed by Anglicans and Presbyterians and Methodists who held a combined service. They were followed by Mormons, Ringatu and Pai Marire prayer leaders, Baptists, Russellites, Jehovah's Witnesses, Pentecostal Leaguers, Christian Scientists and Zionists and many others, each adding a new doctrine to the welter of ideas and revelations and interpretations of scripture which became the material of speculation and theological discussion on the Ratana marae.
— Jim McLeod Henderson, *Ratana: The Man, the Church, the Political Movement*, 1972

Between two books
The events emanating from Ratana Pā, while praised by many as a positive step for Māori, were increasingly challenged by the mainstream churches, which had difficulty reconciling Ratana's popularity, his healing powers and some of the theology that was allowed to develop.

Initially, Ratana had the support of most denominations. The gospel he preached was largely in line with traditional Christianity. Some of his followers were ordained Methodist or Anglican ministers, others were trained as lay readers, or were in line for leadership roles.

Despite the rise of itinerant healing ministries around the world there was still a tendency to dismiss healing as no longer available or relevant in such 'enlightened' times. The Reverend Joseph Kemp, founder of the Bible Training Institute of New Zealand, who had arrived from Edinburgh in 1920 to pastor the Auckland Baptist Tabernacle, was so impressed with Ratana he warned against the trend to dismiss the supernatural.

T. W. Ratana travelled extensively during 1920 and 1921 preaching the Christian gospel, offering practical health guidelines, healing people from their physical illnesses and looking at ways to address their 'land sickness'. *Uri Whakatupuranga (Ratana Archives)*.

In recent years there has been a significant revival of the ministry of healing in the Church throughout the world and we cannot ignore a problem in which the mass of men are so vitally interested. Moreover a careful study of the New Testament would lead us back to believe that not only did our Lord and Saviour himself heal the sick but he taught his disciples to heal; and never was divine healing doubted until zeal to overthrow what was called 'the Faith Cure Delusion' led to rash attempts to prove the permanent passing of all supernatural signs. At the present moment there is a quickened interest in the teachings the Christ still fulfils in Christian experience [through] his powers to give life and give it more abundantly . . . His presence is capable of creating a heightened vitality of Spirit which strengthens and sustains the life of the body.

At the annual conference of the Methodist Church in Wellington in March 1920, Reverend Robert Haddon had likened Ratana's work of healing to that of the apostles. It began with a period of seclusion and fasting during which 'the new power came to him, and immediately by prayer and laying-on of hands' he cured a sick child. 'His teaching was out-and-out Christianity. He opposes all that injures the Maori – tohungaism, drink and other vices.' Haddon said Ratana did not claim to be a god; he was merely a man, a finger pointing people to God their Creator, and Christ their Saviour.

Ratana and his party stayed at the Waipapa Hostel in Auckland during their 1922 North Island tour. The Māori hostel between present-day Parnell and the old Auckland railway station was the site of the original Parliament buildings when Auckland was for a short time the capital of New Zealand. The photo was taken in September 1922 by caretaker Mrs Ghent. *Uri Whakatupuranga (Ratana Archives).*

Salvation Army officer Lieutenant-Colonel Carmichael visited Ratana and made an attempt to assess his work. In his booklet *Ratana the Healer* (1921), he declared there were important lessons to be learned from the ministry of Ratana: 'Simplicity of faith in God was something that would bring the Maori people back to the faith of their fathers, to accept the word of God as a reality, and to accept the promises of God literally, and believe in God for the saving of souls and the healing of bodies also.'

In an article in the *Greymouth Evening Star*, Carmichael listed some of the more outstanding cures: 'A child's sight restored, a woman suffering from a paralytic stroke, a Maori boy from New Plymouth badly deformed and walking on crutches, a boy from Hawera suffering from infantile paralysis.'

Ratana's āpotoro had been travelling to different tribal areas bringing the good news of the healing ministry and the message of unity, and ākonga – students or those training to be apostles – were selected to help them. During 1921 about 19,000 Māori had signed Ratana's covenant asserting they would believe in the Father, Son and Holy Ghost and the Faithful Angels, and forsake all superstitions and belief in tohunga. The covenant remained open during the Christmas hui with new signatures added daily.

It was clear a new religious movement was on the rise, but there had been no attempts to formalise this – even though Ratana Pā had its own church building and enthusiastic mōrehu had already built churches at Te Kumi (north of Te

Kūiti), and near Helensville. While those residing permanently at Ratana Pā had a strong desire to have their own church movement, and frequently discussed this when Ratana was away on tour, Ratana himself continued to insist they remain with their own churches.

Doctrinal divisions

The Ratana Pā mission church, Piki Te Ora, was open to all denominations. Inside there were pictures of the crucifixion and a large image of Christ. While vestments were not worn by the clergy, services were typically held in the Māori language using a form similar to the Anglican evensong. Ministers from the different denominations urged followers of Ratana to 'seek the light'. During the Christmas 1921 celebrations, Canon Wilfred Williams, who supervised Anglican mission work between Wanganui and Wellington, celebrated the Eucharist for around 300 communicants, and open discussion on religious issues was encouraged.

According to Jim McLeod Henderson:

> Seventh Day Adventists on Saturday were followed by Anglicans and Presbyterians and Methodists who held a combined service. They were followed by Mormons, Ringatu and Pai Marire prayer leaders, Baptists, Russellites, Jehovah's Witnesses, Pentecostal Leaguers, Christian Scientists and Zionists and many others, each adding a new doctrine to the welter of ideas and revelations and interpretations of scripture which became the material of speculation and theological discussion on the Ratana marae.

The Church of England, initially believing Ratana's healing ministry aligned with its own goals, had provided staff to help with Sunday School and services at the Pā. The Venerable H. W. Williams and his nephew, the Canon Wilfred Williams, after interviewing Ratana for two and a half hours, had concluded his doctrine was sound, and his approach based largely on the *Book of Common Prayer* and the *Methodist Hymnal*. The Anglican hierarchy, however, had become less comfortable as growing numbers from its own Māori flock were drawn into the Ratana camp, and as the talk of questionable theology grew.

The Roman Catholic Church, after expressing concerns about the doctrine of the 'the holy angels and the faithful angels' and claims that theological issues were being decided by vote, was the first to officially withdraw support. The recalling of Reverend Piri Munro by the Anglican Bishop during Ratana's 1921 South Island tour was further evidence of growing opposition.

However Munro said he never saw the slightest hint of 'Maoriism', a term used to describe faith in the old gods of paganism. 'I think Ratana is being used to free the native mind from the influence of Maoriism or tohungaism and his gift of healing is only given to impress the people.' Munro had first-hand experience of the old ways. His own great-grandfather was 'one of the last of the high priests and oracles of Maori paganism' that had been passed to him until his conversion to Christianity.

> It is often disheartening to see native boys and girls, after receiving a good education and being well placed in the world, suddenly go wrong and make a mess of the whole thing. Their failure must be attributed to the Maori mind which some time or other takes charge of the psychological position and diverts the steps. We Maori clergy have failed to overcome the handicap of the Maori mind, but Ratana has been raised up by God to do so.

While Ratana gave all the glory to God, some of his followers were placing him on a pedestal – which wasn't helped by his own description of himself as Māngai (a mouthpiece of God). The inclusion of the Anahera Pono (faithful or holy angels) in prayers and on the flags and banners alongside the Holy Trinity was further evidence to some of his detractors that he was taking his people back into polytheism.

Through a misreading of the biblical record that Christ's return would be a 'coming in the clouds' (Matthew 24:30–31, 26:64), some came to believe that this referred to events of 8 November 1918 when Ratana experienced his first encounter as a cloud came towards him from the ocean. Some used scriptural references to support the use of the term Māngai, including Luke 21 where Jesus tells his followers: 'For I will give you a mouth and such utterance and wisdom that all your enemies combined will be unable to stand against or refute'. While the scriptures themselves make it plain this referred to the presence of 'the Comforter' or the Holy Spirit following Christ's death and resurrection, some took this as a direct reference to Ratana.

The term Māngai had been used by a number of Māori prophets when they were inspired by a force outside themselves. An inspired revelation from the lips of a prophet, or from one believer to another, is often described as 'a word' (he kupu). Ratana saw himself as a voice Ihoa could use; when the Spirit of God sought expression he was the physical body through which the message could be broadcast to the world.

Māngai, as adopted by Ratana, meant in its simplest form 'the giver of words'. It is also seen as his way of bridging the old, traditional Māori worship of Io (said by some to be Ihoa or Jehovah), the supreme God – unapproachable except through tohunga and the highest-ranking chiefs – and the European understanding of the Creator, who could be approached directly through Tama, the Son or Jesus the Christ.

Ratana's reasons for including the angels in prayers and referring to them so

There were concerns that the angelic hosts were being given too much reverence – stories of strange lights appearing around Ratana Pā and the angel in the graveyard shedding tears when money was placed in its hands didn't help. The angel tears in this photo, however, are simply evidence that it had been raining. *Newman Collection, 1986.*

often were complex. It was through angelic visitation that his original encounter at the old farmhouse was confirmed, and in his subsequent testing and trials angels provided guidance and conveyed messages from Ihoa. The angels were never considered equal to, or part of, the Holy Trinity; just members of the extended divine family. Ratana had made a clear distinction between the fallen angels (those opposed to the divine plan), and the faithful and holy angels, whose role was to facilitate the climax of the old age and help usher in the new.

He had often quoted Bible stories where angels ministered between God and man and protected believers in times of trouble, and he assured his people – when they feared his mana (influence/authority) would disappear as he moved into outlying tribal areas – that he would also be protected by the angels. As a result, the mōrehu sought to honour Ihoa's messengers and thank them for their work in watching over them.

Ratana believed he was proclaiming what had already been foretold by Christ: the time of the end when the angels would come from heaven and pour out judgements on the wicked, the greedy, the corrupt and those who damaged the earth. Among Ratana's main reference points was the Book of Revelation; he often spoke of the angels placing a seal on the faithful as protection against the troubled times ahead (Revelation 7:4 and 14.1–5).

Political eyebrows raised

As Ratana travelled tirelessly to almost every marae around the country, he saw first-hand the plight of his people, and became convinced of an urgent need for social and political reforms alongside spiritual awakening. He engaged in strenuous debate over the issues facing each tribe, asking them to tell the story of how they had lost their lands and in the process gathered letters, sworn statements, photographs and maps.

Through his connections with prominent politicians, Ratana believed he had struck an agreement with the government to establish a Treaty Commission to look into the various claims. Many Māori leaders had attempted to address land grievances with the government, even travelling to England to appeal to the Crown. Their pleas had been rejected, and now the question was being asked, was Ratana the one to deliver the people from te māuiui o te oneone (land sickness) and restore their mana motuhake.

Apart from the so-called theological deviations, and the threat Ratana posed to Māori attendance at mainstream churches, political eyebrows were now being raised. The potent mix of religion and politics brewing among his followers brought resentment from those who felt their own goals threatened, including existing Māori members of Parliament.

The Reverend A. J. Seamer, however, could see that the bigger picture had biblical parallels. 'One can no more separate the religion and politics of the folk who flocked to Ratana, than one can the politics and religion of the Israelites in the days of the Judges prior to Saul.'

Ratana had set aside 6 February as a special day to reflect on the Treaty of Waitangi. To the mōrehu, the treaty had given the Crown absolute right to govern or rule the Māori people, in return for certain undertakings:

1. Māori would reserve the right to fish and hunt as in the past;
2. Māori would be permitted to govern themselves in certain circumstances;
3. Māori would have equal rights with the Pākehā, and the Crown would do all in its power to protect those rights.

It seemed logical to many around the country that Ratana's growing influence could be put to good use in the political arena. In April 1922, a meeting of over 3000 Māori asked him to accept nomination or nominate candidates for the various parliamentary seats. He insisted that his movement wasn't political, and that voters should follow their conscience; although several followers did put themselves forward as independent candidates that year.

In his bid to remove the obstacles to Māori unity, Ratana continued to believe in an accord with the King movement in the Waikato. With the backing of this influential body he would be assured of gaining the government's full attention

Haami Tokouru Ratana stood as a Ratana Independent against longstanding Waikato-backed candidate Maui Pomare in 1923, winning a surprisingly high percentage of the vote. *Uri Whakatupuranga (Ratana Archives).*

to deal with outstanding treaty issues for all Māori. However, Te Puea Herangi – who had revived the King movement and re-established its base at Ngāruawāhia after the First World War and the death of her grandfather King Tawhiao – was highly protective of King Te Rata.

She didn't want any connection with Ratana, and was offended that senior members of the movement – including Tupu Taingakawa, Reweti Te Whena, and the only surviving son of King Tawhiao, Haunui Tawhiao – had defected to Ratana. It was no surprise, then, that Te Rata wouldn't sign Ratana's covenant. Prominent Māori statesmen Maui Pomare and Apirana Ngata also refused to back his call for a united Māoridom.

The rift deepened in October 1922 when Ratana travelled with 300 of his followers to the king's marae at Waahi Pā, near Huntly, leaving the speaking to Pita Moko, who failed to address the king in the appropriate manner and ignored other protocols. This offended Te Rata, who was at the head of his people with his elders. While the visitors were given hospitality for the night, the king left his home quietly without speaking to Ratana, believing his mana had been undermined. Ratana was also offended and allowed his eldest son, Haami Tokouru, to stand against Waikato-backed Pomare in the Western Māori seat as an Independent Ratana candidate, polling 3037 votes, proving he could flex political muscle if needed.

During 1922 Ratana continued his healing activity, visiting marae and locations important to Māori history and prophecy, adding signatures to his petition

The Marsden cross erected at Oihi Bay in the Bay of Islands where the first sermon was preached by Samuel Marsden on Christmas Day 1814, beginning 'Behold, I bring you glad tidings of great joy', the angelic message which had heralded the birth of Christ. The original cross, that was severely damaged by a storm in 1918, was eventually moved to Matauri Bay.
Newman Collection, 2007.

and urging people to put aside tribal barriers and work together to have the treaty legally recognised.

While in the Bay of Islands he visited Oihi Bay. Standing at the foot of the stone Celtic cross marking the spot where Samuel Marsden had preached the first sermon on Christmas Day 1814, Ratana saw a portion had been broken off. He knelt among the weeds at the foot of the monument, and found the missing piece. He claimed the mauri (life force or spirit) of Marsden's first prayers and sermons, and that piece of the cross found its way back to Ratana Pā where it is today secured in front of the Arepa tower at the entrance to the Ratana Temple.

He also visited the memorial stone at Te Tii Marae at Waitangi where Aperahama Taonui had, in 1881, attempted a re-enactment of the Treaty of Waitangi signing and made his famous prophecy:

> Oh Chiefs of Ngapuhi, do not cover your taonga the Treaty of Waitangi with the flag of England, but rather, you must cover it with your own cloak, the cloak of this nation . . . because you have chosen not to take heed, this House

will become inhabited by spiders and cobwebs . . . There is a child coming who will bear in his right hand the Holy Bible, and in his left hand the Treaty of Waitangi, listen to him.

Ratana researcher Ruia Aperahama says the majority of the United Confederation of Tribes – the first to sign the treaty – originated from the 'House of Ngapuhi' and the Ngapuhi Federation, and were divided in their support for the Crown. Taonui, an active member of both factions, signed the treaty under the name Tautoro, but believed there was still an opportunity for a pan-tribal Māori parliament including a Māori variation of the Christian church as an alternative to the Westminster system of governance and its strong Church of England links. He warned both houses that there would be problems if a strong Māori body didn't watch over post-treaty events.

Taonui was involved in the opening of the meeting house at Te Tii, Waitangi, in March 1881. A monument bearing the Māori text of the treaty was to be covered with a Māori cloak then a Union Jack, and unveiled by Governor-General Arthur Gordon. He planned this ceremony as a statement of unity between Pākehā and Māori, and drew up a proposal from the north for a separate Māori parliament, which was to be presented at the meeting. However, Gordon did not attend, the Māori parliament movement failed to gain European sympathy and Taonui – already ostracised by his own people and ridiculed for his claim to be 'the younger brother of Christ' – died the following year.

While at Waitangi, it is claimed, Ratana sent several members of his party to examine the old Treaty House, the original Busby residence erected in 1833–34. The building was in great disrepair. When they finally prised the door open, the interior was found to be thick with cobwebs. The Ratana group, so the oral tradition goes, cleaned out the building, but in the back of their minds was the memory of the prophecy made about a spider inhabiting the house where the treaty had lain.

Taking it to the top

Ratana's efforts to record the stories of how various tribes had lost their land resulted in 34,000 signatures – an incredible number considering the total Māori population at the time was only around 57,000.

Despite the overwhelming desire of the people to have the Treaty of Waitangi honoured, the government, including its Māori members, ignored the petition. The Native Department, responsible for listening to the voice of Māoridom, retained its hostile attitude towards Ratana. A more direct approach was needed. Ratana would take the petition and copies of the Māori version of the treaty, along with reams of supporting documentation, to England. He would present it to King George, asking him to intervene and put things right.

Several Māori leaders had appealed to the government and even gone to England to try and get a hearing for their land grievances. King Te Rata (left), Tupu Taingakawa (seated), Mita Karaka and Hori Tirau Paora, representing the Kīngitanga, were referred back to the New Zealand Government when they sought a meeting with King George V in London in 1914 to try and halt further land being seized. *Uri Whakatupuranga (Ratana Archives).*

The Ratana movement was growing in size and complexity, and it was agreed that a new organisational structure was necessary to co-ordinate the efforts of various committees around the country, share the workload and maintain focus. The Kotahitanga Council was established at Ratana Pā before the impending first world tour in April 1924.

The council would take responsibility for farming the land at Ratana, investigate land claims and take care of health, education and fundraising. Also established were a number of sports, cultural, educational and musical groups and committees. Ratana was attempting to shift the focus from himself and give more responsibility to those who would act wisely on behalf of the growing Ratana community and, ultimately, all Māoridom.

However, one of the society's first decisions was possibly its worst. It determined to create an investment society known as the Bank of the Kotahitanga, or the Savings Bank of the United Maori Welfare League of the Northern, Southern and Chatham Islands. It claimed it could raise £37 million for the 'advancement and good of the people'. The grand mission statement indicated it would, through encouraging people to save and spend wisely, be able to assist farmers and landowners, help with marae and building improvements, lend money to those wishing to purchase land for farming, help those facing financial difficulties (including widows and orphans), equip the movement's children for the future, and help people repay mortgages.

Ratana was surprised that things had so quickly become focused on finance. He warned the council that it did not fully understand its own 'power and authority or jurisdiction' or the full impact of what it was proposing. After Christmas 1923 he remained troubled at the plans to enter the banking industry, telling the organisers they would ultimately be held responsible for the downfall of the 'treasures' they had charge over.

> Today, I see you have sold me. For four years now I have carried the burdens of the people, and of this whole land, and now it seems the work I have done may come to nothing. This is me, my body standing here, my work, my hopes . . . gone. This is because you choose to seek after silver and gold. I tell you, although just one of you chooses to go this way, you will all end up being guilty. This is what bothers me at this time. Know this, maybe I am only a mere human being but my work is aimed at building treasures in heaven.

There was great excitement at the Christmas gathering and much work to tie up the loose ends for the ambitious plan to visit 'the United Kingdom, France, the United States of America and Japan'. The 'world tour' would attend the Empire Exhibition in London and ultimately present the Treaty of Waitangi petition, including signatures from two-thirds of Māori, to King George V.

In the touring party would be Ratana's wife Te Whaea and children Tokouru, Matiu, Arepa, Omeka, Piki and Maata, along with two performing troupes of twelve young people. A small administrative team would join them, along with a group of elders, including the main organiser and spokesman Pita Moko, the prime minister of the Kīngitanga Māori Parliament Tupu Taingakawa, another senior King movement representative Reweti Te Whena, and Ratana's friend and business adviser Pepene Eketone, who would act as Māori interpreter.

The first issue of the Ratana newspaper, *Te Whetu Marama o Te Kotahitanga* appeared on 15 March 1924 with enthusiastic coverage of Ratana's 'world tour' plans and the formation of the Kotahitanga Bank. Meanwhile, the relatively straightforward arrangements to gain official approval for the Ratana troupe to leave the country were complicated by government fears about Ratana's motives. The formal application 'to leave for England to view the exhibition' was referred to Cabinet. The Honourable J. G. Coates laid out stringent conditions, requiring sufficient funds (£1600) be deposited with the Internal

Affairs Department for return fares and accommodation in England. Cabinet delayed any decision until the last minute. Even after Ratana asked two sitting members of Parliament to try and speed things up as time was running out, he was told again passports would not be issued unless the deposit was made.

The amount was eventually dropped to £1000 and payment made. On 4 April, less than a week before they were to depart, Pita Moko, in announcing the passports had finally been released, complained this was the first Māori party to travel overseas that had been hobbled by such conditions. He blamed the delays on certain 'political natives' who sought to undermine Ratana's plans. Then Dr Peter Buck (Te Rangi Hiroa), at the direction of Sir Maui Pomare, the Minister of Health, turned up at Ratana Pā to vaccinate the people and give them a health check. While some claim this was a further stalling tactic, Pomare insisted he was helping the troupe after learning some members were afflicted with hakihaki (itch).

Meanwhile, Ratana and his family visited Mount Taranaki, and beside Te Rere o Kapuni (Dawson Falls), the waterfall of the prophets, he sensed a voice repeating the words of the prophet Titokowaru: 'Ahakoa iti taku iti ka tu ahau ki te aroaro o nga iwi nunui o te ao. Even though I be but a small tiny nation, I shall stand before the presence of the world's great nations.' They moved on to the Parihaka settlement, once the largest Māori village in the country, where the prophet Te Whiti had conducted his peaceful resistance against the government land grab in the late 1870s.

There the villagers had been encouraged to peaceful resistance, by continuing to farm land being confiscated by the government. On 5 November 1881 around 2000 people sat quietly on the marae as a group of singing children greeted an army of 1500 militia and armed constabulary. The Riot Act was read and an hour later the leaders, Te Whiti o Rongomai and Tohu Kakahi, were arrested and led away. The village was demolished, and in the following months crops were destroyed, livestock killed and people from other tribal regions forced to leave the province.

As Ratana recalled the events of only three decades earlier he was deeply moved. It was near midnight on 18 March, the anniversary of the return to the village by Te Whiti after his release from prison in 1883. The celebrations had died down, and as Ratana looked around he saw an old woman standing by her house. He approached and asked what she was thinking. 'My boy,' she said, 'I am reminiscing upon the prophecy that Whiti and Tohu left behind, "Not until this village, Parihaka, has been reclaimed by the bush and overgrown and not until one surviving old woman is left within this village, that a young child shall come and lift this old woman bearing her into the new revelations of Jehovah, the Living God".'

Ratana's visit to the waterfall and his encounter with the old woman at the historic village gave him strength and confirmed his plans. He believed Te Whiti and Tohu had foretold the day when he would take his spiritual message to the wider world. As a symbol of his conviction he took with him a bottle of water from Te Rere o Kapuni.

Ratana had asked successive governments whether the treaty was dead, and, while the official answer had been unsatisfactory, he believed Ihoa had shown him it was still alive. He would take his mandate directly from the people of the land. He was convinced that the petition, representing strong support from Māori across all tribes in the nation, was the root of a tree that would bear much fruit. 'I tell you this tree is beginning to bloom, soon to bear fruit, but don't shake it, lest those fruits fall to the ground.'

The interior of the Whare Mauri. *William Hall-Raines, Alexander Turnbull Library, Wellington.*

For many years the curious could enter Whare Herehere or the 'Devil House' or peer through the bars on a small window and see the evidence of the amazing healings that had taken place at Ratana Pā. This was where the walking sticks, wheelchairs, crutches and glasses from those who had been healed were kept, and a safe place (or prison) for once-tapu stones, statues, carvings, taiaha and other items, once Ratana had lifted mākutu, or curses, placed by tohunga. This was the only building at Ratana Pā that had traditional Māori carvings. Many items were restored in the 1980s, although some books, papers and other items were unable to be saved from water damage. The building now remains locked. An inventory located in 2005 showed 40 taiaha, often carved and entwined with human hair, 74 pairs of crutches, 181 ornate walking or talking sticks, 50 pairs of spectacles, badges, pendants, medals and detailed whakapapa of 165 of the elders who stood with Ratana. Many important pieces of New Zealand history remain there including Te Kooti's Ringatū bells, Te Maiharoa's gun and sword gifted to Ratana and the large greenstone that was part of the curse at Ngā Tau e Waru meeting house in Masterton. *All images Ans Westra unless stated otherwise.*

SIX

ROYAL REJECTION

On this day I have led the morehu across the seas of the world (Te Whitinga o te Ao) to . . . see our father (King George V) and present to him the cries of his children for justice, as I stand at this door that is closed to us, you see before you an orphan, I have no home here.

—T. W. Ratana, London, 1924

I will stand upon the land of Japan and their government, and when I reach Japan I will reveal to them all hidden things [spiritual] and let the fire be set alight. The whole world will soon come to know of this war and will come to know the significance of your claims and cause.

—T. W. Ratana, on his way to Japan, 1924

War warnings escalate

Ever since the signing of the Treaty of Waitangi, Māori chiefs and pan-tribal groups had petitioned the government for a stronger voice in their own affairs, to have the 'sacred' document honoured and confiscated lands returned. They felt they had a right to appeal directly to the Crown as they had technically been granted 'the rights and privileges of British subjects'.

Although the United Confederation of Tribes, which had signed the Declaration of Independence in 1835, had been promised regular meetings with the government to address ongoing issues, this never eventuated. Lobbying for political representation for Māori continued to be rejected. Tamihana Te Rauparaha, who preached peace and reconciliation to many former enemies of his father, chief Te Rauparaha, was presented to Queen Victoria by Archdeacon

T. W. Ratana (centre) with 'world tour' band members, including his sons Arepa (at his left), Omeka (front right) and his whāngaied son Dan Reremoana (front left). *Uri Whakatupuranga (Ratana Archives).*

William Williams in 1852. This visit helped to convince him that Māori needed to have their own king to represent them in dealings with the Crown.

In 1866 Wiremu Tamihana's petition to Parliament to return confiscated lands was rejected, although Parliament did agree during that period to create four Māori seats. Previously, only men who owned property had been eligible to vote, and because Māori property was owned communally the land-holding requirement was dropped. Māori men won the right to vote in 1867, and they were able to exercise this the following year, fifteen years before European men who did not own property.

Frederick Nene Russell, Mete Kingi Te Rangi Paetahi, Tareha Te Moananui and John Paterson were the first Māori members of Parliament. Te Moananui was the first to speak, urging the government to enact wise laws to promote good, and for Māori and Pākehā to work together. The speech was in Māori, and an interpreter was arranged only at the last minute. This language difficulty meant many early attempts at representation were ineffective.

Having seen little evidence that the New Zealand Government was delivering on the promises made by the British, Māori had begun sending petitions and deputations directly to London, requesting that the Treaty of Waitangi be honoured. Hirini Taiwhanga travelled to England in 1882 representing Ngāpuhi, but failed to get an audience with Queen Victoria. King Tawhiao visited

England in 1884 with several other chiefs to petition the queen over the Treaty of Waitangi, but was refused access. He then put Māori grievances before the Secretary of State for Colonies, Lord Derby, to no avail.

Meanwhile, elders and chiefs continued to motivate the people and broker intertribal hui, or gatherings, where family and tribal connections could be strengthened and alliances forged. Discussions were held on how to uplift the people, restore their mana and celebrate their arts, crafts, music, and cultural and religious beliefs and systems. The Kotahitanga movement, which originated in the Bay of Islands, was determined to push for Māori unity and have the conditions of the treaty fulfilled. It attracted membership from throughout the North Island and began staging its own Māori Parliament meetings from 1892 to 1902. There was a strong following in the Wairarapa and Hawke's Bay.

Both the Kotahitanga movement and the Kīngitanga had gained widespread influence by the 1890s. However, Premier Richard Seddon remarked the Māori Parliament was really only a rūnanga (assembly, place of debate). There was 'only one parliament in New Zealand, and it would never give up control of the Maoris or their lands'.

In 1895, a national boycott of the Native Land Court by the Māori Parliament was defeated because Crown officials could always find someone to lodge an application for blocks that the Crown was interested in buying. After the boycott failed, the Kotahitanga movement lost much of its influence, until its membership and those in the King movement began to take guidance from a new breed of young leaders who had worked their way up through the European education system. The Young Māori Party, believing Māori should take the best from the European world and influence government from within, included Maui Pomare, Apirana Ngata and Te Rangi Hiroa (Peter Buck).

Pomare and Buck were both medical officers before ultimately entering Parliament, and Ngata had trained as a lawyer. They pursued a policy of social and religious reform, urging Māori to adopt the technology and practices of Western culture, including health and hygiene, literacy, farming and the 'Protestant work ethic'. They urged Māori to wean themselves off reliance on the tohunga and old customs.

From 1900 there was a shift to consultation and the creation of individual tribal policy. The Kingitanga Parliament continued to discuss land grievances, the Treaty of Waitangi, mana motuhake and competing claims for chiefly authority. In 1907, King Mahuta drafted a petition to King Edward asking that Māori be put on the same footing as Pākehā, and in 1914 King Te Rata and his party, including his uncle Tupu Taingakawa, visited England to seek an audience with King George V asking that the British Government intercede to stop further land being taken. Both were referred back to the New Zealand Government.

On behalf of the people

T. W. Ratana had publicly committed himself to a political programme for the first time in a speech at Ratana Pā during the Christmas hui of 1923; he would go to London and take with him the Bible and the Treaty of Waitangi, symbolic of the spiritual and social sides of his mission.

In the past he had turned down offers of up to £50,000 to go to England and America, believing he would lose his power if he accepted. Instead he began raising his own funds to take a core group of followers with him. He had told the people, 'You see my body standing here but my spirit is far away seeking your welfare . . . in Samoa and in England, and has reached the British Exhibition'. He hoped to shake hands with King George and lay New Zealand's foundational document before him. 'I will ask him, "This is the Treaty you have made. What do you think of it?" He will not be able to deny it.'

The touring group – including a well-rehearsed concert party of dancers, singers and musicians who would draw crowds and raise funds along the way – left Ratana Pā for Wellington on 9 April 1924. A local newspaper reported the party were taking with them many documents and exhibits to substantiate Ratana's claim to healing power. 'Among them is the steel frame worn by Miss Lammas of Nelson, before Ratana's intervention.' The party carried with them aboard the *Maheno* mere (clubs), greenstone ornaments, wood carving and taiaha, and about 150 kākahu (cloaks), incorporating kiwi, native pigeon, tui, kākā and weka feathers.

A fortnight later they steamed into Sydney. The *Sydney Sun* newspaper, under the heading 'Miracle Man – Ratana in Sydney', reported on their brief stopover.

> Tahu Wiremu Ratana looks more like a prosperous tradesman than a famous miracle man. Well built and plump, without being stout, he is good-looking, with a light brown complexion. Except for a light moustache, Ratana is clean shaven, and he looks about 40, although he is nearer 52. Unlike other faith healers, he travels without a blare of trumpets and there are never any bands to welcome him, not because there are not bands ready to do that, but because his movements are always kept something of a secret. Six years ago Ratana was a prosperous and well-to-do farmer. Always religiously inclined, he was a stout Presbyterian, and he seldom read anything but the Bible. His favourite passage was the 'healing doctrine' as explained in the ninth chapter of the Gospel of St Matthew, and so interested in it did he become that he started to practise it. Many cures were performed by the dusky faith-healer, and as church committee after church committee reported favourably on his work even the sceptical Pakeha was convinced . . . To Ratana's credit a number have been investigated and found to be existent. Several cured of blindness or partial

Above left: Ratana travelled around Durban and Capetown to see how the people lived, and he had his photo taken with a rickshaw driver on discovering he was a Zulu chief. He wanted to express his concern that a man of such high ranking was being treated like a slave. *Uri Whakatupuranga (Ratana Archives). Above right:* Ratana and his troupe were dismayed at the way black dock workers were treated and so arranged secretly to hold a picnic for them, prophesying that a time would come when they would take charge of their own country again. *Uri Whakatupuranga (Ratana Archives).*

paralysis were watched for a considerable period and after months there was no sign of relapse.

The journey continued aboard the P&O liner SS *Barrabool*. When the ship neared its berth in Capetown, South Africa, the Ratana troupe, looking through the portholes, saw 'thousands and thousands of feet . . . [and] thousands more slaves with baskets of coal'. Ratana was moved to compassion and asked if the black dock workers could board the ship under the pretence that they would be cleaning the quarters of his troupe. Instead he and his people cooked up a feast and spread it out before them. Ratana prayed, then prophesied a day was coming when the mighty hand of God would lift up and liberate this black nation. A time was coming, he said, when 'the head would become the tail and the tail would be the head':

> Listen carefully oh morehu and our children [touring party], I have seen and indeed witnessed these black-skinned people treated like dogs, I am hurt by

this. Yet it shall come to pass, that in Jehovah's time and place, he shall lift these people up . . .

Ratana believed his mission was not only to seek redress for Māori land confiscations, but to represent his country, show off the talents of his performing troupe, preach the gospel, and learn about other nations and peoples at every port of call. On arrival in England, Ratana also held a feast on board the ship for the black dock workers there.

WHETŪ MĀRAMA TOHU

In the early hours of the morning, as the SS *Barrabool* passed close to the Mediterranean Sea, Ratana woke the members of his troupe and called them onto the deck, pointing to a stunning crescent moon with a bright star between its edges shining out from the velvet backdrop of the night sky.

He explained this was the tohu (mark, sign or proof) that was guiding them on their journey, and was to be their emblem: 'This was the star that rose in the east and led the three wise men to witness the birth of Jesus Christ. We will follow this star like the wise men of old, as we make our way around the world.' Then he explained that the crescent moon with the star was symbolic of completion and would later signify the coming together of all people throughout the world. A full whakamoemiti, or prayer and worship service, was then conducted.

When they arrived in London, Ratana sent his secretary to a jeweller to have badges made with the four-pointed star and crescent moon. The topmost point of the star was blue (The Father), the right point was white (The Son), the left point red (Holy Spirit) and the lowest point purple (The Angels). The crescent moon was blue. Initially the whetū mārama had a ribbon with a cross in the middle and two ribbons attached below and was given to each of the 39 members of the 1924 world tour party. On their return a growing number of followers wanted to wear the symbol, and many created their own from the lids of old tobacco tins.

A second five-pointed star was introduced in 1925. It had a circle in the middle and the lower left point in pink. The colour pink, previously set aside as representing humanity, was adopted by Ratana himself. It was seen particularly in reference to his role as Piri Wiri Tua, 'the campaigner' in his efforts to bring the Treaty of Waitangi into law. This is the emblem worn by Ratana followers today.

Sidelined at exhibition

When they reached London, Tupu Taingakawa made contact with Barclays, the firm of lawyers he had contacted during his visits to England in 1884 when he had come with King Tawhiao and in 1914 with King Te Rata. Old man Barclay had since passed away, but partners A. Peacock, a Mr Goddard and Walter Andrew were contracted for the sum of £500 to prepare the claims to be presented to the British Parliament, to Premier Ramsay McDonald and to King George V or his son Edward, the Prince of Wales.

Ratana and his party were early arrivals at the Empire Exhibition and immediately became disturbed at the way Māori culture was being portrayed, in particular the dilapidated meeting house at the New Zealand Pavilion, which had originally been presented to Queen Victoria, and pulled out of storage after nearly 50 years.

Pita Moko described it as a disgrace. While the carving was intact, and a good example of Māori craftsmanship, the panelling was 'an eyesore' and all European. As for the mats, he would not have them on his own doorstep. He maintained that if the authorities intended to represent Māori, they should have made a display that was creditable to the race. 'We were the only coloured race under the British flag that did not have proper representation at the exhibition.' He found that coldness strange, 'seeing that the Maori boys had proved themselves as such good fellows during the wartime at home and were respected'. In comparison with the Burma hut, he said, the display suggested that Māori were 'low down in the scale of native races'.

According to Ratana apostle Kereama Pene, on seeing the state of the meeting house and the Māori exhibits, Ratana quickly took control.

> He and his troupe set about designing and rebuilding the stage. The troupe plaited, weaved, painted and redid the whole meeting house exhibition. Later the party, which included some of New Zealand's top cultural musicians and performers, delivered a presentation on their own set. Prior to this most people had no idea about the Maori people. They had only seen those who had made their way to England virtually as slaves or kitchen help.

The news reached New Zealand via telegraph on 22 May that the royal party had visited the New Zealand Pavilion at the Empire Exhibition, including the Māori House.

> Major Dansey explained the house carvings. King George V had remarked, 'I have a great admiration for the Maori; they are a most courageous race.' The whole party was photographed outside the house. They then entered the magnificent rimu panelled reception room of the New Zealand Pavilion where they signed the visitor's book and the Queen was presented with a New Zealand rug.

T. W. Ratana and his wife Te Whaea (centre) with members of the combined band that toured with them to the UK and Japan. *Tirikatene-Sullivan Collection.*

Ratana and Te Whaea with the 1924 world tour girls' band.
Uri Whakatupuranga (Ratana Archives).

While the New Zealand Government decided to leverage the fact that the Ratana troupe were at the exhibition, their recognition came far too late. At the request of Sir James Allen, the party were issued tickets and asked to give 'an entertainment'. They kept the tickets and paid their own expenses in protest at the way they had been treated. At the exhibition Ratana's wife, Te Urumanao, and their two daughters Piki and Maata, along with Pepene Eketone, Pita

Moko and another member of the party were presented to Princess Helena Victoria. The princess was given a New Zealand travelling rug by Mrs Ratana. Mr Eketone presented a piupiu (dancer's kilt) to Lady Allen, which was to be shown in the Māori House until the end of the exhibition.

Ratana's thoughts on the exhibition reached Whanganui a few days later via telegraph and appeared in a local paper, revealing the party had been treated in a very off-hand manner and while many coloured races were represented at the exhibition at Wembley, 'even the Zulus had their fares paid'.

Second war foreseen

On 17 May 1924 the party crossed Westminster Bridge. Ratana stopped in the middle and began to prophesy: 'As I stand on this bridge and look all around me, I tell you all, the Angel of Death will visit this place, not a stone shall stand upon a stone and the inhabitants of these houses will live under the ground.'

Witnesses from the world tour group reported that he also said: 'When all your castles [stone houses] are destroyed in time to come, then will the carpenters, the blacksmiths and the shoemakers be in power, and I will be the government.' The reference to blacksmiths and shoemakers borrows from a statement made by Tawhiao: 'My friends are the shoemaker, the blacksmith, the watchmaker, the carpenters, orphans and widows . . .'

There is also a reference to a similar statement made when Ratana was speaking to members of his group as they looked out the window of their accommodation: 'Do you all see these stone buildings [castles, churches] standing here? The time is coming when they shall be toppled and brought down, where stone shall never lie upon stone.' Some say in describing the destruction of the stone buildings and referring to Tawhiao's prophecy, Ratana foresaw both the Luftwaffe bombing of London, which reduced the buildings around Westminster to rubble, and the subsequent election of Labour governments in both England and New Zealand.

They saw many poor people in Britain. Conditions seemed to be worse in France and Belgium, while people in Germany appeared prosperous and well fed. Ratana's party was generally well received, with people from every country 'marvelling at him and his party, his sincerity, wisdom and the miraculous healings he performed on the sick and infirm'.

However, the enormity of their task ahead was beginning to take a toll. Ratana and his group, staying at an RSA hall and a hotel near Hyde Park, were beginning to feel the financial pressure and their first two concerts in London were poorly attended. Ratana and Pita Moko, after dealing with concert arrangements, travel plans and answering bags full of correspondence from all over the globe, often collapsed through exhaustion in the early hours of the morning.

Ratana's daughters, Maata and Piki Te Ora, in London wearing kiwi feather cloaks and wielding greenstone mere, in front of the Ratana banner.
Uri Whakatupuranga (Ratana Archives).

All the while, at the forefront of Ratana's mind was his goal of achieving an audience with King George V and Prime Minister Stanley Baldwin, who was in France at the time. There had been no response from the lawyers who were attempting to arrange those meetings, and calls seeking an update seemed to be fobbed off. Meanwhile Moko visited the Japanese Embassy to discuss plans for the return leg of the tour. He also arranged with New Zealand High Commissioner, Sir James Allen, for twelve elders from the Ratana party to meet with Lord Terrington, Lord Arnold, secretary to the House of Lords, and Lord Denham to discuss business arrangements for patent rights owned by members of the party, including one for warning lights on vehicles and another for safer railway crossings.

However, it soon became clear that Sir James Allen was actively undermining support for the Ratana contingent. Apparently, Governor-General Viscount Jellicoe had sent a confidential telegram to the British secretary of state, warning him the Ratana group 'had no representative capacity and should not be encouraged or received by the Government or any Royal personage'. Ratana was furious. He felt betrayed and was overcome by a sense of failure:

> On this day I have led the morehu across the seas of the world (Te Whitinga o te Ao) to . . . see our father (King George V) and present to him the cries of his children for justice, as I stand at this door that is closed to us, you see before you an orphan, I have no home here.

Then a door opened. Tupu Taingakawa was invited to attend the League of Mercy Garden Party on 22 July at St James Palace, hosted by Prince Edward, the Prince of Wales. Tupu, Reweti Te Whena and Tokouru Ratana would attend the event with their lawyer, and present a letter that Ratana had drawn up, along with important symbolic gifts. The letter carefully stated that the prince's lineage back to his great-grandmother Queen Victoria, who had endorsed the declaration of Māori independence (after her predecessor William IV) and the Treaty of Waitangi. The letter also introduced the prince to the 'Chiefs of Maori Tribes of New Zealand, who are on a mission to the Government of England'.

The 'chiefly gentlemen' from New Zealand, accompanied by their lawyer Walter Andrew Esquire, were escorted to a tent at St James Palace and introduced to 'nobles, royalty and gentry'. About 4 p.m. the Prince of Wales made an appearance, and as a line formed, Tupu led the party with their gifts and letter in hand. The prince spoke:

> Kia Ora . . . Arohanui . . . I am pleased to see you again, Tupu, as do I all of you. Indeed when I saw you all in your traditional attire, I was reminded of my Maori people of New Zealand. I know you well, Tupu, since I first saw you (Tupu) and you (Reweti) in Rotorua, but for you (Tokouru) perhaps a first time acquaintance. Yes, indeed, I heard that you had arrived here in London, and I so much wished to meet with you again.

Tupu and Reweti presented the Māori cloaks and gifts first. The prince appeared 'pleased and grateful'. Tokouru presented the letter, which was almost intercepted by the prince's secretary Sir Godfrey Thomas, but Andrew persisted on behalf of his clients, stuffing the letter into the prince's pocket. The gifts were quickly taken to his private chambers. Following this the three 'chiefs' were introduced to Queen Victoria's daughter, Princess Louise, Duchess of Argyll.

After a prolonged wait for a response from the prince and the British Government, a letter was sent to their lawyers demanding to know why everything was taking so long. Andrew seemed affronted, claiming progress was being made, but more time was needed along with another $1000 to finance their case for the next sitting of Parliament. Ratana said this was unacceptable. Their finances were already thin, they were living in cramped conditions and tensions were growing between troupe members.

Then, on 7 August, they received a letter from Sir James Allen advising that the cloaks and letter given to Prince Edward would be 'returned at once'. This was seen as a further mark of disrespect. During the evening prayer meeting, Ratana held up a £10 note and set it alight with a match, prophesying the fall of the monarchy and saying the end of Britain's holy covenant with God was drawing near.

Attempts to gain an interview with the Minister of the Colonies, Mr Thomas, were politely rejected. Andrew sought an explanation as to why the party, which had travelled 15,000 miles for this meeting, 'should be denied a privilege granted so many other Colonial Deputations and Visitors'. The response came: 'any representation which members of the Maori race desire to make with regard to their affairs should be made not to His Majesty's Government but to the Government and Parliament of New Zealand in which the Maoris are directly and specially represented.'

Then it was learned that the bureaucratic response: 'unless forwarded through the usual channels and recommended by the Government of New Zealand', rejecting the gifts given to the Prince of Wales, had come from the prince's own representative. It was now painfully clear; the New Zealand Government, the British Government and the Crown were all refusing to deal with the Māori claims. While the London law firm run by lords Terrington and Thomas was interested in acquiring the patents owned by members of the party, Ratana now withdrew the offer. If the British Government wouldn't do business with him he wasn't about to have business dealings with it, or its Lords.

His mission was falling apart, the promises he had made to the troupe and the people back home were in tatters, and important decisions had to be made. There was discussion about sending half the team home, joining with other performing groups to reduce the costs, or splitting up and doing different concerts to meet their commitments. On 14 August, one group set off for Edinburgh in Scotland while Ratana, Moko, Tokouru and others travelled to Belfast, Ireland.

A week later they all met back in London for a combined concert, as a fundraiser for several hospitals before 7000 people at Groveland Park, and another before lords, ladies and celebrities at Hampstead Conservatoire with proceeds, ironically, going to the League of Mercy. A further public concert was held at St Georges Hall where the audience witnessed the best the troupe had to offer, including musical items, poi dancing and haka. The *London Evening Standard* reported on the Hampstead concert:

> Prior to the musical programme Peter Moko, Ratana's secretary, explained why the party were in England. First he said it was to disseminate the Power and Glory of God and secondly to place before the Imperial Government their grievances. Almost from the first he said, the Treaty of Waitangi was not venerated, and as the years went on it became more and more apparent that it was not being fulfilled. The Maori party had come to England as representatives of their race, to entreat England to rectify the injustice. He had hoped when they arrived in this country to receive recognition from the Christian element, but he regretted this was not so.

The 'three chiefs' who met with Prince Edward and presented their petitions and gifts on behalf of Māori people, only to have them returned and their petition referred back to the New Zealand Government. From left: Haami Tokouru Ratana, Tupu Taingakawa and Ratana's daughter Maata (Te Reo) to Huia (Boyce) Whenuaroa (at right). *Uri Whakatupuranga (Ratana Archives).*

Entrances blocked

While Ratana was being ignored in the official arena, the awareness of his presence in the United Kingdom was growing. A special unit at the Post Office in London was required to handle the influx of correspondence for the miracle man, some of it redirected from New Zealand but the bulk pouring in from around the United Kingdom and Europe. As Ratana and his party prepared to travel to Geneva, the newspapers in London reported that since his arrival he 'had received 5000 letters from people who had heard of his reputation and remarkable success in faith healing . . . 3500 from people who state they have been cured'.

On 26 August another letter arrived, this time from N. E. Archer, the assistant to the Colonial Secretary, stating that the British Government was not responsible for the injustices claimed by Ratana, and that he should place the claim before the New Zealand Government. Mr Andrew attempted to clarify that the Māori contingent had a right to appeal to the British Parliament because New Zealand had chosen not to act accordingly. Ratana and his kaumātua began to consider their options.

Pita Moko spoke to a correspondent for the *Walthamston Guardian* about Ratana's failure to get an audience with the Colonial Office over Treaty of Waitangi claims. He said that Māori felt keenly about the issue and sought compensation for the loss of their land, and the failure to address the issues

Above: Ratana Rugby Club 1955. Back, left to right: A. W. Wiremu, J. K. Kapea, C. B. Pahi, P. A. Gardiner, W. P. Puketohe. Middle row, left to right: O. T. Taiaroa (President), M. A. Taiaroa (Massuer), R. B. Aperahama, J. E. Stewart, H. P. Paki (Chairman and Manager), B. Hadfield, B. H. Tatarangi, O. M. McCalman (Coach), K. K. Taiaroa (Club Captain). Front row, left to right: H. K. Mason, D. T. Nepia, D. H. Huia (Vice Captain), M. W. Hihira (Captain), G. T. Maraku, M. S. Hauparoa. Absent: Mrs P. P. Ratahi (Patron); players absent: G. K. Rangi, T. G. Wereta, W. P. Green, W. T. Rogan, C. H. Temaiparea.
Athalie (McCalman) Price.

Left: Ratana always fielded a strong rugby team to compete in local competitions and an equally strong following of young and old were there to cheer them on. The first rugby team was formed in 1924.
Uri Whakataupuranga (Ratana Archives).

It's estimated about 4000 Ratana mōrehu are involved in regular competitive sports activities around the country from rugby to netball and hockey. The Maramatanga Sports Club at Ratana Pa is the strongest youth-based sporting organisation within the movement. There is also keen involvement of about 4000 members in music and culture, including brass bands and kapa haka and culture groups. In his day, Ratana often took sports, music and cultural teams with him around the country and even offered his own trophies, particularly for rugby games. *All photos Uri Whakatupuranga (Ratana Archives) unless stated otherwise.*

Everything has its time and place. A time to laugh, a time to be sad, a time to talk and to listen, a time to play an instrument or stand respectfully while official proceedings are underway; a time to remember the good old days and to realise that these might be the good old days next year. A time to teach your children and a time to let them discover the world for themselves, a time to be young and full of mischief, to be staunch and proud, to be humble and gracious, to be old and wise. A time to pass on memories and make new ones, and a time to simply chill out. *Photo essay using Ans Westra images from 1963, 1964 and 2005.*

reflected on the honour of England. He hoped to persuade the League of Nations in Geneva to intervene. To get an audience they needed a sponsor. An approach was made to the German Consulate in Geneva and Ratana, along with Pita Moko and Tokouru Ratana, both veterans of the Great War, travelled by train to Berlin to see if they could get a letter of support.

While in Berlin, Ratana continued prophesying that the world was heading rapidly towards a second Great War, with Germany reigniting the fire. 'Heoi ka whakakahangia ano te ngiha o te ahi, whakarongo ano tatou i tenei ra haere ake nei, ka kite koutou, ka mura te ao katoa. The flare of the flame will increase today and after; we must listen carefully, you will see the whole world burn.'

Internal upheavals throughout Germany meant that there would be no support; they were advised to take the claims to the American Embassy in Geneva. Back in London in September, further attempts were made to gain access to the League of Nations through the Japanese, French and Swiss embassies. Pressures were mounting within the Ratana camp; there was uncertainty, confusion, homesickness and disappointment. Cablegrams were sent back home to the Kotahitanga Bank; surely they would be able to help support their people on this most important of missions. No reply.

Ratana was determined to cover every avenue – he would not return without something encouraging for the people who had placed so much trust in him. He had received a positive response from the Japanese Embassy, offering to help the party ahead of its journey home via Japan. He decided now to go direct to the League of Nations. On 11 September at midday the party finally arrived in Geneva where Ratana said: 'I am considering planting the next seed in Japan, just as we have done so here in Geneva.'

First, he wanted his elders to stand in the League of Nations building. Pita Moko and Tokouru arranged to meet with the secretary of the League of Nations at the Palace de Nation. However, an assistant secretary showed up with a by now familiar message, advising their claims should be referred back to the New Zealand Government. The following evening they met at the Metropole Hotel with the Japanese Ambassador, Siko Kusama. Later, Ratana spoke to his people at length about Japan and prophesied that it would unite with Germany for a second world war.

Feathers for the future

Meanwhile Pita Moko worked tirelessly to try to secure passes to a League of Nations conference in Geneva, but only succeeded in gaining access to the buildings for a sightseeing tour. On 13 September, a newspaper article headlined 'Confiscated Lands Controversy' described six of the party wearing blankets (actually Māori cloaks) over their shoulders appearing at the conference of the League of Nations only to discover there was no plenary session. 'It is suspected

Chief Deskaheh, representing the Six Nations People on the Canadian border, had arrived in London the year before Ratana to protest the harsh treatment and betrayal of his people through breaking of their treaty with the British. After being turned away by government and Crown he laid his grievances before the League of Nations only months before Ratana.
Newman Collection.

in informed quarters the Maoris will not neglect the opportunity to revive the confiscated lands controversy.'

On 15 September at midday, the Ratana entourage entered the League of Nations building and its main chambers. While in the building Moko sat in the chair of the president of the League, and on looking around commented that all nations were represented except the Māori. It is said Tupu Taingakawa deposited a copy of the Treaty of Waitangi, the petition from 34,000 Māori and the details of the settlements sought, along with a huia feather and a kiwi cloak, with the indigenous representative of the League of Nations. He asked that the doors be left open, saying that one day a delegation would come wearing huia feathers and cloaks with a mandate to represent the treaty.

This highly symbolic deposit of documents and gifts qualified the Māori as only the second indigenous people to have laid their land grievances before the international body. Levi General, of the Haudenosaunee people of North America, was a spiritual and political statesman and member of the Cayuga council working to gain recognition for the Six Nations people. He had arrived in Geneva the year before, travelling a similar path to Ratana. After the First World War he assumed the ancient name Deskaheh and, in 1921, went to England to appeal to King George V about injustices committed against his people on the Canadian border. He was denied an audience. He then spent over a year in Geneva, preparing petitions, seeking meetings with foreign delegates and speaking out about the injustices Canada had committed against their former Iroquois allies. He persisted with his efforts to get a hearing for his people until his health began to fail him and he left for home late in 1923.

After they had left the important documentation relating to Māori grievances, Tokouru and Moko met again with the Ambassador Kusama and his secretary, T. Okuma, who agreed to support Ratana's claims at the next conference of the League of Nations. However, the Japanese were then warned by High Commissioner Allen not to have anything to do with the Ratana party. Ratana was again shocked at the opposition raised against him by his own government. All he wanted was a voice, a chance to raise the Māori flag in Geneva to present his claims regarding the Treaty of Waitangi. Again he had been cut off.

A consolation came through an invitation from League of Nations executives to a formal dinner at Restaurant Dumon in Paris. Here Ratana and his group were commended for their ambassadorial efforts on behalf of all Māori. Ratana later explained that despite the rejections it was now clear that after being hidden from the world the Māori people were seen to exist: 'thousands saw the Maori people, Maori work and entertainment [and] they saw that what they had heard about the Maori people being loving, and dignified, was indeed correct'.

While the return trip had been pre-paid, accommodation, internal travel and basics such as food were on an extremely tight budget and all eyes were now on the distant shores of Aotearoa. Another cable was sent to the Kotahitanga Bank at Ratana Pā asking for assistance. No reply. There had been problems with their travel plans and some confusion in the arrangements made by Cook Travel, as the party sought to move between Marseilles and Egypt. At least the Japanese were prepared to offer hospitality and keen for Ratana and his party to experience life in their nation before returning home. Arrangements were made to travel aboard the Japanese-owned *Suwa Maru*, heading for the Mediterranean with brief stopovers at Gibraltar, Messina, Italy and Greece.

It is said Ratana was broken-hearted and, while on the Rock of Gibraltar, that 6.5 square kilometre limestone island on the coast of Spain overlooking the Mediterranean Sea, he cried in sheer frustration, as he quoted the prophecies of Te Whiti, Tawhiao and other Māori seers.

> I have explained to you before that another nation would help you, whether that is America or Japan. Today you have been united with Japan and I am so pleased. I care not about the British or New Zealand governments. I will stand upon the land of Japan and their government, and when I reach Japan I will reveal to them all hidden things [spiritual] and let the fire be set alight. The whole world will soon come to know of this war and will come to know the significance of your claims and cause. If the 35,000 Maori are united in their understanding of this, then the war will not come upon the world . . . not until the old covenant has passed away, and a new covenant shall rise, that is the time . . . Ma Taku Tatu atu ra ano ki runga o Hapani katahi ka Mura Te Ahi. Not until I have reached Japan will the fire blaze.

In London Ratana had met a young man training to be a minister under the guidance of Christian Bishop Juji Nakada. Haeretika Kito had introduced Ratana to a Mr Kurasawa, a secretary with the Japanese Embassy in London, who helped make arrangements for the visit to Japan. Kito had become close with a number of the young people in the Ratana contingent and was also on the *Suwa Maru* as it left the United Kingdom.

Kindred spirits

As they approached Tokyo Harbour on 15 October 1924, Ratana pointed to the Japanese 'rising sun' flag on one of the boats, saying, 'I know this is where the missing link is, what the eye can see is a red sun but the missing link lies beyond.' The missing link, he said, connected the Japanese people who occupy the northern hemisphere and his own Māori people from the Pacific who lived in the southern hemisphere. Kito had told his people he was returning with a party of special guests from New Zealand so a great reception awaited them and a special church service was arranged. Ratana toured the three main islands and the group gave occasional performances during what was planned to be a stopover of several days. When it was time to leave, however, a dock strike prevented their departure.

Ratana was eager to get home for the 8 November celebrations commemo-

A friendship struck with a young missionary Haeretika Kito (middle of the top row) in London opened unexpected doors for the Ratana touring party when they ended up staying with his mentor Bishop Juji Nakada after a dock strike shut down the port in Tokyo. Kito is shown between Ratana band members Henare Toka (left) and Morehu Perepe in transit between London and Japan. Kito ended up returning with them to live at Ratana Pā for many months. *Uri Whakatupuranga (Ratana Archives).*

Bishop Juji Nakada, co-founder of the Oriental Mission Society, and T. W. Ratana became close friends, sharing spiritual insights and forming a 'spiritual alliance' between the Japanese and Māori people. They even swapped traditional garments for this photograph. *Tirikatene-Sullivan Collection.*

rating the beginning of his healing ministry. The young missionary Kito sent word to his mentor Nakada, a member of the indigenous Ainu people and a minister of the Japanese Anglican Church, who came in from the outskirts of Tokyo. A year previously the Japanese had suffered a massive earthquake that took 140,000 lives – nearly half of them in Tokyo – and the country was still in turmoil. While they had little to offer, Ratana and his party were invited to stay at Nakada's Bible College and Music School at Kashiwagi.

Tokugawa, Japan's strongest daimyo (powerful samurai) had outlawed Christianity and expelled all missionaries around 1610. Bishop Nakada, home from his base in America, had been converted to Christianity at the age of seventeen, and been instrumental in re-establishing the faith in Japan. Along with famed theologian Oswald Chambers, who had died while serving as chaplain to the ANZAC troops in the Great War, Nakada had helped found the Oriental Mission Society, which had branches throughout Japan, China, Korea and other Asian nations.

Nakada and Ratana became close friends. Both were well versed in their genealogies, cultural traditions and the scriptures, and would sit and talk for hours. Nakada believed both nations had descended from the Tribes of Israel; the Japanese from the house of Benjamin and the Māori from the House of Judah. Ratana observed similarities between the traditions and rituals of Māori, Japanese and ancient Israel.

A dual wedding to cement the 'spiritual marriage' of the Māori and Japanese people was staged while the world tour troupe were staying in Japan. Ratana presided over the marriage of Bishop Juji Nakada's son Ugo and his fiancée Daisy, while Bishop Nakada performed the ceremony marrying Ratana's daughter Maata (Te Reo) to Huia (Boyce) Whenuaroa. *Uri Whakatupuranga (Ratana Archives)*.

Both men believed in the Second Coming of the Son of God and were endowed with prophetic insights, believing their respective nations would have much to do with each other in the future. They spoke about the hidden meaning behind the Japanese flag, agreeing that the rising sun represented Christ. They also thought the angel over the Japanese was Michael and the angel over New Zealand was Gabriel. Nakada referred to Ratana and the Māori people as 'keepers of the southern stars' and to his own people as 'keepers of the northern stars', believing both their nations would be instrumental in heralding the Second Coming of the Christ.

Ratana and Bishop Nakada arranged a double wedding on 8 November 1924, exactly six years after Ratana's 'divine visitation'. Nakada presided over the marriage of Ratana's daughter Maata (Te Reo) to Huia (Boyce) Whenuaroa and Ratana officiated in the marriage of Nakada's son Ugo to a woman named Daisy. All wore traditional Japanese costumes, and Ratana and Nakada swapped their ethnic robes for the occasion. Two cakes were baked and it was said the two peoples had 'entered into the promise', a kind of spiritual marriage.

During the marriage celebrations Ratana was introduced to guests, including ministers of the Japanese Government. Ratana then made a promise to Nakada:

> The seed God has promised my race, I promise to yours. The wedding is not just a marriage between two of our people it is a marriage between our nations, the cake is not just about breaking bread between two people but sharing the same

promises; the same bounty that has been guaranteed to my people. From out of the ashes you shall rise like a phoenix and reach the pinnacle of economic excellence. When you do, don't forget my people.

Ratana was told: 'While we are not in a position to honour your plea now, in the future we will honour you.' Ratana presented Bishop Nakada with cloaks and pendants. In return he was presented with ceremonial swords: a long sword, a half sword and a small blade.

According to the world tour diaries, officials at the Imperial Palace, once learning Ratana was a prophet and healer, invited him to meet with Yoshihito, also known as Taisho, the 123rd emperor, who was very ill. Ratana cooked him a broth from local kūmara and prayed with him. Taisho had been enthroned in 1915 at Kyoto, but because of 'a cerebral illness' had been unable to deal with state affairs, leaving these to crown prince Hirohito who became regent in 1921. Ratana was challenged: 'If you are a prophet, then prophesy over our emperor.'

So Ratana, as the Māngai, told the emperor he needed to give up the titles that accorded him god status or he couldn't help: 'This kingdom, this house you live in, will become a prison. Your status as a god will be taken . . . Your people will be turned to dust when you see two bright lights above you. Give up your godship or God will bring you to your knees.' However, the emperor wouldn't listen. Ratana concluded: 'Have no fear, your nation will rise again. This is meant to be.' Before departing he turned towards Juji Nakada, saying to the emperor and his attendants, that he would leave a gift with this man.

Nakada was a witness to all that was said at the Imperial Palace and wrote everything down. Emperor Taisho died in 1926. The original Imperial Palace, the home of Japan's Imperial family since 1888 and built on the former Edo Castle from the days of the Tokugawa Shogunate, was destroyed during the 1945 air raids.

Only days after the encounter with the emperor, the dock strike was over, and what had become the highlight of the 1924 world tour came to a close as the Ratana party boarded the *Mishima Maru* and headed for home.

SEVEN

DENOMINATIONS CLOSE RANK

Had I agreed for our church to be Anglican, my followers who belong to the Roman Catholic Church and other religions would have been angry. Therefore, in order to make peace among you, your church has been named the Ratana Church.

—T. W. Ratana, 1925

I believe that Jehovah sent His Son in the human form of Jesus Christ to redeem man and to conquer the power of sin, of darkness and of death. Heaven is now Christ's throne and the earth is his footstool, but his chosen dwelling place is in the hearts of those who truly believe in him and have union with him in his victory and glory.

—Clause three of the Ratana Creed

Rumours and restlessness

As the SS *Niagara* steamed into the Waitematā Harbour on 22 December 1924 the large crowd at Queen's Wharf soon heard the familiar strains of the Ratana band playing on deck. While relieved to be home after nine months abroad, Ratana hid among the rest of the party, keeping a low profile until they boarded the train to Ratana Pā the next day.

When he arrived at the small station alongside the Ratana family farm on Christmas Eve 1924, the people were horrified. Here was their leader, the one they had been aching to see, dressed like he'd just come in from the fields. 'I am your servant and labourer returning home from work . . . which is why you see me dressed in working men's clothes, and by this we now know that we have reached the end of working time . . . it is now time to come back home . . . '

While Ratana may have considered his efforts a failure, the people who had been pouring into the Pā for the annual Christmas celebrations were obviously glad to have him back. During the seven-day hui he spoke of the different cultures, customs, laws and philosophies he had encountered on the world tour. While there were many wonderful church buildings, he had witnessed little evidence of a real faith in Ihoa or that any nation knew much about the Māori people. 'My friends,' he said, 'to tell the truth, the peoples of this world have deserted Ihoa and forget that what they know resulted in great benefits for them (and) came from Ihoa. Instead, today it seems they claim that their knowledge or intelligence is something they achieved themselves.'

Ratana had rejected pressure to form a separate church but, in his absence, Otene Paora and Henare Wiri Toka had gone ahead and registered the Church of the Faithful Angels. However, attempts to establish a membership among Ratana followers were undermined when the Reverend A. J. Seamer stepped in, urging the people to remain faithful to Ratana's wishes. In Ratana's absence some of the Methodist missionaries living at the Pā had been bullied by those who were more interested in revering the Māngai as a divine emissary than embracing the Christian message. Ratana immediately deregistered the church and scolded those who were making life hard for his friend.

Then there were business and political issues to deal with. Just as he had feared, the Kotahitanga Bank's grand ideas had got out of control.

> When I was in England I received letters telling me about the great volumes of water that were flowing into our tank . . . Because of this, I decided to try the bank out. Thus, after talking with the elders of my roopu [group], I sent a cable home asking for £3000. However, I didn't see any sign of that. While in Marseilles, I sent a cable home asking for £2000. Getting no satisfaction from that, I decided to try again, this time for £1000, when we reached Singapore. This I did without success, so I tried again in Tokyo, Japan, this time for £500. I met with the same result here, so I spoke again with the elders of the roopu, and we decided to try for one pound. I don't know to this day what happened to that one pound . . .

The management committee had made unwise investments, acquiring expensive property on mortgage arrangements that weren't serviced, even resulting in the land where the Ratana Temple was to be built being heavily mortgaged and the interest unpaid. Some claimed Ratana had spent the money, which deeply hurt him. 'I left the tank full but somebody left the tap running.' He then went inside his home and stayed there. Word went around that he was dying and the people were killing him with their suspicions. When the critics appeared to have been silenced and he felt his reputation was restored, Ratana finally emerged, entered a large car and, propped up with cushions, drove around the marae waving to his people.

Ratana looked into the financial activities of the 'bank', and had the directors sign a statement that he had not used any of the money to cover tour costs, which was then lodged with the Bank of New Zealand. The money had come from the sale of his mother's land, from some wealthier members of the movement, donations from mōrehu and revenue from concerts during the tour. The Crown Law Office, however, thought the bank's activities may have been illegal. Questions were asked in the press and in Parliament, and a constable

Between tours, about December 1924. Back row, from left to right: Te Arepa Ratana (Ngā Rauru, Ngāti Apa), Mikaera Whenuaroa (Ngāti Tūwharetoa), Huia 'Boyce' Whenuaroa (Ngāti Tūwharetoa), Pita T. Moko (Te Arawa), Te Okeroa Whenuaroa (Ngāti Tūwharetoa), Peina Werahiko Tamau (Ngā Rauru), Whiuwhiu Pineaha (Ngāti Kahungunu), Tokouru H. Ratana (Ngā Rauru, Ngāti Apa). Third row, from left to right: Hamuera Uru Te Angina (Ngāti Apa), Ngapae Aropeta Tamumu (Ngāti Apa), Morehu A. Perepe (Te Āti Haunui-ā-Pāpārangi), Paikea Henare Toka (Ngāti Whātua), Waiora P. Moko (Ngāti Tūwharetoa), Timi Hahiwutu Churchwood (Samoa), Tariuha M. Te Awe Awe (Rangitāne, Ngāti Raukawa), Eruera Pairama 'Ted' Kaipara (Ngāti Whātua), Tahiopiripi Moerua (Ngāti Maniapoto). Second row, from left to right: Kimiora Whenuaroa (Ngāti Tūwharetoa), Te Aorangi O. Eketone (Ngāti Maniapoto), Huhana Toka (Ngāti Whātua), Mariana Hekenui (Ngāti Tūwharetoa), Te Urumanao 'Te Whaea' Ratana (Ngā Rauru, Te Āti Haunui-ā-Pāpārangi), Karitua Te Utupoto (Ngāti Apa), Mere Te Kahu (Ngāti Kahungunu), Mihiterina Te Awe Awe (Rangitāne, Ngāti Raukawa), Ripeka Ratana (Ngā Rauru, Ngāti Apa). Front row, from left to right: Taani (Dan) Reremoana (Ngā Rauru, Ngāti Apa), Huiatahi Hawira (Ngāti Maniapoto), Piki Te Ora Ratana (Ngā Rauru, Ngāti Apa), Maata Te Reo Whenuaroa (Ngā Rauru, Ngāti Apa), Iriaka Te Rio (Te Āti Haunui-ā-Pāpārangi), Te Omeka Ratana (Ngā Rauru, Ngāti Apa), Te Akau Tamumu (Ngā Rauru). Caption details: Trevor Paku Carrol, with some corrections. *Frank J. Denton, Tesla Studios Collection, ATL F-17026 1/1 Tesla, Alexander Turnbull Library, Wellington.*

was sent to Ratana Pā to investigate. It was decided that there was not enough evidence to prosecute. An internal investigation was held and the bank was wound up 'with as little fuss as possible', with Ratana and his family settling the remaining debts.

Spies and other lies

Meanwhile, Ratana's exploits in Japan had also fuelled the rumour mill – the talk of a spiritual marriage and samurai swords being gifted caused some to believe that the Japanese were coming to liberate the Māori people. This, along with stories of a Japanese spy at Ratana Pā, resulted in resolutions condemning the visit being signed in Rotorua, Dannevirke, Whanganui and communities along the Whanganui River. Sir Maui Pomare added his concerns in the newspapers and won for himself the support of some of Ratana's followers for a time. There were intense denials by members of the group, and from Ratana himself. The backlash was so widespread that his son Tokouru did not stand for the elections that year.

Ratana was offended that his loyalty to the Crown and the New Zealand Government was being questioned. He responded by publishing a statement in *Whetu Marama*, ironically translated into English by Haeretika Kito, the young Japanese missionary who Ratana had befriended in London. Kito, having trained as an Anglican clergyman under Juji Nakada, lived at Ratana Pā for three years to study the Māori language and become an apostle in the Ratana Church. The statement contained the core of a covenant giving those who had previously pledged support an opportunity to reaffirm their commitment to unite under Ihoa.

> To all men and women of the Maori race who oppose my Covenants, contaminating and exaggerating by saying that we are married to the Japanese nation, I hereby command you to wear your spectacles to enable you to see, read and understand the words written thereon. Since you do not comprehend the meaning of the Covenant, I myself will suffer explanation for your benefit . . . Dear Friends, try and eat honey which is so delicious, to sweeten your mouths.

The statement explained that after being treated indifferently by other nations, Ratana and his party went to Japan where they found three divisions of belief – two native and one Christian. 'I met only one bishop and explained my mission for Jehovah . . . The marriage and the cake haven't been understood. The cake is for the remnants of my people to signify the wedding of the Japanese to the Divine Light only.' When the covenant closed five months later on 21 May 1925 there were 22,941 signatures. He reminded his followers and detractors of the substance of the covenant, and hinted further at the next stage of his mission:

> But remember this, I told you right at the beginning, there is the Bible on one side, and the Treaty of Waitangi on the other. Now that we have been sealed as the children of Ihoa, know this, the same hand that carried the Ture Matua [law of God] will carry the Ture Tangata [law of man]. Very soon you will see. I now have no fears, for the kawenata has been committed before the throne of Ihoa, and the Ture Tangata has been placed in my right hand.

However, the New Zealand Government was not satisfied and began its own inquiry into the Japanese rumours. Governor-General Sir Charles Fergusson wrote to the British in mid-1925 to try to find out what had really gone on: 'Ludicrous as these assertions are, my Government has reason to believe a good number of Maori who are easily led by such promises believe the assertions of Ratana. It is desirable that impression should be destroyed.' Sir Charles' message was marked 'top secret', as was the reply, which was kept under wraps for over 70 years. The confidential reply was that Ratana had not seen any Japanese ministers, 'although his band played at a private party given by the Minister of Agriculture'.

Because that communiqué was top secret the government could not pass on to the public the reassurance it had received or where it had come from, and issued its own statement that Ratana had not been received by the Japanese government. Further inquiries were made with assistance from the British Government, which in turn received a cable from Japan confirming that no promise of any kind of support was given or implied by the Japanese Government.

The anti-Ratana rhetoric was further fuelled when workers helping develop land around the Pā for wheat farming were given a certificate that some claimed was to gain favour with the Japanese when they landed. In fact the certificate entitled the bearers to free games of pool and other benefits at Ratana Pā to thank them for their labour.

Fork in the road

Ratana was deeply hurt when he learned many couples were living together because the mainstream churches were now refusing to marry them or baptise their children. He became more frustrated when he learned some apostles were actually performing marriages; as they weren't registered under the New Zealand Marriage Act and their actions were illegal.

Some among the faithful were deifying the angelic host, and there were frequent reports of mysterious lights appearing in the night sky around the Pā, further straining relationships with the mainstream churches. The Catholics had already severed ties and the relationship with the Anglicans was rapidly cooling. There was open debate about the nature of the angels, and concern was

Confirming the kawenata, Easter Hui, 21 May 1925. Ratana dedicated his 1921 covenant against tohungaism, his 1922 affirmation against sorcery, drawing in the 'short net and long net' for the poor and broken and the rich and wealthy, and his 1923 covenant embracing the Holy and Faithful Angels. All were dedicated to the Son of Peace. *Uri Whakatupuranga (Ratana Archives).*

expressed that some were elevating Ratana to the status of 'divine mediator' or an equal to Christ. Within days of his return it seemed Ratana was facing allegations of heresy. In the midst of the Christmas celebrations he agreed to try and reach a consensus with the churches to affirm key elements of the Christian faith and dispel the rumours and exaggerations. A final hui (meeting) was planned to try and resolve the confusion.

It was agreed Methodist general superintendent the Reverend A. J. Seamer would speak to the people first, and that no one else should have a say until Ratana had supported him. Ahead of the meeting Seamer took his old friend aside and ran through all the doctrinal issues that were to be discussed and agreed on. Ratana was in full accord and ready for this important evening meeting. However, the mood wasn't helped by the belligerent attitude of some church leaders, who were demanding Ratana and his followers join their particular denomination. Ratana saw the division and knew this would break his followers into splinter groups and possibly bring an end to his ministry.

Jim McLeod Henderson recalls the scene from eyewitness accounts.

> There was bright moonlight over the marae on the night of the crucial gathering. On a brilliantly lit platform the ministers were seated. They included the Anglicans: the Reverends F. Bennett, P. Munro, W. G. Williams and Canon A. Williams. Beside them were the Methodists, the Reverend R. T. Haddon and the Reverend Seamer who rose to speak when the short evening service was concluded. In Maori, he outlined the doctrine of the Triune God and then passed on to the question of the status of the angels. He complimented Ratana on his constant emphasis of the fact that they were God's servants, not gods. The term atua [gods] really meant 'of beyond the visible world', and this had caused confusion, for it had been used too loosely in reference to the angels. In fact they were the servants of God. He then turned to Ratana to ask him to speak to his people.

Unfortunately, while the assembly waited calmly for Ratana to speak, one of the Anglican clergy stood up and, believing that the meeting was fully sympathetic, spoke warmly in support of Seamer's remarks. He then quoted scripture against angel worship and the Church's authority on the subject. From all sides came murmurs as the meeting grew restless. A Ringatū speaker aired his views on authority and the orthodox churches, followed by others who stirred up the feelings of the mōrehu. On the platform, Reverend Bennett attempted to pacify the people, but the mind of the meeting had been lost and he was strongly opposed.

During the tumult Seamer quietly stepped aside to the comparatively peaceful verge of the gathering where he was met by Ratana who said: 'I can't address them after that! The church has too many voices and the people are divided. We must go our own way!' When he did speak, however, Ratana's stance grew increasingly independent and from that point he made no further attempt to co-operate with or join the recognised churches. His attitude is perhaps best expressed in the prayer remembered by the late Kingi Tahiwi of Wellington: 'Lord God our Father, protect us in all our doings and certainly protect us from intellectuals!' From that night, theological debates were continuous at Ratana Pā, and although Ratana himself supported the orthodox group, he did allow it to be said that he had declared the arrival of a new era, the Dispensation of the Faithful Angels.

Following the heated debate during the Christmas 1924 hui the mainstream churches stepped back to consider their position just as Ratana was reviewing his. Reverend Seamer was eager to clarify the theological position of the Ratana movement, and was now aware there was little alternative to forming a separate church. He met regularly with Ratana and his elders to prepare a Statement of Faith, to lodge with the authorities for registration under the Marriage Act. With the help of Reverend Dr Harry Ranston he helped prepare and translate the Ratana Creed from Māori before official ministers were chosen.

On the Day of Pentecost, 31 May 1925, Ratana announced his intention to form a separate church but urged the people to wait just a little longer. Then, on 5 July 1925 at 11 a.m. as a misty rain began falling at the Pā, he announced the church had now been 'spiritually' established.

> Minute particles of rain fall from the heavens to reach and mingle with the earth; a cloud of smoke [or steam] rises from the earth to reach and become part of the heavens; likewise I seal and establish your church upon the solid Rock of the Matua, Tama, Wairua Tapu me nga Anahera Pono me te Mangai, from which it shall never be shaken or moved.

Whāngaied to the family

Many who had watched the tiny Pā grow from a ramshackle encampment into a small township, and followed the miracles of the past eight years, felt a strong sense of family. It seemed logical that the name Ratana be applied to the new religious movement.

> Had I agreed for our church to be Anglican, my followers who belong to the Roman Catholic Church and other religions would have been angry. Therefore, in order to make peace among you, your church has been named the Ratana Church. I have already told you that you have all adopted the name Ratana, and that being so, everything you have and treasure will be known by that name.

He further explained that his grandfather had virtually predicted this time during a hui of Ngāti Apa elders where religious matters affecting their people were discussed. After everyone had spoken, Ngahina Pakaru Ratana let his voice be heard:

> Oh elders of Ngati Apa, I greet you and salute you. I have listened to what you have had to say. I have something to tell you, and I want you all to take careful note of what I am about to say. My fellow elders, when you die all memory of you will pass away and be forgotten. But with me, it will be different, for I will never die, because I have three names. If Te Pakaru dies, Ngahina will still be alive; if Ngahina dies, Ratana will live on. Let us leave this statement of mine for our descendants to look at, that they may grasp and understand what I mean.

On 15 July the Ratana Church of New Zealand was registered in Wellington. But even as the official documents for the Ratana Church were with the registrar, debate over the most controversial issues was still raging. There was a strong belief that the angelic host had somehow missed out on their due recognition as part of God's hierarchy, and that through the māramatanga of the Ratana Church they were able to be glorified on earth.

Iwiora Tamaiparea had moved that 'the Ratana Church of the Morehu and of the whole world, be based upon Ihoa of Hosts, Father, Son, Holy Spirit and Their Faithful Angels and ending with the Mangai'. An amendment attempting to make it clear that the Faithful Angels did not come into the same category as the Holy Trinity was lost. On 18 July 1925 the resolution confirming the position of the Holy Angels and the Māngai alongside the Trinity was passed in clear defiance of traditional church theology. In the minds of Anglicans, Catholics and Presbyterians at least, the heresy of Ratana was now officially confirmed.

The Ratana Church Constitution was accepted by the Registrar-General on 21 July. Ratana himself was president and the names of 38 apostles were

T. W. Ratana, Te Whaea and their son Te Omeka with the large family Bible, which Ratana frequently made notes in. On Christmas Day 1925, he said: 'The most important book to me is the Bible. These hymn books are one thing, but the Bible is our real treasure.'
Uri Whakatupuranga (Ratana Archives).

published in accordance with the Marriage Act of 1908. Press reports emerged that Ratana had allegedly asked his followers to leave any clergyman who did not add the angels to the baptism formula or wherever the Trinity was mentioned in a service, and start a branch of the Ratana Church.

The Anglican Synod quickly reacted, labelling the Ratana Church a 'schismatic sect' and, a day before the official constitution was approved, issuing a pastoral letter to the Māori clergy and laity, warning that anyone signing the Ratana covenant was taking 'a very serious step toward excommunicating [themselves] from the Church of Christ'. Three North Island bishops, Archbishop Averill, Bishop Sprott of Wellington and Bishop Sedgwick of Waiapu, issued instructions to the clergy and the people of the Māori race. It was 'not lawful for clergy to give [followers of Ratana] the ministration of the Church in Holy Communion, Marriage or Burial'. They concluded that 'any lay reader who joined the Ratana movement immediately forfeited his licence and must return his badge of office'.

On being informed that they could no longer be members of the mainstream church and a follower of Ratana, many, including those who held positions of leadership, were forced to make a decision.

In response to the Anglican outburst an executive of the Ratana movement,

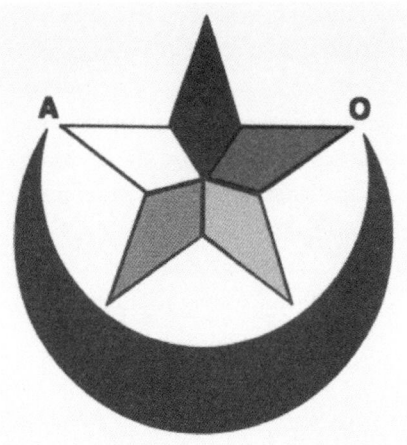 

quoted by *United Press*, said the Ratana Church would continue to be based along lines laid down and approved by the people. 'Services would be shorn of a good deal of "useless flummery" and would be in accordance with the straightforward simple teachings of Christ.'

The formation of the Ratana Church was a cause of much celebration, but the drawn-out arguments with the established churches and subsequent rejection of Ratana followers from among them gave rise to much bitterness that would continue down the years. Māori from a variety of religious backgrounds – including those with an affinity for the old ways – quickly aligned with Ratana, including those who clearly had ideas that were more heretical than anything he had ever expressed. While Ratana tried to give a biblical context for everything he said, he did little either to correct those who offered views contrary to his own or to pull the people back from adoration of the angels.

The Methodists continued their support, hoping to keep things moving along the Christian path, accepting a section at Ratana Pā where a two-room residence was built so deaconesses could continue teaching at the school. Piki Te Ora, the church building, was placed at their disposal so that they could also conduct Sunday school services.

G. I. Laurenson, general superintendent of the Methodist home and Māori missions, wrote there was little time to train the new Ratana ministers who had come from very different traditions.

> Naturally their preaching depended upon the background from which they had individually come. There was not time for them to have gathered a body of teaching which would give some uniform pattern to their work. Hence when they returned to their tribal areas and began their official duties, the type of

thought reflected these various traditions. In the Ratana Creed there appears among other statements this sentence (No 10) which reads: 'I believe that Tahupotiki Wiremu Ratana is a mouthpiece of Jehovah (Mangai), spreading abroad light on the above truths concerning the salvation of the spirit and the vitalising of the body.' Gradually this was brought to the front, and became the dominating emphasis. However, owing to the differences of understanding of the rest of the body of their creed, it became changed in use to 'The Mouthpiece' (Te Mangai) and this is now in general usage of Ratana people. It was not intended in the original form of the statement. With this there came also a change in many of the words of traditional Mission hymns and prayers and orders of service.

Jim McLeod Henderson says various hymns and catechisms written and used in services weren't always authorised, and tended to elevate the status of Ratana. He cites the popular Ratana hymn 'Mā Te Mārie' as perhaps being the closest to a true Ratana theology:

> May the peace of God the Father
> Son and Holy Ghost
> With the Holy Angels
> Guard and watch over all of us.
> May the Holy Guide as well
> Lead us in the right way
> In truth and righteousness
> To the Throne of Jehovah.

The formation of the Ratana Church quickly resulted in many locally based Māori churches folding; the trickle leaving the established churches turned into a stream. Ratana asked the Kōmiti Hāhi Matua, the church governing body, to ensure there was a proper form for services, to provide the appropriate books and to 'work out' a proper theology while he was away on the next phase of his world tour in the United States.

After much discussion, the committee agreed to print the procedure for church services based on the Methodist Prayer Book, with appropriate changes such as replacing the word Atua with Matua to avoid confusion with the old gods (atua), and including the Faithful Angels where it was appropriate to do so. The Kotahitanga executive, still getting its bearings after the failed Ratana Bank debacle, would look after affairs at the Pā and ensure the newly formed church was properly established.

EIGHT

AMERICAN EXPEDITION

Oh Morehu, you know not the reason of my way for I shall say to you all, there I shall acquire the Olive branch.
—T. W. Ratana, ahead of his United States tour, 1925

Twins of Babylon will stand in this city. The beginning and the end are here on this street. The twins, Sodom and Gomorrah, will fall.
—T. W. Ratana, prophesying on Wall Street in downtown Manhattan, 1925

Signs for modern times
The American tour was intended to further showcase Māori to the world, and to gain a better understanding of economic and social issues by establishing relationships with key businesspeople and indigenous communities. As expected, there was also a deeper thread, which would only later become evident in Ratana's prophecies and the symbolic nature of some of his actions.

Although the Ratana touring group had only recently returned from overseas, they were again forced to jump through government hoops to get clearance, including depositing money to cover accommodation and return fares. The Ministry of Internal Affairs insisted: 'All members of his party will [be required] to make fresh applications for passports, irrespective of the fact that they already have passports.'

Eventually Ratana and a smaller party of performers and advisers left New Zealand on 19 August 1925 to travel through the South Pacific via Rarotonga and Tahiti before heading on to America. Ratana's stopovers in Rarotonga and Tahiti came through his relationship with Dr Rangi Hiroa (Peter Buck),

Above left: Six-shooters and saloons. 'Shorty' Dan Reremoana (left) and Henare Toka get a taste of the old west in California, 1925. *Above right:* Ratana party friends step back in time on a night out during the 1925 American tour. *Uri Whakatupuranga (Ratana Archives).*

the health and welfare officer who cleared the party to travel, who had strong connections in the Pacific Islands. Ratana is said to have healed many people, in particular members of the royal families, and undertaken research to re-establish Polynesian genealogical ties. Ratana apostle Ruia Aperahama says Ratana was also keen to encourage trade and industry, including the import and export of fruit and seafood under the Kotahitanga organisation.

Ratana explained that the American trip had special spiritual significance. 'Oh Morehu, you know not the reason of my way for I shall say to you all, there I shall acquire the Olive branch.' He spoke about gifts he would take to America, in particular film footage of life at Ratana Pā. After a time he said these gifts would 'reveal prosperity and fruits'.

The tour took Ratana and his party through several cities and states, including California, New York, Texas, Arizona, Columbus in Ohio, Utah including Great Salt Lake City, Cheyenne, Wyoming, Pennsylvania, Indiana, Missouri, Kansas City and, in Canada, Ontario and Calgary.

A large feature in the *San Francisco Examiner* in October 1925 was both a review of spiritual healing practitioners of the times and testament to the public relations skills of Pita Moko. The article was headlined 'Ratana, Invisible Maori Healer Works Cures Here', with the strap line 'Famous praying tribesman from

New Zealand with 26 followers camped in San Francisco; accepts no money and has received 287,000 letters'. That must have caught the attention of many readers.

After a long preamble about faith healers and Ratana's mission the *Examiner* writer recounted the story of how Ratana 'found his gift', the healing of his son Omeka after the 'needle incident', and the cure of Fannie Lammas. It also quoted several letters from San Francisco residents who had been healed; including one from a person who could now 'read a newspaper without glasses for the first time in 25 years'. A further testimony came from a woman who had been ill for a year after an accident and was now able to walk. The writer of the article contacted the woman to confirm the content of her letter and was assured that the details were correct.

On his visit to Salt Lake City, Ratana allegedly became the first dark-skinned person to go into the Holy of Holies in the Mormon Tabernacle, and there it is said he healed one of the patriarchs. Ratana asked them as a mark of respect to add a principle to their church laws to enable dark-skinned people to become patriarchs in the Mormon Church. It is not clear whether this had any impact on the movement, which maintained conflicting views about the place of 'coloured people'; some even perpetuated the erroneous nonsense that they were 'from the Devil', had sinned in their 'pre-mortal existence as spirits', and were a cursed race springing from the union of Cain. While many Asians, American Indians and Fijians and indeed Māori were admitted as elders in the church over the years, an edict to remove all racist terminology from official documentation was not made until 1976. According to apostle Kereama Pene, Ratana stood on a soap box outside the Mormon Tabernacle in Salt Lake City, preaching about the amazing things that dark-skinned people would do in the future.

The Ratana kaumātua met with representatives of the wheat industry, 'the American Trades Council' (possibly the American Federation of Labour) and car maker Henry Ford, who proposed Ratana become the South Pacific distributor of Ford motor vehicles. Ford would help underwrite a production factory providing jobs in New Zealand. It was also proposed that Ratana become the New Zealand agent for American Express and he was given an open cheque, which he accepted but never filled in.

In his further adventures in the United States it is claimed Ratana, on a visit to New York, found himself standing on Wall Street in downtown Manhattan. There he allegedly made an announcement to the people who were with him, including his young sons Arepa and Omeka: 'Twins of Babylon will stand in this city. The beginning and the end are here on this street. The twins, Sodom and Gomorrah, will fall.' Obviously, he could not have known he was standing near the future site of the Twin Towers in the financial district, which would control much of the movement of money throughout the world.

Arranged marriage

Shortly after the Ratana Church was officially established, Ratana, with the encouragement of his wife Te Urumanao, had taken a second, much younger, 'spiritual' wife. He had evoked an ancient chiefly right, believing his actions were an important part of his unfolding mission. Some say he was influenced by Mormon practices or that he had taken a page from the Old Testament patriarchs David and Solomon who married multiple wives, allegedly to bring together previously warring peoples.

The arranged 'second marriage' was to Iriaka Te Rio, a young violin player and singer who had travelled with Ratana on the 1924 world tour. She was from the chiefly line of a respected Whanganui River hapū (tribal group). Her own mother died when she was young and there was some sense of taking responsibility for her and her destiny. Ratana had first seen her at a Catholic convent along the Whanganui River. The people of her tribe had decided she would become part of T. W. Ratana's household and a tono (request) was made for Iriaka. 'It was a spiritual thing, something sacred, done ceremonially according to the old traditions. The people admired her for it and she knew she had a role to fulfil to do with the māramatanga,' said a family spokesperson.

From this time Ratana's wife Te Urumanao took the title Te Whaea o te Katoa (mother of all), a name she had first been given after an encounter with the Holy Spirit while Ratana was still facing his testing, eight years previously. Iriaka became known as Iriaka T. W. Ratana or Te Whaea Iti (little or humble mother). Her first child died at birth and was, according to the World Tour Journal kept by Ratana's son Tokouru, buried in a cemetery described as 'a garden of clovers' in Calgary, Canada. Ratana named the child Piri Wiri Tua ('the campaigner'), or one who bores through to the other side, a name he would increasingly use of himself in the years ahead as he focused more on the political side of his mission.

Ratana had perhaps seen this premature death in a foreign land as symbolic of his own frustrated mission to have Māori unified with a single voice, the Treaty of Waitangi recognised and land grievances resolved. He is reported to have said: 'Stay for a time . . . then you shall rise together with the nations of America. For I shall fetch you near and observe and raise you up.' It is said the prophecy of the 'nations of America' has to do with the rise of the indigenous or first nation peoples throughout the Americas. Ratana then 'secured a Guardian' or an angel to stay with the child until it was time for the 'spirit' to be returned. It is said that when the Treaty of Waitangi 'speaks for itself' without the aid of men, then the spirit of what was lost will be gathered up and returned home to New Zealand.

The party returned home to New Zealand on 22 December aboard the SS *Niagara*. Ratana showed his people the open cheque given to him by American Express as an example of the blessings that were available under

Above left: Tuheka Hetet was Ratana's project foreman on Te Temepara Tapu o Ihoa, basing the construction on an old Baptist church and ideas brought back from his world tour. When initial costs of an architect and building material proved out of the movement's budget it was agreed mōrehu would do most of the work. The foundation stone was laid on 4 April 1926. Tuheka Hetet's wife, Rangimarie, later became a dame and was given an honorary doctorate for her great skill as a weaver and traditional cloak maker. *Above right:* Ihaka Te Tai was the first editor of the *Whetu Marama* newspaper (1924–27) and looked after spiritual matters, including developing the church structure and vestments, when Ratana was overseas.
Uri Whakatupuranga (Ratana Archives).

his māramatanga. However, he quoted the biblical story of Esau who sold his birthright for a meal of pottage (thick soup), saying that he would not sell out his māramatanga for money. The cheque remained pinned to a sheet in Ratana's office for many years.

Spiritual centre

Before his three-month American tour Ratana had approved plans to build Te Temepara Tapu o Ihoa, the Holy Temple of Jehovah, on a tract of land at the eastern edge of the marae. In a vision he had seen 'a magnificent temple' representing the mana and symbolism of his ministry, embodying deep spiritual truths from the Bible along with his own revelations. The design would be based on what he had seen in Japan with ideas now added from his American trip.

Nga Akoranga, the internal training books first published in 1982, state that the temple was intended to convey 'something greater and nobler than what can be seen by the human eye' – the unification of the Māori people through a true and strong faith in Ihoa o ngā Mano and the principles, policies and guidelines of the māramatanga. Ratana was determined that the temple would be the best he and his people could build. Construction would take priority, and mōrehu were encouraged to make personal donations of at least 5 shillings each.

To facilitate the construction and further streamline the movement's affairs around the country, the Kotahitanga organisation was again restructured with better management skills and greater accountability. Under Ratana's presidency,

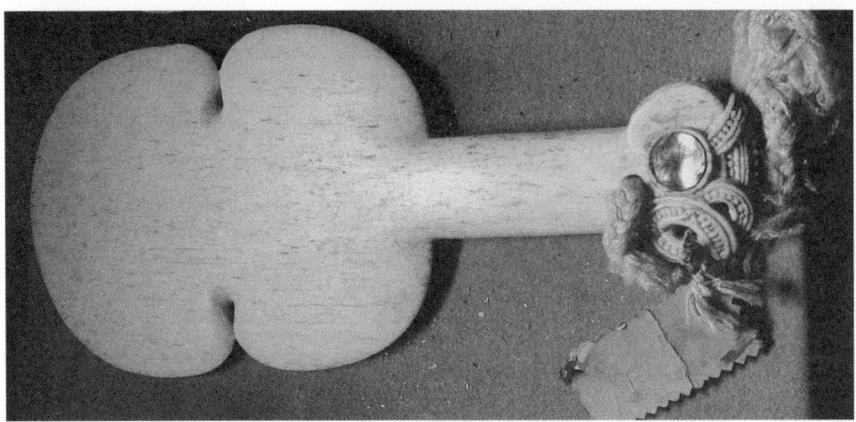

The whalebone mere, passed down to Paraire Paikea from his ancestor Paikea Te Hekeua, paramount chief of Ngāti Whātua, was given to T. W. Ratana as a symbol of loyalty from the people of the north. *Kereama Pene.*

an elected committee would run affairs at Ratana Pā, and there would Komiti Takiwa (regional committees) in Tai Tokerau, Tairāwhiti, Tai Hauauru and Waipounamu.

By the end of 1925, Ratana's registered church membership included 11,567 Māori – about 18 per cent of the Māori population – and 193 Pākehā. The only denomination with more Māori members was Anglican. There were 110 āpotoro, 500 ākonga (students) and 500 āwhina (supporters and carers) involved in church work.

During 1926 the Ratana faith gained many new members, including a strong commitment from the Uri-o-Hau hapū of Kaipara, who had staunchly resisted the messianic Māori religions in favour of Christianity. They were still reeling from the underhanded deals of Methodist missionary William Gittos, who facilitated the sale of much of their tribal land, when one of their own helped restore confidence. Paraire Paikea, descended from Paikea Te Hekeua, a paramount chief of Ngāti Whātua and related to many of the leading tribes of Northland, was ordained a Methodist minister in 1920 and rapidly become a key person in the Ratana movement. He was there when Ratana had performed his miracles at Otamatea and, along with many of the locals, was thoroughly convinced this man could help change the destiny of Māori.

Under the guidance of the Reverend A. J. Seamer, Paikea had made frequent visits to Ratana Pā, helping develop the Ratana Creed, conducting marriages and offering religious advice soon after the church was formed. The Methodist Board had also authorised three other ministers to become registered as Ratana apostles. By the end of 1926, Paikea was working closely with Ratana in a secretarial capacity, and most of his family and tribal members had joined the movement.

Another endorsement of Ratana as a legitimate successor of the Christian-based Māori prophetic movement came when his aunty, the highly influential Mere Rikiriki, donated two buildings to Ratana Pā in 1924, then signed his covenant two years later on 4 February 1926. When she died from a stroke five weeks later aged 72, Ratana and 200 of his followers attended her tangi. Many came by car and truck while others took the traditional route from Ratana Pā along the beach to her home at Parewanui.

Mere Rikiriki had inherited the mantle of the Māori prophetic movement and was a major influence in bringing a new spiritual understanding of one God and the healing work, and comforting power and guidance of the Holy Spirit. She had chosen Ratana as her successor and he became an advocate for the māramatanga, a term she had coined. Ratana was convinced Ihoa desired to have a relationship with the Māori people. If unity could be achieved then the spiritual, physical and social needs of the people could be better addressed.

Ratana was comforted by the fact that his attempts to petition the Crown had encouraged Sir Maui Pomare to push for the long-promised Royal Commission of Inquiry into confiscated land. Pomare had convinced Prime Minister Gordon Coates to back the plan, and encouraged Māori dairy farmers to donate money to ensure it got the attention it deserved. The commission, established during 1926 with restricted resources, time frame and terms of reference, recommended limited compensation where confiscation was found to have been excessive.

While he respected the tribal nature of Māori, Ratana also saw this was a source of pride and division that kept them powerless. He continued to meet opposition from Ringatū on the East Coast and the King movement in the Waikato. His attempts to engage with King Te Rata had been misunderstood, and he couldn't get near Te Puea, who remained the driving force in the movement because of Te Rata's ongoing illness. Te Puea considered Ratana 'an undistinguished charlatan and a usurper of traditional loyalties', an enemy of the Kīngitanga and a threat to Te Rata's leadership. She was annoyed that many Maniapoto people of Tainui were turning to Ratana despite having reached an accord with the King movement, warning they could not serve two masters.

In April 1926, Ratana announced he would no longer address the people according to tribes or sub-tribes. He looked back to November 1918, when he had been told to spread the good news, heal the Māori people of their infirmities, and call his followers mōrehu. 'It doesn't matter where you come from in this land, those of you who are in this maramatanga will be welcomed as morehu, for that is what the chosen people are called.'

Before a major gathering or hui, or departing for a tour, Ratana would spend over a week in meditation, study and prayers, and only when he felt the time was right would he appear before the mōrehu with encouragement or guidance

Labourers worked tirelessly to complete the Ratana Temple within eighteen months so it could be opened during Christmas 1927. *Uri Whakatupuranga (Ratana Archives).*

about the task ahead. Many of his pronouncements on the marae were based on biblical texts and often regarded as prophetic. During most gatherings there was some announcement or 'prophecy'. Ratana would invariably remain among the crowd or seated on the veranda of his homestead until he felt the time was right to resolve a debate, or introduce some revelation.

He frequently delegated public speaking, particularly where there was a ceremonial role requiring great oratory skills or knowledge of Māori protocol. It was this approach that was misunderstood by King Te Rata's advisers in 1922 after Ratana failed to appear at the head of his party, leaving the formalities to his secretary, Pita Moko. Despite the ongoing difficulties with the Māori royal family, Ratana was determined to find common ground. He feared that the people would blame him if he did not make an effort to include the King movement in his plans to rally Māoridom as a political force to deal with Māori issues.

The stand-off was both political and spiritual. Te Puea was firmly entrenched in the Pai Mārire movement that had inspired her grandfather, and while it included Old Testament elements it still embraced Māoritanga and its plurality of gods and ancestral worship. She was also caught in a political bind with both Apirana Ngata, who had at this time been in Parliament for 22 years, and Reform Party Prime Minister Gordon Coates, who relied on her support. They feared the rise of the Labour Party which, with the support of Ratana, could displace them both.

Drowning the pain

As the year progressed, Ratana began to take the disappointments and rejection personally. Civil and church leaders had taken every opportunity to discredit and mock him. Anglican Bishop Sedgwick, addressing the Waiapu Diocesan Synod, claimed Ratana's faith-healing era was over, he was losing his mana among the people and the movement was declining. Archbishop Averill predicted he would be stranded like Rua, the prophet from Te Urewera. Sir Apirana Ngata said at a conference at Arohanui Pā, near Whanganui, that he'd been waiting a long time for Māori to see 'the unwisdom' of joining Ratana.

Ratana was weary; there were financial problems, and the growing responsibility of motivating his movement and shouldering the burden of his work as well as his role as president of the Kotahitanga was taking its toll. He increasingly took refuge at the seaside with his immediate family or drove to Te Poi near Matamata to escape the growing pressures and the constant demands of the people at the Pā. As the Kōmiti Hāhi Matua took over more of the church-related business, Ratana again became prone to 'immoderate drinking'.

As the Depression bit harder many people were laid off from their jobs, and when seasonal employment at the freezing works ended, many Māori would arrive at Ratana Pā, where there was often excessive use of alcohol. On one of those occasions a light aircraft landed on the marae offering rides for a fee. Jim McLeod Henderson wrote that one of the first on board was Ratana.

> As the plane circled over the marae the prophet appeared carrying gin, whisky and beer bottles which he dropped to the ground. When he drank, he said he did so to show the morehu that he was entirely human, not divine. Unable to sustain the role forced on him by the people, of magician, reincarnation or 'younger brother of Christ' and inaugurator of a new era, 'the dispensation of the Faithful Angels', he appeared as very human when he said that he was not 'like a parson all the time'. Sometimes he was the Mangai, inspired of God, inhabited by the wairua [spirit] of the prophets, and at other times he was just Bill Ratana who wanted everyone to have a drink and be happy. After an orgy [drinking binge] in Wanganui or Marton he would return to set to work to improve the appearance of the Pa.

Another example has Ratana drinking a bottle of whisky in front of the assembled people at the Pā. Tossing aside the empty bottle he apparently said, 'Now that's the Devil, and I, your Mangai, have taken him inside myself so that you, the morehu, will not be harmed. Don't touch the stuff.' At times he would load his small car up with children and take a ride into the hotel at Turakina for an hour or two. While sitting outside waiting for him, the children made up an action song:

> Motu kaa iti rawa ee
> Ko Piri Wiri Tua te taraiwa ee
> Tangi ana te koongo
> Ooga! Ooga! Ooga!
> Goodbye e te iwi ee.

Ans Westra, at the time working for the Maori Affairs Department publication *Te Ao Hou*, managed to capture the atmosphere in the Ratana Temple during a 1962 service by crouching on a balcony above the people. From this time on she regularly captured historic images at the annual Ratana celebrations. *Ans Westra*.

'In the little motor car with Piri Wiri Tua as the driver, the horn going Ooga! Ooga! Ooga!' they sang as they rattled back to the marae to buy ice creams and 'keep quiet about where they had been'. After one of his binges that year, Ratana was convicted of drunken driving and driving without a licence. Name suppression was refused. News of his lapse only gave his detractors further ammunition, undermining his authority within the movement and the wider community. Ratana's problems with alcohol could in part be seen as representative of an epidemic among Māori; it is claimed as many as 80 per cent of Māori men were struggling with the waipiro (poisoned or stinking water).

After his brush with the law Ratana offered to resign leadership of the church, but no one could agree on a successor. His wife Te Urumanao convinced him to resume his position. A decade after his original vision, Ratana appeared before the people, humbled by his recent state of mind and conscious of the great burden that lay on his shoulders.

Greetings to you all on this day, the 8th of November . . . I am here before you all without a collar and tie, without a white shirt and my clothes well worn and tattered. This was my appearance when the enlightenment descended upon me. Before today I wasn't known as a respectable man, I was likened to an animal . . . I who had no relatives, no friends, nobody took any notice of me. Only those who drank liquor with me, and the animals of course. Yes in these days I wasn't a good person to know. I drank liquor, became a drunkard and even an alcoholic. If I was to tell you the physical pain I suffered under the Holy Spirit you will not believe me. I stand here before you bearing the scars of my physical ordeal. But today as I stand enlightened I am called a man . . . by whom? By Ihoa o nga Mano, Matua, Tama, Wairua Tapu me nga Anahera Pono. They covered me with the cloak of enlightenment and then you who are known as the morehu. Therefore I greet the morehu within the enlightenment because you promoted me to this position for which I am now recognised as a man on this day the 8th of November. May you all receive the blessings you have prayed for.

The shaky foundation of his relationship with the traditional churches continued to crumble. Apirana Ngata, who was feeling political pressure from the Ratana movement, also had influence within the Anglican Church, and in 1928 persuaded it to establish a Māori bishopric of Aotearoa. There were also logistical problems in some rural areas where Ratana had shared buildings with other churches. At Pāmapūria, near Kaitaia, a fence was built down the centre of a graveyard. And in Te Kao a meeting house was literally cut in half with axes in a conflict between 'white sheep and black sheep', a division that continued for many years, according to Jim McLeod Henderson.

While the other denominations had deserted, the Methodists continued to emphasise tact and patience, careful not to unduly subvert 'the marvellous reawakening of racial consciousness and the desire of the people to organise and control their own religious activities'. The Methodist Board had decided that 'the interests of the Kingdom of God and the development of the Maori race must ever be put before purely denominational considerations'.

Despite the ongoing criticism from political and so-called spiritual circles, the Ratana movement itself was growing at an astonishing rate. It was estimated by Ngata in parliamentary questions in 1927 that it had more than 21,500 members, about one-third of the Māori population.

NINE

GOOD NEWS FROM AFAR

> Your temple is now like a ladder, reaching from earth to heaven . . . Heaven is Ihoa's throne, and the earth is Ihoa's footstool, thus on this day the foot of Ihoa is drawn here to this marae, never again will you have to wonder, where is Ihoa . . . the angels which the people of the world fear to mention, are continually descending to this earth and ascending to heaven . . . I am with the angels; the Son is with the angels and the angels are among you also.
> —T. W. Ratana at the opening of Te Temepara Tapu o Ihoa, 1927

Theology of the temple

There were many events competing for Ratana's attention as 1927 drew to a close, including the completion of Te Temepara Tapu o Ihoa and the imminent arrival of his old friend Bishop Juji Nakada, who had confirmed he would be crossing the 'waves of the great ocean to Aotearoa' for the opening. He wrote quoting Proverbs 25:25: 'Good news from a far off land is like cold water to a thirsty soul.' The platform for his visit would be 'faith, hope and love', including the love shared in Japan in 1924 when Ratana and his rōpū (group) had been welcome guests at his school of music in Kashiwagi.

He was greeted by Ratana and members of the 1924 world tour party outside the newly completed temple on 21 December, then escorted by the Ratana band onto the marae where about 2000 people were waiting. Bishop Nakada brought greetings from the Christians in Japan, explaining that he and his people continued to observe and celebrate Ratana's special day, 8 November. 'Indeed, may I say we are of one family, of one blood, even as we are joined together as are all Christians in the blood of Christ, Son of the Living God.' He was near tears as he concluded:

Bishop Juji Nakada arrived in time for the official opening of the Ratana Temple and the driving in of the 'last nail', which symbolised completion and reaffirmed the symbolic 'marriage' between the Japanese and Māori people. *Uri Whakatupuranga (Ratana Archives)*.

You, who live under the star of the south, have been blessed with the gift of divine light and enlightenment. We, who live under the star of the north, have not yet been blessed with that divine gift. I therefore urge you to strongly and earnestly pray that we, too, be blessed with the divine light that shines upon you.

It had been a rough year. Ratana had been challenged by politicians, preachers and his own people. Here at last here was an occasion to celebrate. The great temple of his vision was built on time and to budget. Most of the funding had come from the mōrehu, as had much of the labour, for which he was grateful.

During these past years, it was predicted by the critics . . . that it would not take long, that you the bearers, Nga Pou, will fall together with your maramatanga. However, because the gospel, that you preach today, is the gospel of Revelation according to St John, the gospel of the Father and of the Son, and of the Holy Spirit and Faithful Angels . . . you will not fall down in the storm and criticism of man . . . All those who uplift the work for the Glory of Ihoa, know . . . that this enlightenment you uplift today will not dissolve. To those who are steadfast, and hold fast to my teaching, I greet you, for I can not pay you for your undertaking, but may the Holy Trinity reward you.

He urged the people not to take notice of ignorant words regarding their māramatanga. 'Leave them to fly around, but unite the morehu, and hold fast

The official opening of the Ratana Temple, January 1928. *Uri Whakatupuranga* (Ratana Archives).

to peace, where-in lies the power of the Father, of the Son, of the Holy Spirit, of the Faithful Angels and Te Mangai.' He spoke of the temple as a refuge for the mōrehu, a place where 'the breath of [the] Holy Spirit . . . [had] been spilled from heaven, that morehu may drink thereof, and be spiritually nourished':

> Your temple is now like a ladder, reaching from earth to heaven . . . Heaven is Ihoa's throne, and the earth is Ihoa's footstool, thus on this day the foot of Ihoa is drawn here to this marae, never again will you have to wonder, where is Ihoa . . . the angels which the people of the world fear to mention, are continually descending to this earth and ascending to heaven . . . I am with the angels; the Son is with the angels and the angels are among you also.

He remained concerned some were departing from the teachings, reminding them that the truths and the healing had been sought by many outside Māoridom. He prophesied, like the Old Testament prophet Amos, of a time when there would be a great hunger for the words of God, but because they didn't accept them when they were given, many would wander 'from sea to sea' and not find what they were looking for. He warned that if his people did not take advantage of his māramatanga, which was now represented in the temple, others would seek it out: 'For what is written here . . . is the accomplishment and fruition of great things. [If it was not for] the revelation of this enlightenment by the Tama to the Mangai o nga Ariki the miracles would not have happened . . . also the great works set out in these days have been fulfilled.'

Temple opening

Bishop Nakada returned to Ratana Pā after a short trip to Auckland where he preached at Methodist and Anglican churches. On 25 January 1928 he was present for T. W. Ratana's 55th birthday celebrations, and the official opening and consecration of the temple. There were 110 apostles, 60 ākonga and 70 āwhina in attendance.

Ratana's sermon addressed some of the most controversial and misunder-

Above left: The stained glass imagery above the pulpit or 'throne' is the Seal of God (Te Hīri o Ihoa). The white circle background represents the Son of God and the five-pointed star in the foreground features the Tokotoru Tapu (Holy Trinity) in the three upward points of the stars, with the two purple base points symbolising the angelic host pointing downwards. Above this image is the centre point where all things are linked together by chains that encircle the building interior. *Above right:* The chains around the interior of the Ratana Temple link Matua, Tama, Wairua Tapu, Anahera Pono, the Māngai and Ratana in the wider cosmology of the Ratana faith and give Ihu Karaiti (Tama, the Son) pride of place at the front. For many years the exotic collection of potplants around the walls were all imported from other nations, indicating the Ratana Temple was for all nations and peoples.
Uri Whakatupuranga (Ratana Archives).

stood elements of his theology, now woven into the tapestry of symbolism in the temple. He said Ihoa was there at the creation of the universe and space, as was the enemy Satan. From the beginning, 'Ihoa was one with the Father, the Son and the Holy Spirit and Ihoa was one with the Faithful Angels'. The words and symbols in the temple showed the nature of the Father and the coming of the Son, who descended from the Throne of Ihoa, was conceived in the womb of Mary and born into this world as a physical man named Jesus Christ, to fulfil scriptural prophecy.

He was saddened the name Jesus Christ was used extensively by the Pākehā as a swear word.

> Just recently I heard one saying: 'By Jesus Christ I'll kill you!' This is not the only way this name is blasphemed, or used wrongfully, there are many others . . . let us leave this name Christ aside in peace and understanding, for others to use; let us, instead, adhere to the Son, a name we have yet to hear blasphemed or used as a swear word.
>
> I do not deny the Christ; I agree and believe in the Christ and his mission of this earth. However, now he has risen into heaven, and is known as the Son of the Living Father, the name pronounced at the beginning of creation. The Christ said I was (born) even before Abraham and the prophets. The question

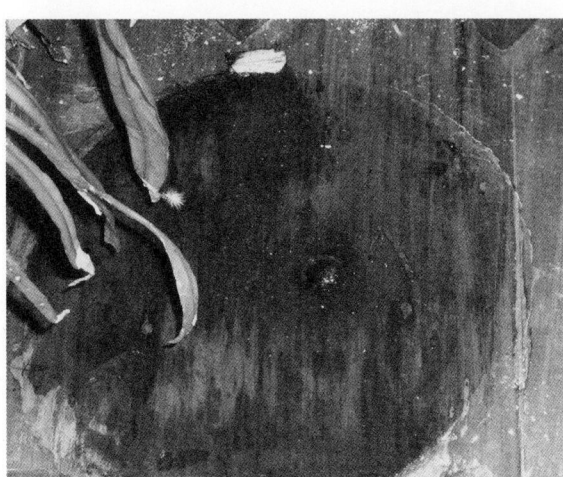

The empty space and impression left by the Japanese 'last nail' coin placed inside the Ratana Temple by Bishop Nakada in 1928. It was stolen in 2000. *Kereama Pene.*

then arises, whose birth (or existence) was the Christ referring to? Let me tell you – it was not the birth of his body but rather that of the Spiritual Son.

After Christ had been baptised he went out into the desert and Satan appeared to tempt and test him. Satan said: 'If you are the Son of God, command these stones to become loaves of bread' (Matthew 4:3). Therefore, said Ratana, it was clear that Satan knew 'the Son' was Christ's original name. 'Truly the Son did descend into the womb of Mary, and when born into this world and living on this earth, he was called Jesus Christ. It also follows logically that his name should now be the Son, as he has risen into heaven.'

And he used Christ's last word to his disciples:

Go therefore and make disciples of all nations, baptising them in the name of the Father, and of the Son, and of the Holy Spirit' (Matthew 28:19). Jesus did not say 'in the name of the Father, and of the Christ, and of the Holy Spirit'. Today we include in our prayers the Faithful Angels, and so complete that which was left us by Christ, thus adding strength to our faith.

Ratana said that he had not invented these things thoughtlessly, and urged the Māori people to unite as one under the powerful hand of Ihoa, the Father, the Son, the Holy Spirit and the Faithful Angels. He would not allow God's word and māramatanga to be twisted or spoilt, to please or benefit the physical person; only the Spirit preaches good and truth: 'I shall not preach in a manner designed just for the sake of pleasing (people) or to gain rewards for myself. If I were thinking of personal gain, or seeking a high place for myself, I would have sold myself to the world long ago.'

Eruera Tirikatene captured the first of the Ratana political seats. He was also a registered apostle in the church, having been taught personally by T. W. Ratana. He was often asked to remove angel statues and images of Ratana that were placed in the temple by those who adored the teacher more than his teachings. *Ans Westra.*

After Ratana delivered his sermon in front of the temple, Bishop Nakada addressed the congregation: 'I believe the work in which Ratana is engaged is for the good of the Maori people throughout this land . . . I will pray for Ratana in all his good works . . . that the blessings of the Great One, the Father, be forever upon him, and that in all his work the true Spirit of Jesus Christ be with you'. He asked the mōrehu who 'are blessed with God's gift of Divine Light' to pray for the 70 million Japanese people that they too may be given 'the power and authority to stamp out idolatry and evil in the name of God Almighty'.

After a third hymn, Ratana ended the service with a prayer and then drove te nēra whakamutunga (the 'last nail') through a Japanese yen coin provided by Bishop Nakada, into the area in front of the tumuaki's throne. The last nail symbolised the coming together of the spiritual and physical elements of Ratana's mission, sealing the promises of the future spiritual blessings that would come to the Japanese people and the economic help that they would provide to the Māori people in the future.

Bishop Nakada had previously shipped out to New Zealand stained glass for the windows in the temple, particularly blue and purple colours that had been unavailable locally. Another gift had been the large 'clock mechanism', which had been meticulously planted around with colourful flowers at the front of the temple.

When the Ratana troupe had performed at his music school and in concerts in Japan Nakada had been so impressed by the songs and hymns that he had

noted them down, written sheet music and trained his people to sing them. He presented Ratana with the book of musical arrangements for the choirs and bands.

Ratana apostle Kereama Pene says that the church had never had written music before. Most of the hymns were based on the style of the old-time American Methodist preacher and singer Ira Sankey. Nakada's gift enabled the choirs to move to another level. Of the transcribed hymns, six were 'inspired pieces' known as takutai moana (foreshore) hymns, believed to have come through the direct inspiration of the Holy Spirit and the angels as Ratana meditated at the mouth of the Whangaehu River. He would hear the music, Paraire Paikea would transcribe what Ratana sang and women choir members would help sing and remember the tunes.

TEMPLE SYMBOLISM

Today Temepara Tapu o Ihoa, restored to its original design with white stone walls, red-tiled roof and twin green-topped bell towers remains the centre of religious worship at Ratana Pā. The 100 wooden pews, capable of seating up to 2000 people, are filled with faithful during the founder's birthday service and on other church occasions.

As well as being a type of the Old Testament temple where the children of Israel worshipped Jehovah, the Ratana Temple is symbolic of the salvation of the people and the New Testament promise of the Holy Spirit dwelling in the believer, in the inner temple of the human heart. The rich symbolism is intended to represent the entire cosmology of Ratana's belief system inside and out – from the Holy Trinity held sacred by mainstream churches to the 'Sun of God' on the apex of the outer building and the Eye of God (kanohi) just inside the entrance. The symbols, words and colour schemes are designed to lift the people above their worldly cares to marvel at the God of heaven and his promises to the people.

The main stained glass window, directly above the throne, features the Seal of God (Te Hīri o Ihoa mentioned in Revelation 7:2), as a large five-pointed star in a white circle background, which is Te Tama o Ihoa (the White Sun or Son of God). This symbol, created in 1926, features the Tokotoru Tapu (Holy Trinity) in the colours of the three upward points of the stars, with the two purple base points representing the angelic host. The Trinity gets all the praise and credit while the angelic messengers are said to come and go in a manner reminiscent of Jacob's dream, where he saw a ladder to heaven and the angels ascending and descending, marking that place as holy.

In the Ratana theology there are two groups of angels: Anahera Pono, the

Faithful Angels led by Kapariera (Gabriel); and the Anahera Tapu, the Holy Angels led by Mikaera (Michael). The seal is surrounded by the seven angels mentioned in Revelation. The name Ihu Karaiti (Jesus Christ) is given a place of reverence at the front of the temple.

The main Ratana symbol, the whetū mārama (star and moon), represents the Kingdom of Light or Māramatanga, standing firm against Satan and the forces of darkness or mākutu. This tohu or symbol – a five-pointed star and a crescent moon – is repeated at equal spacing around the interior joined by five chains. These whetū mārama all have gold as the downward point, signifying enlightenment, with the colours representing the Father (blue) and the Son (white) pointing upwards and the angels (purple) and Holy Spirit (red) pointing outwards. On the crescent moon under the stars appears the name T. W. Ratana. It is the work of the angels and the Wairua Tapu to draw all people to Ihoa, and it was Ratana's work to unite Māori under Ihoa o ngā Mano.

The chains linking the symbols around the walls of the temple represent unity in the heavenly order. They link Ihoa to the Son, the Son to the Holy Spirit, the Holy Spirit to the angels and, beneath them, Tama and the Māngai are also linked, emphasising the distinction between Christ's earthly mission in a physical body and his risen, perfected form as the Son. It is said these versions of the whetū mārama, and there are many variants around Ratana Pā, represent Ihoa and the Son establishing a tūrangawaewae (strong foundation) on earth, and the anointing of God's Word, which is to be spoken out through the Ratana māramatanga.

The five-pointed star and crescent moon symbol is also used on the two bell tower domes and on the rear ridge of the temple. The three stars on the temple (two at the front and one at the rear) have the crescent moon (enlightenment) touching the blue (Father) and purple (the angels), with red (Wairua Tapu) pointing towards the sea (Te Takutai Moana o Whangaehu) in the direction from which the cloud appeared on that afternoon of 8 November 1918. If you follow the lines on the map from the Ratana Temple as they stretch out across the world, it is said they align with Israel.

Different drought

On Saturday 11 February 1928, Ratana gathered the people to the temple. Ever since Christmas, he had felt a growing sense of unease. To make things worse there hadn't been rain for over a month and the water tanks were drying up. High winds were ranging across the ground and dust was flying everywhere.

When the temple bells stopped ringing, he spoke of opposing forces at work

in the Pā and wondered whether this was why prayers weren't being answered and why 'the gates of heaven remain closed and refuse to let rain fall upon us'. He concluded that it was because people were 'backbiting and belittling' him and not getting on with the works he had asked of them.

He again put out the challenge for unity in following his message and the plans he had prepared, including the work of the Pā. He said the path ahead would soon become clear, and he went inside to pray and consider the way forward. At midnight, after everyone had returned to their homes, it began to rain. A reporter from *Whetu Marama* saw Ratana and Te Whaea and their family standing on the veranda of their home giving thanks to 'the Holy Trinity, the Faithful Angels and the Mangai'.

During the opening ceremony a fortnight earlier Ratana had stood at the front of the temple between the two bell towers and declared again that his spiritual works were complete, saying much of that responsibility would now rest with the apostles and officers of the Ratana Church. The temple would become the central symbol of the movement. 'As I stand here, the Mangai remains and will abide in the temple. My name henceforth shall be Piri Wiri Tua. I shall plough the land and till the earth.'

TEN

THE PHYSICAL WORKS

I have told you, you have not yet seen the glory of Ihoa; human knowledge cannot reveal it to you, because it has not yet been seen by man; that is why we do not fear; however the day is coming when those who do not see will see, when those who do not hear will hear, and those who do not fear will fear. It will be then that the faithful will have their faith endorsed. There are too many people who are waiting for fire to come down from heaven to hear the thunder and to see the lightning; never mind, oh Morehu, don't worry, for you are Ihoa's footstool.

—T. W. Ratana, 18 December 1926

I shall divide my 'body' into four quarters and I alone shall put it together again . . . While I do this work I shall be known as Wiremu, a human being just like you. Why must it be so? Lest the people become startled as they are when they call me Mangai.

—T. W. Ratana at Te Kūiti in 1928, announcing his intention to contest the Māori seats

Ploughing the land

While Ratana's ministry is often simplistically split into spiritual and political periods, the Ture Wairua and the Ture Tangata were clearly inseparable aspects of the work he was engaged in. Like the Christian ethos of faith being wasted without works and works ineffectual without faith, he needed both pillars to remain strong.

His claim to be representing not only the Māori people but Ihoa o ngā Mano

and the political and spiritual heritage of his forebears had given him the mana to motivate and indeed lead the people into the next stage. The powerful events at the outset of his ministry had already laid out a much grander plan than any politician on the hustings could muster.

While he was fishing with his family in 1918 two large whales had surfed to the shore in an extraordinary spectacle. The first whale lay quietly on the sand resigned to its fate, representing the Ture Wairua – the spiritual works which embraced the Bible, the challenge to tohungaism and an extraordinary healing ministry. The second whale, symbolising the Ture Tangata or physical works, had thrashed about violently then allegedly escaped back to the ocean. This represented Ratana's redoubled effort to deal with Māori land grievances through the Treaty of Waitangi. Having been rejected by politicians and royalty, he would now work towards becoming the government and creating change from within.

Ratana knew that it was time to sort out affairs in his own backyard, literally turning his hand to matters of the land and farming his own acreage at Ratana Pā, and figuratively 'ploughing' the nation to determine the support for his new role as Piri Wiri Tua, the 'treaty campaigner'.

The Kotahitanga executive had purchased an additional 700-acre farm bordering the Pā between the main Whanganui-Palmerston North highway and Rangatahi Road, but without the necessary effort to deliver a return it had been forced into bankruptcy. Ratana called the people together to prevent the land from being sold and encouraged visitors and locals to take a communal approach to sowing, tending and harvesting.

After discussions with Sir James Carroll, the Kotahitanga was further restructured in December 1927 under the guidance of Paraire Paikea and Eruera Tirikatene. Tirikatene was put in charge of the machinery and reclaiming the full 1200 acres. On the farm, which began on a hill overlooking the Pā, were two houses and a large building known as the Maunga Hinai (Mount Sinai) workshop, used as a granary and a storehouse. In it he set up a blacksmith's shop, and a machinery workshop where a fitter could maintain and repair the second-hand farm equipment, which included twelve tractors.

Some of the more affluent mōrehu were encouraged to bring in their tractors and machinery to clear the land of gorse, blackberry and scrub, and prepare 1000 acres for the wheat farm. The remaining 200 acres were to be set aside so that families living at the Pā could have their own vegetable gardens. The residents – including tractor drivers, lorry drivers, labourers, those who looked after the horses in the stables, mechanics, cooks, a blacksmith, a carpenter and bootmaker, along with frequent visitors – all pulled together to make the community self-supporting and pay off the debt. Workers were paid in cigarettes, tickets to dances and access to the pool tables at the Pā.

Tirikatene made arrangements for harvesting, while Paikea took over the

Above left: The stained glass imagery above the pulpit or 'throne' is the Seal of God (Te Hīri o Ihoa). The white circle background represents the Son of God and the five-pointed star in the foreground features the Tokotoru Tapu (Holy Trinity) in the three upward points of the stars, with the two purple base points symbolising the angelic host pointing downwards. Above this image is the centre point where all things are linked together by chains that encircle the building interior. *Above right:* The chains around the interior of the Ratana Temple link Matua, Tama, Wairua Tapu, Anahera Pono, the Māngai and Ratana in the wider cosmology of the Ratana faith and give Ihu Karaiti (Tama, the Son) pride of place at the front. For many years the exotic collection of potplants around the walls were all imported from other nations, indicating the Ratana Temple was for all nations and peoples.
Uri Whakatupuranga (Ratana Archives).

stood elements of his theology, now woven into the tapestry of symbolism in the temple. He said Ihoa was there at the creation of the universe and space, as was the enemy Satan. From the beginning, 'Ihoa was one with the Father, the Son and the Holy Spirit and Ihoa was one with the Faithful Angels'. The words and symbols in the temple showed the nature of the Father and the coming of the Son, who descended from the Throne of Ihoa, was conceived in the womb of Mary and born into this world as a physical man named Jesus Christ, to fulfil scriptural prophecy.

He was saddened the name Jesus Christ was used extensively by the Pākehā as a swear word.

> Just recently I heard one saying: 'By Jesus Christ I'll kill you!' This is not the only way this name is blasphemed, or used wrongfully, there are many others . . . let us leave this name Christ aside in peace and understanding, for others to use; let us, instead, adhere to the Son, a name we have yet to hear blasphemed or used as a swear word.
>
> I do not deny the Christ; I agree and believe in the Christ and his mission of this earth. However, now he has risen into heaven, and is known as the Son of the Living Father, the name pronounced at the beginning of creation. The Christ said I was (born) even before Abraham and the prophets. The question

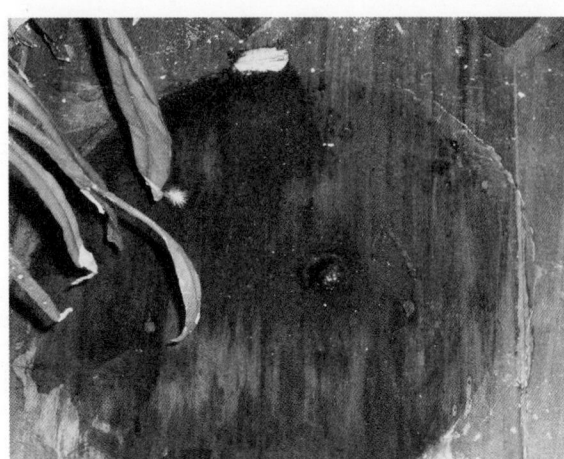

The empty space and impression left by the Japanese 'last nail' coin placed inside the Ratana Temple by Bishop Nakada in 1928. It was stolen in 2000. *Kereama Pene.*

then arises, whose birth (or existence) was the Christ referring to? Let me tell you – it was not the birth of his body but rather that of the Spiritual Son.

After Christ had been baptised he went out into the desert and Satan appeared to tempt and test him. Satan said: 'If you are the Son of God, command these stones to become loaves of bread' (Matthew 4:3). Therefore, said Ratana, it was clear that Satan knew 'the Son' was Christ's original name. 'Truly the Son did descend into the womb of Mary, and when born into this world and living on this earth, he was called Jesus Christ. It also follows logically that his name should now be the Son, as he has risen into heaven.'

And he used Christ's last word to his disciples:

Go therefore and make disciples of all nations, baptising them in the name of the Father, and of the Son, and of the Holy Spirit' (Matthew 28:19). Jesus did not say 'in the name of the Father, and of the Christ, and of the Holy Spirit'. Today we include in our prayers the Faithful Angels, and so complete that which was left us by Christ, thus adding strength to our faith.

Ratana said that he had not invented these things thoughtlessly, and urged the Māori people to unite as one under the powerful hand of Ihoa, the Father, the Son, the Holy Spirit and the Faithful Angels. He would not allow God's word and māramatanga to be twisted or spoilt, to please or benefit the physical person; only the Spirit preaches good and truth: 'I shall not preach in a manner designed just for the sake of pleasing (people) or to gain rewards for myself. If I were thinking of personal gain, or seeking a high place for myself, I would have sold myself to the world long ago.'

Eruera Tirikatene captured the first of the Ratana political seats. He was also a registered apostle in the church, having been taught personally by T. W. Ratana. He was often asked to remove angel statues and images of Ratana that were placed in the temple by those who adored the teacher more than his teachings. *Ans Westra.*

After Ratana delivered his sermon in front of the temple, Bishop Nakada addressed the congregation: 'I believe the work in which Ratana is engaged is for the good of the Maori people throughout this land . . . I will pray for Ratana in all his good works . . . that the blessings of the Great One, the Father, be forever upon him, and that in all his work the true Spirit of Jesus Christ be with you'. He asked the mōrehu who 'are blessed with God's gift of Divine Light' to pray for the 70 million Japanese people that they too may be given 'the power and authority to stamp out idolatry and evil in the name of God Almighty'.

After a third hymn, Ratana ended the service with a prayer and then drove te nēra whakamutunga (the 'last nail') through a Japanese yen coin provided by Bishop Nakada, into the area in front of the tumuaki's throne. The last nail symbolised the coming together of the spiritual and physical elements of Ratana's mission, sealing the promises of the future spiritual blessings that would come to the Japanese people and the economic help that they would provide to the Māori people in the future.

Bishop Nakada had previously shipped out to New Zealand stained glass for the windows in the temple, particularly blue and purple colours that had been unavailable locally. Another gift had been the large 'clock mechanism', which had been meticulously planted around with colourful flowers at the front of the temple.

When the Ratana troupe had performed at his music school and in concerts in Japan Nakada had been so impressed by the songs and hymns that he had

noted them down, written sheet music and trained his people to sing them. He presented Ratana with the book of musical arrangements for the choirs and bands.

Ratana apostle Kereama Pene says that the church had never had written music before. Most of the hymns were based on the style of the old-time American Methodist preacher and singer Ira Sankey. Nakada's gift enabled the choirs to move to another level. Of the transcribed hymns, six were 'inspired pieces' known as takutai moana (foreshore) hymns, believed to have come through the direct inspiration of the Holy Spirit and the angels as Ratana meditated at the mouth of the Whangaehu River. He would hear the music, Paraire Paikea would transcribe what Ratana sang and women choir members would help sing and remember the tunes.

TEMPLE SYMBOLISM

Today Temepara Tapu o Ihoa, restored to its original design with white stone walls, red-tiled roof and twin green-topped bell towers remains the centre of religious worship at Ratana Pā. The 100 wooden pews, capable of seating up to 2000 people, are filled with faithful during the founder's birthday service and on other church occasions.

As well as being a type of the Old Testament temple where the children of Israel worshipped Jehovah, the Ratana Temple is symbolic of the salvation of the people and the New Testament promise of the Holy Spirit dwelling in the believer, in the inner temple of the human heart. The rich symbolism is intended to represent the entire cosmology of Ratana's belief system inside and out – from the Holy Trinity held sacred by mainstream churches to the 'Sun of God' on the apex of the outer building and the Eye of God (kanohi) just inside the entrance. The symbols, words and colour schemes are designed to lift the people above their worldly cares to marvel at the God of heaven and his promises to the people.

The main stained glass window, directly above the throne, features the Seal of God (Te Hīri o Ihoa mentioned in Revelation 7:2), as a large five-pointed star in a white circle background, which is Te Tama o Ihoa (the White Sun or Son of God). This symbol, created in 1926, features the Tokotoru Tapu (Holy Trinity) in the colours of the three upward points of the stars, with the two purple base points representing the angelic host. The Trinity gets all the praise and credit while the angelic messengers are said to come and go in a manner reminiscent of Jacob's dream, where he saw a ladder to heaven and the angels ascending and descending, marking that place as holy.

In the Ratana theology there are two groups of angels: Anahera Pono, the

Faithful Angels led by Kapariera (Gabriel); and the Anahera Tapu, the Holy Angels led by Mikaera (Michael). The seal is surrounded by the seven angels mentioned in Revelation. The name Ihu Karaiti (Jesus Christ) is given a place of reverence at the front of the temple.

The main Ratana symbol, the whetū mārama (star and moon), represents the Kingdom of Light or Māramatanga, standing firm against Satan and the forces of darkness or mākutu. This tohu or symbol – a five-pointed star and a crescent moon – is repeated at equal spacing around the interior joined by five chains. These whetū mārama all have gold as the downward point, signifying enlightenment, with the colours representing the Father (blue) and the Son (white) pointing upwards and the angels (purple) and Holy Spirit (red) pointing outwards. On the crescent moon under the stars appears the name T. W. Ratana. It is the work of the angels and the Wairua Tapu to draw all people to Ihoa, and it was Ratana's work to unite Māori under Ihoa o ngā Mano.

The chains linking the symbols around the walls of the temple represent unity in the heavenly order. They link Ihoa to the Son, the Son to the Holy Spirit, the Holy Spirit to the angels and, beneath them, Tama and the Māngai are also linked, emphasising the distinction between Christ's earthly mission in a physical body and his risen, perfected form as the Son. It is said these versions of the whetū mārama, and there are many variants around Ratana Pā, represent Ihoa and the Son establishing a tūrangawaewae (strong foundation) on earth, and the anointing of God's Word, which is to be spoken out through the Ratana māramatanga.

The five-pointed star and crescent moon symbol is also used on the two bell tower domes and on the rear ridge of the temple. The three stars on the temple (two at the front and one at the rear) have the crescent moon (enlightenment) touching the blue (Father) and purple (the angels), with red (Wairua Tapu) pointing towards the sea (Te Takutai Moana o Whangaehu) in the direction from which the cloud appeared on that afternoon of 8 November 1918. If you follow the lines on the map from the Ratana Temple as they stretch out across the world, it is said they align with Israel.

Different drought

On Saturday 11 February 1928, Ratana gathered the people to the temple. Ever since Christmas, he had felt a growing sense of unease. To make things worse there hadn't been rain for over a month and the water tanks were drying up. High winds were ranging across the ground and dust was flying everywhere.

When the temple bells stopped ringing, he spoke of opposing forces at work

in the Pā and wondered whether this was why prayers weren't being answered and why 'the gates of heaven remain closed and refuse to let rain fall upon us'. He concluded that it was because people were 'backbiting and belittling' him and not getting on with the works he had asked of them.

He again put out the challenge for unity in following his message and the plans he had prepared, including the work of the Pā. He said the path ahead would soon become clear, and he went inside to pray and consider the way forward. At midnight, after everyone had returned to their homes, it began to rain. A reporter from *Whetu Marama* saw Ratana and Te Whaea and their family standing on the veranda of their home giving thanks to 'the Holy Trinity, the Faithful Angels and the Mangai'.

During the opening ceremony a fortnight earlier Ratana had stood at the front of the temple between the two bell towers and declared again that his spiritual works were complete, saying much of that responsibility would now rest with the apostles and officers of the Ratana Church. The temple would become the central symbol of the movement. 'As I stand here, the Mangai remains and will abide in the temple. My name henceforth shall be Piri Wiri Tua. I shall plough the land and till the earth.'

TEN

THE PHYSICAL WORKS

I have told you, you have not yet seen the glory of Ihoa; human knowledge cannot reveal it to you, because it has not yet been seen by man; that is why we do not fear; however the day is coming when those who do not see will see, when those who do not hear will hear, and those who do not fear will fear. It will be then that the faithful will have their faith endorsed. There are too many people who are waiting for fire to come down from heaven to hear the thunder and to see the lightning; never mind, oh Morehu, don't worry, for you are Ihoa's footstool.

—T. W. Ratana, 18 December 1926

I shall divide my 'body' into four quarters and I alone shall put it together again . . . While I do this work I shall be known as Wiremu, a human being just like you. Why must it be so? Lest the people become startled as they are when they call me Mangai.

—T. W. Ratana at Te Kūiti in 1928, announcing his intention to contest the Māori seats

Ploughing the land

While Ratana's ministry is often simplistically split into spiritual and political periods, the Ture Wairua and the Ture Tangata were clearly inseparable aspects of the work he was engaged in. Like the Christian ethos of faith being wasted without works and works ineffectual without faith, he needed both pillars to remain strong.

His claim to be representing not only the Māori people but Ihoa o ngā Mano

and the political and spiritual heritage of his forebears had given him the mana to motivate and indeed lead the people into the next stage. The powerful events at the outset of his ministry had already laid out a much grander plan than any politician on the hustings could muster.

While he was fishing with his family in 1918 two large whales had surfed to the shore in an extraordinary spectacle. The first whale lay quietly on the sand resigned to its fate, representing the Ture Wairua – the spiritual works which embraced the Bible, the challenge to tohungaism and an extraordinary healing ministry. The second whale, symbolising the Ture Tangata or physical works, had thrashed about violently then allegedly escaped back to the ocean. This represented Ratana's redoubled effort to deal with Māori land grievances through the Treaty of Waitangi. Having been rejected by politicians and royalty, he would now work towards becoming the government and creating change from within.

Ratana knew that it was time to sort out affairs in his own backyard, literally turning his hand to matters of the land and farming his own acreage at Ratana Pā, and figuratively 'ploughing' the nation to determine the support for his new role as Piri Wiri Tua, the 'treaty campaigner'.

The Kotahitanga executive had purchased an additional 700-acre farm bordering the Pā between the main Whanganui-Palmerston North highway and Rangatahi Road, but without the necessary effort to deliver a return it had been forced into bankruptcy. Ratana called the people together to prevent the land from being sold and encouraged visitors and locals to take a communal approach to sowing, tending and harvesting.

After discussions with Sir James Carroll, the Kotahitanga was further restructured in December 1927 under the guidance of Paraire Paikea and Eruera Tirikatene. Tirikatene was put in charge of the machinery and reclaiming the full 1200 acres. On the farm, which began on a hill overlooking the Pā, were two houses and a large building known as the Maunga Hinai (Mount Sinai) workshop, used as a granary and a storehouse. In it he set up a blacksmith's shop, and a machinery workshop where a fitter could maintain and repair the second-hand farm equipment, which included twelve tractors.

Some of the more affluent mōrehu were encouraged to bring in their tractors and machinery to clear the land of gorse, blackberry and scrub, and prepare 1000 acres for the wheat farm. The remaining 200 acres were to be set aside so that families living at the Pā could have their own vegetable gardens. The residents – including tractor drivers, lorry drivers, labourers, those who looked after the horses in the stables, mechanics, cooks, a blacksmith, a carpenter and bootmaker, along with frequent visitors – all pulled together to make the community self-supporting and pay off the debt. Workers were paid in cigarettes, tickets to dances and access to the pool tables at the Pā.

Tirikatene made arrangements for harvesting, while Paikea took over the

Above left: The stained glass imagery above the pulpit or 'throne' is the Seal of God (Te Hīri o Ihoa). The white circle background represents the Son of God and the five-pointed star in the foreground features the Tokotoru Tapu (Holy Trinity) in the three upward points of the stars, with the two purple base points symbolising the angelic host pointing downwards. Above this image is the centre point where all things are linked together by chains that encircle the building interior. *Above right:* The chains around the interior of the Ratana Temple link Matua, Tama, Wairua Tapu, Anahera Pono, the Māngai and Ratana in the wider cosmology of the Ratana faith and give Ihu Karaiti (Tama, the Son) pride of place at the front. For many years the exotic collection of potplants around the walls were all imported from other nations, indicating the Ratana Temple was for all nations and peoples.
Uri Whakatupuranga (Ratana Archives).

stood elements of his theology, now woven into the tapestry of symbolism in the temple. He said Ihoa was there at the creation of the universe and space, as was the enemy Satan. From the beginning, 'Ihoa was one with the Father, the Son and the Holy Spirit and Ihoa was one with the Faithful Angels'. The words and symbols in the temple showed the nature of the Father and the coming of the Son, who descended from the Throne of Ihoa, was conceived in the womb of Mary and born into this world as a physical man named Jesus Christ, to fulfil scriptural prophecy.

He was saddened the name Jesus Christ was used extensively by the Pākehā as a swear word.

> Just recently I heard one saying: 'By Jesus Christ I'll kill you!' This is not the only way this name is blasphemed, or used wrongfully, there are many others ... let us leave this name Christ aside in peace and understanding, for others to use; let us, instead, adhere to the Son, a name we have yet to hear blasphemed or used as a swear word.
>
> I do not deny the Christ; I agree and believe in the Christ and his mission of this earth. However, now he has risen into heaven, and is known as the Son of the Living Father, the name pronounced at the beginning of creation. The Christ said I was (born) even before Abraham and the prophets. The question

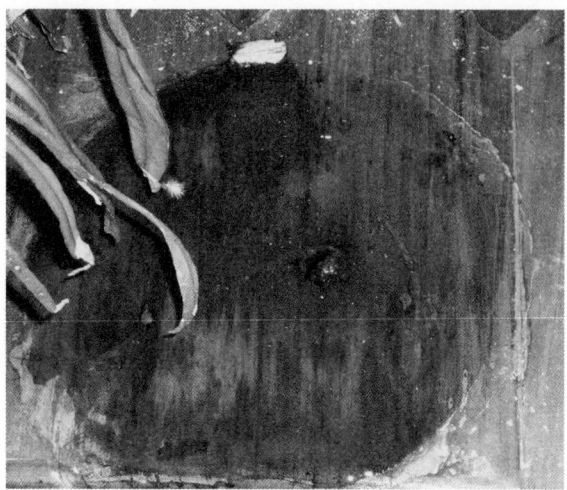

The empty space and impression left by the Japanese 'last nail' coin placed inside the Ratana Temple by Bishop Nakada in 1928. It was stolen in 2000.
Kereama Pene.

then arises, whose birth (or existence) was the Christ referring to? Let me tell you – it was not the birth of his body but rather that of the Spiritual Son.

After Christ had been baptised he went out into the desert and Satan appeared to tempt and test him. Satan said: 'If you are the Son of God, command these stones to become loaves of bread' (Matthew 4:3). Therefore, said Ratana, it was clear that Satan knew 'the Son' was Christ's original name. 'Truly the Son did descend into the womb of Mary, and when born into this world and living on this earth, he was called Jesus Christ. It also follows logically that his name should now be the Son, as he has risen into heaven.'

And he used Christ's last word to his disciples:

> Go therefore and make disciples of all nations, baptising them in the name of the Father, and of the Son, and of the Holy Spirit' (Matthew 28:19). Jesus did not say 'in the name of the Father, and of the Christ, and of the Holy Spirit'. Today we include in our prayers the Faithful Angels, and so complete that which was left us by Christ, thus adding strength to our faith.

Ratana said that he had not invented these things thoughtlessly, and urged the Māori people to unite as one under the powerful hand of Ihoa, the Father, the Son, the Holy Spirit and the Faithful Angels. He would not allow God's word and māramatanga to be twisted or spoilt, to please or benefit the physical person; only the Spirit preaches good and truth: 'I shall not preach in a manner designed just for the sake of pleasing (people) or to gain rewards for myself. If I were thinking of personal gain, or seeking a high place for myself, I would have sold myself to the world long ago.'

Eruera Tirikatene captured the first of the Ratana political seats. He was also a registered apostle in the church, having been taught personally by T. W. Ratana. He was often asked to remove angel statues and images of Ratana that were placed in the temple by those who adored the teacher more than his teachings. *Ans Westra.*

After Ratana delivered his sermon in front of the temple, Bishop Nakada addressed the congregation: 'I believe the work in which Ratana is engaged is for the good of the Maori people throughout this land . . . I will pray for Ratana in all his good works . . . that the blessings of the Great One, the Father, be forever upon him, and that in all his work the true Spirit of Jesus Christ be with you'. He asked the mōrehu who 'are blessed with God's gift of Divine Light' to pray for the 70 million Japanese people that they too may be given 'the power and authority to stamp out idolatry and evil in the name of God Almighty'.

After a third hymn, Ratana ended the service with a prayer and then drove te nēra whakamutunga (the 'last nail') through a Japanese yen coin provided by Bishop Nakada, into the area in front of the tumuaki's throne. The last nail symbolised the coming together of the spiritual and physical elements of Ratana's mission, sealing the promises of the future spiritual blessings that would come to the Japanese people and the economic help that they would provide to the Māori people in the future.

Bishop Nakada had previously shipped out to New Zealand stained glass for the windows in the temple, particularly blue and purple colours that had been unavailable locally. Another gift had been the large 'clock mechanism', which had been meticulously planted around with colourful flowers at the front of the temple.

When the Ratana troupe had performed at his music school and in concerts in Japan Nakada had been so impressed by the songs and hymns that he had

noted them down, written sheet music and trained his people to sing them. He presented Ratana with the book of musical arrangements for the choirs and bands.

Ratana apostle Kereama Pene says that the church had never had written music before. Most of the hymns were based on the style of the old-time American Methodist preacher and singer Ira Sankey. Nakada's gift enabled the choirs to move to another level. Of the transcribed hymns, six were 'inspired pieces' known as takutai moana (foreshore) hymns, believed to have come through the direct inspiration of the Holy Spirit and the angels as Ratana meditated at the mouth of the Whangaehu River. He would hear the music, Paraire Paikea would transcribe what Ratana sang and women choir members would help sing and remember the tunes.

TEMPLE SYMBOLISM

Today Temepara Tapu o Ihoa, restored to its original design with white stone walls, red-tiled roof and twin green-topped bell towers remains the centre of religious worship at Ratana Pā. The 100 wooden pews, capable of seating up to 2000 people, are filled with faithful during the founder's birthday service and on other church occasions.

As well as being a type of the Old Testament temple where the children of Israel worshipped Jehovah, the Ratana Temple is symbolic of the salvation of the people and the New Testament promise of the Holy Spirit dwelling in the believer, in the inner temple of the human heart. The rich symbolism is intended to represent the entire cosmology of Ratana's belief system inside and out – from the Holy Trinity held sacred by mainstream churches to the 'Sun of God' on the apex of the outer building and the Eye of God (kanohi) just inside the entrance. The symbols, words and colour schemes are designed to lift the people above their worldly cares to marvel at the God of heaven and his promises to the people.

The main stained glass window, directly above the throne, features the Seal of God (Te Hīri o Ihoa mentioned in Revelation 7:2), as a large five-pointed star in a white circle background, which is Te Tama o Ihoa (the White Sun or Son of God). This symbol, created in 1926, features the Tokotoru Tapu (Holy Trinity) in the colours of the three upward points of the stars, with the two purple base points representing the angelic host. The Trinity gets all the praise and credit while the angelic messengers are said to come and go in a manner reminiscent of Jacob's dream, where he saw a ladder to heaven and the angels ascending and descending, marking that place as holy.

In the Ratana theology there are two groups of angels: Anahera Pono, the

Faithful Angels led by Kapariera (Gabriel); and the Anahera Tapu, the Holy Angels led by Mikaera (Michael). The seal is surrounded by the seven angels mentioned in Revelation. The name Ihu Karaiti (Jesus Christ) is given a place of reverence at the front of the temple.

The main Ratana symbol, the whetū mārama (star and moon), represents the Kingdom of Light or Māramatanga, standing firm against Satan and the forces of darkness or mākutu. This tohu or symbol – a five-pointed star and a crescent moon – is repeated at equal spacing around the interior joined by five chains. These whetū mārama all have gold as the downward point, signifying enlightenment, with the colours representing the Father (blue) and the Son (white) pointing upwards and the angels (purple) and Holy Spirit (red) pointing outwards. On the crescent moon under the stars appears the name T. W. Ratana. It is the work of the angels and the Wairua Tapu to draw all people to Ihoa, and it was Ratana's work to unite Māori under Ihoa o ngā Mano.

The chains linking the symbols around the walls of the temple represent unity in the heavenly order. They link Ihoa to the Son, the Son to the Holy Spirit, the Holy Spirit to the angels and, beneath them, Tama and the Māngai are also linked, emphasising the distinction between Christ's earthly mission in a physical body and his risen, perfected form as the Son. It is said these versions of the whetū mārama, and there are many variants around Ratana Pā, represent Ihoa and the Son establishing a tūrangawaewae (strong foundation) on earth, and the anointing of God's Word, which is to be spoken out through the Ratana māramatanga.

The five-pointed star and crescent moon symbol is also used on the two bell tower domes and on the rear ridge of the temple. The three stars on the temple (two at the front and one at the rear) have the crescent moon (enlightenment) touching the blue (Father) and purple (the angels), with red (Wairua Tapu) pointing towards the sea (Te Takutai Moana o Whangaehu) in the direction from which the cloud appeared on that afternoon of 8 November 1918. If you follow the lines on the map from the Ratana Temple as they stretch out across the world, it is said they align with Israel.

Different drought

On Saturday 11 February 1928, Ratana gathered the people to the temple. Ever since Christmas, he had felt a growing sense of unease. To make things worse there hadn't been rain for over a month and the water tanks were drying up. High winds were ranging across the ground and dust was flying everywhere.

When the temple bells stopped ringing, he spoke of opposing forces at work

in the Pā and wondered whether this was why prayers weren't being answered and why 'the gates of heaven remain closed and refuse to let rain fall upon us'. He concluded that it was because people were 'backbiting and belittling' him and not getting on with the works he had asked of them.

He again put out the challenge for unity in following his message and the plans he had prepared, including the work of the Pā. He said the path ahead would soon become clear, and he went inside to pray and consider the way forward. At midnight, after everyone had returned to their homes, it began to rain. A reporter from *Whetu Marama* saw Ratana and Te Whaea and their family standing on the veranda of their home giving thanks to 'the Holy Trinity, the Faithful Angels and the Mangai'.

During the opening ceremony a fortnight earlier Ratana had stood at the front of the temple between the two bell towers and declared again that his spiritual works were complete, saying much of that responsibility would now rest with the apostles and officers of the Ratana Church. The temple would become the central symbol of the movement. 'As I stand here, the Mangai remains and will abide in the temple. My name henceforth shall be Piri Wiri Tua. I shall plough the land and till the earth.'

TEN

THE PHYSICAL WORKS

I have told you, you have not yet seen the glory of Ihoa; human knowledge cannot reveal it to you, because it has not yet been seen by man; that is why we do not fear; however the day is coming when those who do not see will see, when those who do not hear will hear, and those who do not fear will fear. It will be then that the faithful will have their faith endorsed. There are too many people who are waiting for fire to come down from heaven to hear the thunder and to see the lightning; never mind, oh Morehu, don't worry, for you are Ihoa's footstool.

—T. W. Ratana, 18 December 1926

I shall divide my 'body' into four quarters and I alone shall put it together again . . . While I do this work I shall be known as Wiremu, a human being just like you. Why must it be so? Lest the people become startled as they are when they call me Mangai.

—T. W. Ratana at Te Kūiti in 1928, announcing his intention to contest the Māori seats

Ploughing the land

While Ratana's ministry is often simplistically split into spiritual and political periods, the Ture Wairua and the Ture Tangata were clearly inseparable aspects of the work he was engaged in. Like the Christian ethos of faith being wasted without works and works ineffectual without faith, he needed both pillars to remain strong.

His claim to be representing not only the Māori people but Ihoa o ngā Mano

and the political and spiritual heritage of his forebears had given him the mana to motivate and indeed lead the people into the next stage. The powerful events at the outset of his ministry had already laid out a much grander plan than any politician on the hustings could muster.

While he was fishing with his family in 1918 two large whales had surfed to the shore in an extraordinary spectacle. The first whale lay quietly on the sand resigned to its fate, representing the Ture Wairua – the spiritual works which embraced the Bible, the challenge to tohungaism and an extraordinary healing ministry. The second whale, symbolising the Ture Tangata or physical works, had thrashed about violently then allegedly escaped back to the ocean. This represented Ratana's redoubled effort to deal with Māori land grievances through the Treaty of Waitangi. Having been rejected by politicians and royalty, he would now work towards becoming the government and creating change from within.

Ratana knew that it was time to sort out affairs in his own backyard, literally turning his hand to matters of the land and farming his own acreage at Ratana Pā, and figuratively 'ploughing' the nation to determine the support for his new role as Piri Wiri Tua, the 'treaty campaigner'.

The Kotahitanga executive had purchased an additional 700-acre farm bordering the Pā between the main Whanganui-Palmerston North highway and Rangatahi Road, but without the necessary effort to deliver a return it had been forced into bankruptcy. Ratana called the people together to prevent the land from being sold and encouraged visitors and locals to take a communal approach to sowing, tending and harvesting.

After discussions with Sir James Carroll, the Kotahitanga was further restructured in December 1927 under the guidance of Paraire Paikea and Eruera Tirikatene. Tirikatene was put in charge of the machinery and reclaiming the full 1200 acres. On the farm, which began on a hill overlooking the Pā, were two houses and a large building known as the Maunga Hinai (Mount Sinai) workshop, used as a granary and a storehouse. In it he set up a blacksmith's shop, and a machinery workshop where a fitter could maintain and repair the second-hand farm equipment, which included twelve tractors.

Some of the more affluent mōrehu were encouraged to bring in their tractors and machinery to clear the land of gorse, blackberry and scrub, and prepare 1000 acres for the wheat farm. The remaining 200 acres were to be set aside so that families living at the Pā could have their own vegetable gardens. The residents – including tractor drivers, lorry drivers, labourers, those who looked after the horses in the stables, mechanics, cooks, a blacksmith, a carpenter and bootmaker, along with frequent visitors – all pulled together to make the community self-supporting and pay off the debt. Workers were paid in cigarettes, tickets to dances and access to the pool tables at the Pā.

Tirikatene made arrangements for harvesting, while Paikea took over the

accounts and ensured grain from the farm was sent off to the Manawatu Mill in Palmerston North. They grew 100 acres of potatoes and other vegetables, and a similar acreage of barley and oats. Kamokamo (marrow) and corn were also grown and sold at market to support those living at the Pā. The Ratana wheat farm, with a total of 500 acres sown, proved to be a profitable and successful enterprise for several years. In fact, it was lauded by the government as one of the best wheat farms in the country and an example of how Māori could pull together to improve their own lot.

Ratana Pā now had 600 permanent residents, and plans were made to extend the facilities to enable it to operate more efficiently as a haven for the people. Mōrehu from different tribal areas were allocated sections to build homes and meeting houses, but after a conflict with the Rangitikei County Council, the tiny township was declared a separate borough with its own local by-laws, rules and regulations.

There were two butcher shops, four general stores, a billiard room and a bakery producing up to 150 loaves of bread each day. The roads were sealed, a makeshift electricity system was built by Tirikatene, and a generator provided by Ratana powered the buildings and street lights. A loudspeaker system broadcast news, public notices or sports results around the marae. Contractors from outside the Pā had previously run 'moving pictures', but now Ratana himself invested in a projector and invited a film-maker to record activities at the Pā, including poi and haka, and to teach others to operate the camera.

To provide for the annual hui, beasts were killed and portioned in the abattoir, then steam-cooked and served with potatoes, pūhā and boiled karengo (seaweed). There were Māori concerts, brass band performances and, in the seven large halls, lively discussions followed by church services, along with accounts of Ratana's miracles retold in story and song. A work programme was begun for the growing number of restless unemployed who were swelling the transient population. Paikea set up various committees around the country to manage work relating to the church, the people, the Treaty of Waitangi and Māori land claims. Security officers, nurses and apostles were appointed to look after the work and train up others. The line of reporting went all the way back to the Kotahitanga Management Committee.

Work schemes applauded

During 1928 the economic and social depression and the subsequent level of unemployment had hit the country so hard that Labour leader Harry Holland declared it was a national emergency, 'as urgent as that of war'. Public and private charitable organisations couldn't cope, and wage cuts, mass layoffs and tougher work conditions imposed as part of the government solution only worsened the problem.

Above and top of facing page: Ratana led by example, literally preparing his own land before again taking up the land claims of Māori as he stepped into his more political role as Piri Wiri Tua. Even the government was forced to admit he was one of the best wheat farmers in the country. His communal approach in the midst of the Great Depression had provided employment for hundreds of people and ensured that Ratana Pā could support its own growing population. At harvest time everyone pitched in. However, requests for assistance to expand Ratana's welfare schemes were rejected, and one political opponent even spread the rumour that the fields were being prepared as a racecourse so that people could bet on horses.

Uri Whakatupuranga (Ratana Archives).

When he worked in a spiritual way, Ratana said it was as if he piloted his aeroplane into the clouds as the Māngai. When he worked among the people in the physical works, his role was more like a taxi driver carrying Māori to any destination they chose. *Kereama Pene.*

The prophets Te Kere and Potangaroa had both spoken of one who would come to take up the mantle to lead Māori into a new era. Te Kere's mantle had passed on to Ratana's aunty, Mere Rikiriki. He and Te Potangaroa had collaborated on the meeting house at Te Oreore Marae in Masterton, but after they had a falling out a curse was placed there in 1881. This memorial honours Ratana's actions in lifting that curse and fulfilling Potangaroa's prophecy 45 years later. *Bronwyn Elsmore.*

Over half the unemployed were Māori who, after leaving their homes in the rural areas to work at freezing works or in forests, farms and in other labour-intensive industries, suddenly found themselves jobless. There was little or no government assistance. The prevailing attitude seemed to be that Māori could live off the land; in reality the best Māori land had already been taken. Māori leaders, elders and the people looked to Ratana for direction. He urged them to remain faithful while he considered the options.

By opening up the Pā, creating communal work and repaying people with food, accommodation and entertainment, Ratana had effectively established his own welfare scheme. As times got tougher he petitioned the government for financial aid. While Ratana's efforts were being applauded by the government as a fine example of Māori entrepreneurship, his requests for assistance were ignored. There even seemed to be a deliberate agenda to undermine him; Western Māori member of Parliament Taite Te Tomo went so far as to accuse Ratana in the House of planning a gambling and horse-racing operation at Ratana Pā.

Despite Ratana's efforts to inspire Māori to new and visionary heights, obstacles remained: tribal barriers, resentments, hidden agendas, and the ongoing speculation in the media about his fading powers and troubled private life. Even among his own people Ratana was aware of apathy; they wanted more miracles, signs in the heavens and words from the Māngai. Only a faithful few were prepared to put their hand to the plough and push forward.

> I have told you, every man, woman and child old enough to understand this maramatanga . . . you have been too lazy to keep alight the lamp that has been given to you. It is not for me to answer or to prove wrong what the newspapers say; it is you, the morehu, who must do this, because, over the past nine years, the teachings and principles of this maramatanga have all been told to you . . . I have given to each of you the power and enlightenment. I agree with what the newspapers say, for you have each been given a task to perform.

Much of the grumbling came from those who were waiting for Ratana to take up the political reins. When asked specifically about political matters, he still spoke about the need for kotahitanga. Mā te wā, he would say, everything had a time and a season, and Ratana felt his had not yet come. In hindsight, a series of tragic but significant events were about to unfold before the movement could come into its own as a powerful force for social change. Despite speculation that Ratana's spiritual powers were fading, some of the greatest interventions in that other realm happened during this period.

Mākutu at Masterton

When responding to a call for help from a tribe or family, there were still occasions when Ratana would step back under the mantle of the Māngai; a spiritual warrior battling the vestiges of a darker age of superstition, and the mākutu that continued to plague Māori.

When invited to drive out evil or cleanse certain areas, he would take with him a group of faithful believers. After the 'exorcism' he would transport objects back to the Whare Māori or the 'jail house' at Ratana Pā to display alongside the walking sticks, wheelchairs and spectacles donated by those he had previously healed. When he went on such demanding missions, his small son Hamuera (Samuel) would often become ill, breaking out in large boils on his neck, arms and legs. When his father returned to the Pā, the boils disappeared just as quickly, leaving pitted scars on his body.

A petition signed by 500 people from the Ngāti Kahungunu iwi of Wairarapa urged Ratana to come to Te Ore Ore marae at Masterton, and expose the 'Mauri stone' placed in the meeting house on 16 March 1881 by the Wairarapa prophet and tohunga Paora Te Potangaroa. Several priests had died in the attempt, and children who had touched the marble statue above it had also died or become ill.

Te Potangaroa, along with the Whanganui prophet and master carver Te Kere, had undertaken to build a large (30 m x 9 m) carved house at Te Kaitekateka (later known as Te Ore Ore), but after an argument Te Kere withdrew, telling Te Potangaroa, 'E kore tenei whare e whakamutua i roto i nga tau e waru. This house will not be finished within eight years.' It was finished in three years and named Ngā Tau e Waru (The Eight Years) in mockery of the failed prophecy.

The building was adorned with unusual S-shaped carvings similar to swastikas, and inside was a stone believed to be a medium for communication with the world of gods and spirits. Te Kere had also carved above the door a representation of male and female genitalia in the sexual act to remove the tapu of chiefs entering the building.

When the house was being carved Te Potangaroa was at the height of his influence, and had recently converted to Christianity. Before he died, he made predictions about the coming of a new church that would meet the needs of Māori. A covenant was drawn up by the scribe Ranginui Kingi, setting out his prophecies, which were then sealed, along with various artefacts, beneath a marble memorial stone inside Ngā Tau e Waru house.

Te Potangaroa had prophesied: 'There is a religious denomination coming for us; perhaps it will come from there, perhaps it will emerge here. Secondly, let the churches into the house – there will be a time when a religion will emerge for you and I and the Maori people.' He predicted that a number of signs over the next 40 years would inform Wairarapa Māori when this would be. Shortly after, missionaries of the Church of Latter Day Saints (Mormons) arrived and many local Māori joined them and still believe today the words pointed to their movement. Over the years other churches, including Ringatū and the Church of the Seven Rules of Jehovah, claimed it was their arrival that had been predicted. It was to this location that Ratana was called 47 years later, in 1928.

Before his departure for Wairarapa, Ratana explained that the journey would be a peaceful one but, with his tongue firmly in his cheek, said he would be travelling with his coffin because he heard all who attempted to remove the stone had died. 'You should all know, oh morehu, this stone being the reason of our trip; outside is sheep's clothing but inside is a ravenous wolf.'

On 14 April 1928, 144 people from Ratana Pā made the journey, including Mete Keepa, editor of the *Whetu Marama* newspaper. After the official welcome onto the marae, Ratana prayed that the devil's work of 'powerful spells' and the powers causing death be deflected. After an evening meal and church service, Ratana wanted to ensure all the descendants of Te Potangaroa were in complete agreement about the removal of the stone and the spiritual cleansing. *Whetu Marama* editor Keepa made a thorough (27-page) documentation of the discussions and debate that followed, including the history of the building, the stone and statue. Ratana confirmed to him this was 'the most powerful of curses throughout the country'.

Ratana declared he had come to this place with the purpose of uniting 'the fish' (Te Ika a Māui) as there were representatives from all parts of the country present. 'It has been nine years now since I have called for the whole country to unite under the protection of Ihoa o nga Mano. Yet there are some who still remain aloof, outside watching this "revelation" with curiosity.'

The people of the Wairarapa had, during the period of the Musket Wars, fled north to the East Coast, taking refuge at Nukutaurua near Mahia where they had first heard the Christian gospel from former slaves who had returned from Northland in 1839. They had returned home to Masterton in 1841 and made a collective commitment to the gospel. While the elders of the marae had in the past had a strong foundation of truth based in Jehovah, Ratana said they added their own mixture of sorcery and their faith had become defiled.

> It backfired against its own descendants, yes indeed [it was] defiled and mixed with that of the flesh thus becoming spoiled; mixed up and confused with animalistic dogmas like fish, owls, dogs and swine. This is why we are dying this very day because the sins of the parents have been passed on to the second and third generations.

Ratana reminded the people of the words spoken by their ancestor Te Potangaroa: 'One foot of Jehovah stands in England, the other stands here in

New Zealand, but if you seek earnestly and in truth that other foot will return here to New Zealand.' He then explained the evil did not lie in the stone he intended to remove, but in human intervention. The statements made by the elders in the past were 'prophecies forecasting the climate and landscape of this country which are here held in the palm of my hand this very day'. He then set forth a challenge to the priests, sorcerers and intellectuals who had twisted or dismissed the truths of Jehovah:

> To all intellects and academics, come let us talk and share. To all you the sorcerers, come let us talk. Come while the sun shines. Let the stars and moon observe us from the night. It was Jehovah that created all these things to express and demonstrate his glory, that is why I have said come all and let us talk and share. You should all hear and know that there is no other appropriate way for the Maori nation beyond and after this revelation that Jehovah has granted you. What then are the real benefits of our priests and sorcerers amongst us the Maori nation? I will say to you all that their works are an abomination and totally disgusting exceeding beyond evil.

What was about to happen would be a sign for the people and the nation, but required their full agreement. 'This is why I call you all who have yet to convert to come together in one waka [canoe] that we may be in unison in paddling towards a quick recovery.' Once he had recovered the stone he said he would not be smashing or destroying it but removing it to the outside so the people would no longer have fears or worries. And as for himself, after the revealing he would no longer refer to those who had not converted as 'outsiders'; 'both morehu and non-morehu I shall claim as mine'. This was a further indication of the move to embrace everyone in the emerging political and social sides of his ministry. The Ratana band then played the hymn 'Pā Mai Te Reo', and Ratana closed in prayer.

On Monday 16 April, Ratana prayed for the men who were to assist him. Inside the meeting house they first lifted the marble statue, and as they carried it outside he explained its history and called on the assistance of the angels. He then began sawing through the floorboards where the statue had stood. He located a vault containing a large glass bottle sealed with wax. When he reached in to lift the bottle up it disintegrated, leaving behind a sheepskin with writing on it, copper coins, a sixpence and a gold coin, along with the remains of three skeletons. The writing on the folded sheepskin had faded, but under the sheepskin he found what he came for – a 100-pound pounamu (greenstone) slab which was lifted from the hole in the floor.

As soon as he began to touch the objects, a heaviness came over him.

As soon as I touched the bottle this sensation continued up to my left shoulder. When I eventually reached and touched the greenstone, this suppressing sensation increased through my arm consuming my whole body. And then it moved to my head and felt like it was squeezing and pressing it down. While being affected this way, I called to the faithful angels to protect from harm the young boys working . . .

The faded writing on the sheepskin was a covenant giving details of Paora Te Potangaroa's prophecies, and a covenant outlining the coming of an anointed national church. The coins were believed to be symbolic of kaihoko whenua, the buying and sale of Ngāti Kahungunu land in Wairarapa. The covenant placed under the monument was damaged beyond recognition by the time Ratana uplifted it. However, a photograph taken in 1881 and preserved by a local family down through the years as a 'sacred document' is revealed by Bronwyn Elsmore in her book *Mana from Heaven*. It states:

We are the lost tribes of Israel, we will learn of the Sceptre of Judah of Shilo and the King of Peace of the Judgement of the King of heaven, of the Sacred Church with a large wall surrounding, of the increase of the race, of faith, love, peace, patience, judgement, unity. All of this plan contained in the covenant will be fulfilled by the people of Nga[t]i Kahungunu during the next 40 years.

The three skeletal remains, according to Ratana, had been placed there as food for the pounamu, and the karakia (prayers) of the elders of the time had placed a powerful force that had backfired on Te Potangaroa's descendants. It is said that Ratana slept for fifteen hours after his ordeal, although his actions in removing the stone increased his mana in the eyes of Wairarapa Māori, and many joined his movement. The statue, which was moved outside, is still there today but now has a plaque commemorating Ratana's success at removing the stone and the curse.

Testing the political soil

Ratana continued travelling around various marae on his fact-finding mission, measuring the mood and loyalty of the people and speaking with various elders. At Hutoia Marae (in the Hokianga) on 29 April 1928, he was asked point blank whether he intended to nominate a candidate.

His response was that he hadn't come to talk about politics, he was already a member of 'the Parliament of Ihoa', however, he made it plain that his māramatanga was not just for healing the ills or ailments of the body. 'It can also help you heal the ills and troubles that beset you where your land claims are concerned.' If Māori were united, they would have no trouble getting the government to attend to their claims. He spoke of his trip to England and his attempts to have Treaty of Waitangi claims heard, and of his sense of betrayal when the Māori politicians had worked to undermine him.

> It is because of this sort of thing that you are having difficulty today. One of you can take a petition to Parliament, but right behind you would be another, intent on discrediting you. That is why you are unable to accomplish anything . . . you're not united.

Ahead of a visit to Te Kūiti, he said the Māngai and Tama would be left in the temple and on this trip he would be known as Wiremu Wiriwiri. This statement that he was now 'trembling William' was a further indicator that his political, social and economic mission was about to begin in earnest. Another interpretation of the word wiriwiri had to do with the shaking, earthquakes and tremors he said would come as confirmation of the next phase of his journey as Piri Wiri Tua, the campaigner, one who would 'drill, bore or plough through to the other side' in his determination to make a political impact.

He spoke of the spiritual and economic changes, including the Depression, which were affecting Māori and the world, and hinted at the great global devastation to come. As long as Māori had land to work so that they could feed their families, money wasn't necessary; the major impact would be on those who weren't used to living without money.

In Te Kūiti, where Te Kooti lived for many years and had presented the local people with the intricately carved Te Tokanganui-a-Noho meeting house, Ratana announced for the first time his specific intention to enter politics. He coined the now-famous phrase, 'Ka wahia taku tinana kia wha nga koata', indicating he would seek candidates from four quarters to represent his body. After watching a game of rugby between Maniapoto and Hauraki, he mused on why he had turned back to farming the land. 'I now realise that in working on the land, my job will not only be to turn the black soil up on to the top of the ground, but to keep digging until I reach red soil.' This meant he would not only continue working the land at Ratana Pā but 'ploughing up the whole of New Zealand'.

Now that the temple was completed, the church established and the Ture Wairua 'properly set out and planned', he was free to focus on his political strategy of having the 'four quarters' of Tai Tokerau, Tairāwhiti, Tai Hauauru and Waipounamu represented in Parliament.

> I shall divide my 'body' into four quarters and I alone shall put it together again . . . While I do this work I shall be known as Wiremu, a human being just like you. Why must it be so? Lest the people become startled as they are when they call me Mangai.

He stressed again his one constant theme: 'First unite under Ihoa, then turn your attention to the Treaty of Waitangi'. His next stop was Pakipaki in Hawke's Bay, where he would attend the tangi of one of his most faithful followers, Mohi Te Atahikoia, a Ngāti Kahungunu leader, politician and a strong advocate of the Kotahitanga movement that had lobbied for an independent Māori parliament. After the tangi Ratana found himself engaged in a debate where he explained the distinction between his spiritual role as Māngai and the newly adopted title of Piri Wiri Tua.

He told the story of his two vehicles: the aeroplane and the motor car. When he worked in a spiritual way or piloted his plane into the clouds as the Māngai, the people become uncomfortable and could not handle the winds, and so they called T. W. Ratana to come down to work among them in the Ture Tangata as Piri Wiri Tua. His new role was like a taxi driver and this vehicle, like his aeroplane, was free and could carry all the Māori people to any destination they desired in the world . . . even to Parliament or England.

He explained to his travelling party that there had been a change in the way Ihoa spoke to him.

> When I worked in the Ture Wairua alone my instructions were to place before the people all the facts, nothing more, and to let each one of them choose for themselves the measure of what I said to them. Today it is different now that I have to speak about the Ture Tangata. I am now not only given the facts to place before the people but also whatever explanations are necessary in order that they will clearly see both the pathway to success and the pathway to failure.

Ratana gave assurances that his candidates would be thoroughly investigated, and if they were successful at the coming elections the Treaty of Waitangi would come alive again. A special committee would be set up to handle the many grievances. 'The candidates to represent us must be of a peaceful and humble nature, and they must not accept money from the government.'

> No one but I shall choose my koata, as I want to be sure they will obey me; and I, myself will stitch up their pockets. Ehara ma tetahi atu tangata hei tohu i aaku Koata, engari maaku ano, kia mohio ai ahau ka whakarongo ratou ki a au, a, maaku ano hei tuitui a ratou paakete.

In October 1928, Ratana was invited to visit the people of Taranaki. His first stop was Te Rere o Kapuni waterfall beside Mount Taranaki, where he received further inspiration before going out among the people to spell out his intentions. 'My kaupapa [plan] includes attention to the problems of all of the people of this land, beginning with those that came before the signing of the treaty, and from the time of the signing of the treaty to this day.' He declared he would be not be working for one section of the people but for all, and he wanted his four candidates to be united in their thoughts and aims and to listen to the people.

> I do not want our representatives to accept money from the Government. I want them to give what the Government pays them to the committee that is to be set up for the purpose of investigating the many claims of our people. You see, I don't want these men to have pockets in their trousers. This is what is wrong with our politicians, 'they have pockets in their trousers'. Now I ask you, can you show me a person who will be willing to work as a Member of Parliament without pay? I doubt it!

Echoing the words of Taranaki prophet Te Whiti o Rongomai, 'Ta te rino i tukituki ai, ma te rino ano e hanga' or 'what the iron (rod) destroys, that same iron must rebuild', Ratana said he had now entered the arena of the law of the land, 'that we might use that law to right the wrongs that have been done to our people'.

He had previously informed the people of Taranaki that he would stand aside and let King Te Rata select a candidate, possibly his younger brother Tumate Mahuta. When he learned that Pomare had been selected as Te Rata's Western Māori candidate, Ratana felt compelled to stand his own candidate. After considerable discussion with the people, Ratana set about establishing his political arm and chose four candidates: his son Haami Tokouru Ratana, Western Māori (Tai Hauauru), Pita Te Turuki Moko, Eastern Māori (Tairāwhiti), Paraire Paikea, Northern Māori (Taitokerau) and Eruera Tihema Tirikatene, Southern Māori (Te Waipounamu).

They would be known as Ratana Independent. Ngā Koata e Wha (the four quarters) and their wives were called to Ratana's house on the edge of the marae and in a formal ceremony signed the covenant that they would totally dedicate themselves to gaining a place in Parliament, accept no bribes or payment or pursue personal gain; the wives would fully support their husbands and be equally as dedicated, and they would work mō te iwi Māori, for all Māori, without concern for tribal or other affiliations.

Ratana confidently declared his intention to capture all four Māori seats at the November 1928 elections, having received petitions from more than 20,000 people, about a third of Māori. However, there was little in the way of campaigning and none of his candidates were successful.

Māori voting was still a fairly basic affair. There was no Māori electoral roll, and voting took place with each individual informing the returning officer and one witness, who he wished to vote for. The voter was not required to write anything down or mark a ballot paper, and no ballot box was used. For Tirikatene in particular, the crucial time on the hustings coincided with harvesting on the Ratana wheat farm, preventing him from raising his profile. His entire family, and two dozen of his Southern Māori supporters working on the essential seasonal tasks, were denied the right to cast an absentee vote, even though Pākehā voters had been able to cast such votes since 1905.

Ironically, all it would have taken was a single tick and Tirikatene would have unseated Tuiti Makitanara, the United member for Southern Māori. He only lost by the returning officer's casting vote. Paraire Paikea polled second out of seven candidates in Northern Māori, Pita Moko polled 1846 votes against Ngata's 4950, and in Western Māori it was a two-way contest between Pomare (4674) and Tokouru Ratana (3075).

T. W. Ratana appeared philosophical, aware that in good time the fruits of his efforts would be known. He was, however, concerned that so many had deserted him in his hour of need. By May he said he would make a more determined effort to return to politics, and once again travelled to every marae to hear the voice of the people.

ELEVEN

A LABOURED ALLIANCE

That the Treaty of Waitangi be embodied in the Statute Book of the Dominion of New Zealand, of the Dominions of the British Commonwealth and of the British Government respectively, in order that all may know that the Treaty of Waitangi is operative, also to preserve the ties of brotherhood between Pakeha and Maori for all time.
—Eruera Tirikatene, on tabling in Parliament Ratana's petition to have the Treaty of Waitangi recognised, 25 November 1932

Pain and the price paid

Ratana knew he had pulling power at the polls, but was also aware of the effort required to displace existing Māori politicians with those who would work tirelessly for broader Māori issues. In a change of tack, he would over the next three years adopt a more conciliatory approach, attempting to work with existing politicians to achieve his goals.

His announcement that he was prepared to put all his campaign issues in the hands of the government under the Prime Minister Joseph Ward came as a surprise to his supporters. He was either tired of holding the reins or playing out a cunning ruse to see what was really in the hearts of the country's politicians.

Despite invitations to Ward and senior politicians from the major parties, he was frequently disappointed when they only 'sent their legs'. The only political faces at the 1928 Christmas hui were William Veitch of the United Party (Liberal) and Tuiti Makitanara, the member of Parliament for Southern Māori who had so narrowly retained his seat in the Ratana challenge. Ratana explained to Veitch that, if he was willing to help, the concerns of the people would be placed in his care. Veitch said that the government would advise him of its plans for Māori in due course.

In response to Makitanara's curiosity about what he wanted in return, Ratana said he wanted the government to help establish a proper water supply and electricity system, to move the Ratana railway station so passengers didn't have to walk back over the line when they arrived, and to have a stationmaster. He also offered a quarter acre of land on which to build a proper post office, as the present one was located at his own home.

Messengers were sent around the country seeking support for this new approach, and the hand was again extended to Prime Minister Ward with an invitation to attend the 25 January hui, when Ratana's generous offer would be placed before him. If he accepted, Ratana would no longer plead with the people about mana motuhake and the Treaty of Waitangi.

Only Makitanara turned up, so Ratana reiterated his previous requests. The response, however, was that the government was not interested in having the remaining Māori lands under its care and direction. Makitanara instead informed Ratana of new legislation that would enable Māori landowners to apply for government loans to help develop their lands. 'I want to make it clear to you all that the tribes who will be given loans are Ngati-Workaholics and Ngati-Stickability. Ngati-Lazy and Ngati-Sit-on-their-bums will get nothing.'

Ratana continued to test the waters on basic issues. He would present another covenant from 4 February 1929 where he would seek to lead the people in all matters pertaining to their land claims. In signing they would be granting him unconditional power and authority to act on their behalf to win back their mana motuhake and have the Treaty of Waitangi brought into law.

Early in March, Ratana and his people were invited by King Te Rata to attend a hui at Ngāruawāhia where Māori leaders, members of Parliament, youth leaders and leaders of various churches would make submissions before the people. Ratana backed off at the last minute, sensing the event was being rigged by Ngata. When his people reported back he was astonished to learn Ngata had indeed dominated the event and spent much effort slamming Ratana, claiming his work was nothing but tohungaism and stating the time of miracles had ended with Christ. Ratana's long-time supporter, the Reverend A. J. Seamer, confirmed the hui had indeed been controlled by Ngata: 'There were lots of people, and lots of kai [food]. However, the thing that struck me most was the absence from that hui of the two greatest leaders of the Maori people. One was King Te Rata Mahuta, and the other was Wiremu Ratana.'

Following the Easter hui at Ratana Pā, 13,477 people had signed the kawenata supporting Ratana's political platform. At the gathering Tuiti Makitanara again made an appearance but when reminded of the request for government assistance for an adequate water supply, he responded that a petition should be put to the government.

Honey from a lion?

Following the hui Ratana announced he would ask the government for assistance in clearing the balance of the debt on the land around the Pā that was being farmed by the mōrehu. At the end of April he and several elders headed for Wellington. On the way to their meeting they stopped by the geranium that had been planted in the grounds of Parliament Buildings in 1919.

> You have all heard and seen in scripture the story about Samson going to fight something mighty. That is the lion. The jaw of the lion was opened wide by Samson and after some time Samson returned and found the lion's mouth infested by a bees' nest with such tasty honey of which he took for himself to eat. So Samson phrased the riddle to his people: what is something sweet coming from something mighty?

Samson, noted Nazarite strongman, was attacked by a lion while walking along a track and, under the influence of the Holy Spirit, killed it with his bare hands. Later when he passed that way again, he saw the lion's carcass swarmed by bees which had made a hive there. He tried the honey and found it sweet. At his own wedding feast he told a riddle about the carcass and the honey, and asked for an

The Arepa Brass Band and cultural group with T. W. Ratana (centre) between his southern koata Eruera Tirikatene (left) and his northern koata Paraire Paikea (right).
Uri Whakatupuranga (Ratana Archives).

interpretation, promising a great reward to anyone who could find the answer. 'Out of the eater came forth meat, and out of the strong came forth sweetness.' The Philistine guests were unable to answer the riddle for seven days, and then only when they forced it from Samson's new wife by threatening to kill her and her family. They replied: 'What is sweeter than honey? And what is stronger than a lion?' Samson was aroused to great anger and responded, 'If you had not ploughed with my heifer, you would not have found out my riddle.'

In Ratana's case the lion, the position of strength or 'the eater', certainly represented his struggles with the British Crown and the New Zealand Government to have the treaty recognised. The honey is seen by Ratana faithful as the treasures that will one day come from having that document recognised by law. Ironically, the geranium Ratana planted from the old family homestead a decade earlier, was at the time thriving in the exact location of the present-day 'Beehive', part of the Parliament complex.

On entering Parliament Ratana and his elders were met by Tuiti Makitanara, who introduced them to Prime Minister Joseph Ward. Ratana was convinced much of the debt on the land had been paid off, but all Ward offered was a further loan at the going rate with the land at Ratana Pā as collateral. Despite Ratana's efforts to partner with the government, there was little evidence that anyone really wanted to help. Long-standing concerns such as water, a better electricity system and moving of the railway station were still not attended to.

A *watchful eye*

Ratana and his supporters made every effort to keep the wheat farming enterprise alive, but Depression conditions were worsening, and they struggled to get high enough prices to maintain profitability. What was worse, the government was now allowing wheat to be imported from Australia, further undermining his business. His attempts at partnering with the government had borne no fruit. 'I will put my trust in the government, one of my eyes will sleep, the other will be ever watchful, looking at what the government is going to do for the benefit of the Maori people.'

Meanwhile, he urged the people to take special notice of what happened over the next nine months as he continued travelling to various marae. 'By living in peace, you the morehu will be blessed and prosper; without peace your lives and works will be full of violence and turmoil, like the waves of the ocean crashing upon the sea shore.'

During the Christmas 1929 hui, Ratana challenged the visiting politicians. If the treaty was still alive, why did the Department of Maori Affairs seem to despise him and the Māori people? Member of Parliament Veitch insisted the treaty still lived and the government only had 'a good and peaceful disposition' towards the Māori people. However he quickly changed the topic to the

Tommy Ratana (Te Arepa) passed away as the temple bells tolled the start of the New Year, 1932. *Uri Whakatupuranga (Ratana Archives)*.

£100,000 set aside through new legislation for Māori land development, which he insisted would bring far greater benefits than the treaty. Veitch was reluctant to put his reassurances that the treaty was still alive in writing, saying Ratana should write to the Prime Minister.

On the departure of the politicians, Ratana asked the 5400 people assembled at the marae to prepare a kaupapa on behalf of the 'United Maori People of Aotearoa, Te Waipounamu and Whare Kauri' that would ultimately be taken to the government. The agreement, known as 'The United Assembly for the Rights and Privileges of the Maori People Under the Treaty of Waitangi', summarised a list of injustices that had resulted from the treaty being dishonoured. It requested a review both of specific Māori land confiscations, and of the laws that allowed confiscation of Māori land and contributed to undermining traditional rights and customs. The English and Māori texts of the treaty were part of the supporting documentation.

By Easter 1930, Ratana had 26,407 signatures on his petition, which became the main topic of discussion by Māori across the country. Apirana Ngata, however, objected to Ratana's list of grievances, stating that there were no issues with the treaty; it was being honoured and if anyone had a problem they should go through the Minister of Maori Affairs.

Another opportunity to gain a seat in Parliament – created through the death in the United States of long-serving member for Western Maori, Sir Maui Pomare – saw Ratana's son Tokouru defeated by Taite Te Tomo in the by-election. Further tweaking of the Ratana political machine was obviously needed to rally the people. The seven Kotahitanga committees agreed to stand down, so members living at Ratana Pā could provide stronger support for Paikea, Moko, Tokouru Ratana and Tirikatene, who would again stand on the Ratana Independent platform in the December 1931 elections.

Tribal leaders from all over the country, including Pākehā and Māori politicians, were in attendance at Ratana Pā in January 1931 for the first of a series of hui to drum up support. The petition now had 35,000 names, yet, despite being invited, party leaders Coates and Holland had again sent their 'legs'. Ratana doubted that anyone in power was willing to take up the issues, and in the mind of the government at least, he believed the treaty was already dead.

> It wasn't the government of England that killed it, but the government in Wellington. Look here, I have been fined for netting flounders in the Whanganui River, and I was fined for shooting pigeons at Manaia, although I was shooting in my own forest and on my own land. I want the government to tell me, in writing, whether or not the treaty still lives. You know now that I have a petition to take to Parliament at its next sitting, but I can tell you now what the government will do when that time comes, it will say: Taihoa, taihoa [Wait, wait]. The government? Its members won't come here because they are afraid. They are afraid because they know they will be embarrassed by the barrage of questions the people have to hurl at them. Ngata has never been to this marae. He was invited to come here last Christmas, but said any time except for Christmas would be convenient for him. He was then asked to come to this hui, but he's not here. I say he, and the rest of them, are afraid to come because they know that the treaty will be the main topic of discussion.

Māori had been getting by as best they could. Their ties with the land had been challenged by the rapid pace of industry, commerce, farming and the technology used by the Europeans. Even the casual work helping to develop land for the Europeans dried up as the Depression bit deeper. Many Māori moved about the country looking for odd jobs or stayed with relatives, but the rate of poverty continued to escalate. Ratana saw the treaty as a means to address this disparity, but Māori church leaders, elders and even Māori members of Parliament seemed to be sitting on the fence.

Those who had heard Ratana describe himself as Wiremu Wiriwiri, and talk about the trembling or shaking to come, would have sat bolt upright when massive tremors rumbled though Hawke's Bay for three and a half minutes on the morning of Tuesday, 3 February 1931. Nearly all the buildings in Napier were levelled and 258 lost their lives as the earth heaved up in some places and dropped in others. In that devastation, coastal areas around Napier were lifted about two metres and forty square kilometres of seabed became dry land.

Labour link stillborn

Ratana had been quietly monitoring Labour and its policies, and considering the possibilities of an alliance. It was clear that Labour was interested in the four Māori seats, so Ratana sought endorsement for his candidates. A largely Ratana-based Maori Council, acting in conjunction with Labour's executive with ten representatives from the four electorates, was approved. However, a request that Ratana candidates 'vote with Labour on all matters affecting the life of the government' did not go down well, resulting in Labour changing its tack, and campaigning directly against Ratana candidates in the Māori seats.

In an uncanny parallel, Ratana's son Arepa had married Te One Tikao's granddaughter Mihara 'Bess' Huiarei, who worked as a voluntary secretary for Ngā Koata e Whā. They lived opposite T. W. Ratana's home in a newly built cottage at the entrance of Ratana Pā in an area known as Maunga Hinai (Mount Sinai). Shortly after the initial agreement to work in conjunction with Labour, Bess gave birth to their only child, a healthy boy named Reipa (Labour), who died suddenly a few months later.

The 38,000 signatures on Ratana's kawenata again failed to translate into votes. Regardless, his candidates still polled second highest in all four seats, and in Southern Māori Tirikatene was only 25 votes behind the incumbent, Tuiti Makitanara. Ratana was clearly annoyed at the outcome of the elections where only 6391 had voted for his candidates. Why had the people said one thing then contradicted it? 'It was a sacred pledge made before Ihoa . . . the remaining 31,609, where are they? They've gone and got lost . . . for ever.' He was losing heart. 'The fight is over,' he said: 'The people have decided that I, and my koata, should fall . . . You have got what you wanted. I now announce that I have finished with the work of the Ture Tangata and the Treaty of Waitangi and mana motuhake. The Maori People can never claim that I deserted them and our taonga [treasures].'

Tensions in the Ratana camp also saw a shift in the long-standing relationship with Pita Moko, who had been Ratana's faithful supporter from the earliest days of his healing ministry. Moko had been an efficient administrator and highly effective public relations person. He was a charismatic person and one of the few among the Ratana inner circle who had 'the Holy Spirit anointing' to heal people. Behind the scenes, particularly since the 1925 American tour, there had been a growing distance between the two men, particularly over Ratana taking a punarua (second wife), and his failure to sort out confusion over theological issues, including rumours of his divinity. Moko resigned from the movement, although remained living at Ratana Pā.

While Ratana had faced his share of disappointments the worst was yet to come. His 21-year-old son Tommy (Arepa), who symbolically represented the spiritual portion of his ministry, had been battling a long illness. It was as if he recognised the end of an era. As the bells tolled the first minutes of the new year of 1932, Tommy passed away.

Ratana remained in mourning, and those closest to him became concerned for his welfare; his wife, sisters, political representatives and 118 others at the Pā signed a petition urging him to let the people go their own way and to stay on only as their leader. His case for the treaty and unity of the people had been plainly stated, but the people had listened to the talk of 'jealous and bigoted people'. Across the country those who had listened to his appeals for a united Māoridom were concerned he may give up on them, and a counter-petition was underway urging him not to leave the work of the Ture Tangata.

At the January 1932 hui, he commended the growing number of visitors for being brave enough to show their faces. Among them was Princess Piupiu Te Wherowhero, the cousin of Te Puea Herangi and daughter of Te Wherowhero Tawhiao of Ngāti Mahuta, the second son of the second Māori king, Tawhiao Matutaera Potatau Te Wherowhero.

Many times during the hui Ratana made the point Te Rata should remain as king. 'Leave me as I am, a prophet. The work of the prophet is to show the way the king should go.' Western Māori member of Parliament Taite Te Tomo had left the Pā earlier in the day but returned, determined to have his say before the thousands of potential voters. 'I want to talk to the people that they may know that I am in Parliament, that "house of worship" where there is gnashing of teeth.' He made a direct challenge to Piupiu and her elders, that she speak her mind before the people and state openly whether she intended to bring her cousin Te Rata to the Pā. Ratana interjected.

> Taite, here I am, your adversary. Let us talk face to face. It was very wrong of you to go about the country telling lies about me, and behind my back, at that. What wrong have I done you; does the work I do hurt you so much that you do this to me? What have you to offer me, or the morehu?
>
> I'll tell you why you do this, it is because you are envious of me and of my work. During the election campaign you went around telling the people that my reason for nominating candidates for Parliament was so that I might become king. Why did you do this? Was it so that the people of Waikato would not vote for my candidates? You were doing this to win votes ... Taite, you are my elder, but I curse you; I have every right to curse you! You said in Parliament that I have finished sowing wheat, and that I am going to build a racecourse on the land. Look for yourself, the paddocks are all sown in wheat, there is not a bare patch left for a racecourse! You speak nothing but lies.

Ratana asked what Te Tomo or his government had ever done for the mōrehu. 'Your work is all bloody humbug! I therefore say to you, the gates are open, this is my Pā, go, and don't ever come back here with your lies.' Piupiu challenged Te Tomo's claim that he was acting on behalf of her cousin Te Rata.

> You have no right to question me. Your job is to look after the welfare of the Maori people in Parliament, that house of stone, the house responsible for imposing great burdens upon all of us of this land. You have no right whatsoever to be questioning what is going on in our hui on our marae.

Te Tomo stormed off, and then Ratana reiterated his frustrations, and further surprised the gathered mōrehu by offering to pass his political baton to Piupiu. He said his work was for all Māoridom, including Te Rata and his people. By her presence at Ratana Pā, and in particular her time in the temple, Piupiu had entered under the 'shelter' of 'the house' that belonged to her and Te Rata. Piupiu acknowledged the great work Ratana had done and was humbled by his offer. She said the fence between the two movements had now been torn down; she had been sent by Te Rata and he would have come himself if the hui had been at a later date.

> I will now go home and tell my people about what has happened here. I came here to seek someone who would 'work for me' and, as if by chance, I have found you. Ratana, I marvel at you. You work so hard to help our people. Yes, the mauiui (sickness or weariness) of the body is one thing, but the mauiui of our lands is another matter altogether.

An invitation was sent to Te Rata, however Taite Te Tomo found out and immediately went to Waikato to oppose Te Rata visiting Ratana Pā and to prevent the people signing Ratana's petition. Ratana felt betrayed, and vowed never again to disclose his plans publicly. Regardless, the friendship between Piupiu and Ratana continued to grow as they discussed issues relating to the future of the Māori people. They shared a common faith; Ratana even took the liberty of ordaining her in the temple as Queen of the Tai Hauauru (Taranaki-King Country Tribes). 'If the thousands under her and the thousands under me unite as one, we will finish our work. Therefore, Piupiu, the 38,000 Maori, Samoans, Tahitians and others who are my supporters are now under you in the work for the Treaty of Waitangi and the Mana Motuhake.'

Piupiu responded:

> Ratana, although our backs are not large, I am sure we will be able to carry our people through . . . I agree, leave the silver and gold to the clever people. Let us put our trust in Ihoa, maybe Ihoa will help us. We will work together, Ratana and I; not for our own benefit, not for the good of the morehu only, but for the good of all of our people.

Political empathy at last

Labour leader Harry Holland, who had previously visited as a member of Parliament and promised to support Ratana's work, announced he would be at the Easter 1932 hui. This would be the first time any party leader had visited Ratana Pā.

Ratana would present to Holland his most recent petition, containing 19,000 signatures, and raise issues relating to the treaty and the imminent government foreclosure on Māori lands, where Māori were unable to pay rates or repay land development loans to buy machinery and fertilisers because of the Depression. The situation was made worse because many Pākehā farmers weren't paying their leases on Māori land. If Holland failed to deal with these concerns, Ratana suggested the people should simply take their land back. Many of the elders and leaders from around the country favoured this approach.

Ratana formally pledged to hand over to Holland the issues contained in his latest kawenata. Having made it clear that successive governments had betrayed him and not even attended to the little things – like helping provide an adequate water supply to the Pā – he turned to the one issue that was on everyone's mind.

> I hold in my hand a copy of the Treaty of Waitangi. Some say there is lots of good in it, and others say there is nothing but bad in it for the Maori people. This causes many of our people to worry and become undecided as to where they should turn. I therefore give this document to you, that your party might study it and let us know in the near future whether the treaty still lives, or whether it is dead. The people who gave this matter for me to handle, want the government to state in writing what it thinks of the treaty.

He also placed the petition containing the 38,000 signatures of those who had sworn to support him into Holland's hands, along with the related documentation. 'I do this although I know you are not the government, but in the knowledge that when you become the government in 1934, you will already have received the seed, and then you might give me what I ask for.'

In the petition were specific claims that needed resolving, including the return of lands that had been plundered or confiscated in Taranaki, Waikato, Tauranga and Tairāwhiti, the claims of the people of Ngāi Tahu, rating and taxation of Māori land, unpaid leases and rentals on Māori land, a claim for Lake Taupō and 'other cases that might be brought forward under the Treaty of Waitangi'. Another gnawing concern was the failure to pay the promised amounts to Māori who had served in the Great War.

> In respect of the funds set aside for Maori returned servicemen, we all know

> this money was raised by the Maori people of Tairawhiti and other areas. After our sons came home they were asked about this money. They replied that they knew nothing about it, or about what had happened to that money.

He explained to Holland that the people wanted all these matters thoroughly investigated and that the only acceptable course was for 'justice [to be] done . . . under the Treaty of Waitangi'. He gave him twelve months. If the matters weren't dealt with satisfactorily, he would go to Parliament and bring the documents back to the Pā and put them before the people again. When it came time for Holland to speak, he congratulated Ratana that his candidates had polled so well at the last elections, describing them as 'real lions' and 'sons of the Maori people'.

> Ratana has given me the petition of kotahitanga of the Maori people, and this pleases me because this makes me conscious of the fact that you have placed your trust in me, that I and my party should spare no effort in dealing properly with all of the matters you have given into my hands.

Holland said he would give his full support and place the matters raised before the Maori Policy Committee. When that time arrived he would ask Ratana to be present. After Holland departed, Ratana said he did not believe his petition would succeed, because neither the Māori people nor the government were in a position to resolve the issues at this time. He had passed on the petition and documentation to ensure they were taken to Parliament so that the people of the land would see, hear and know for certain that these matters affect them all. 'I know he will not succeed.'

Rather than resolving the issues on a tribe-by-tribe basis, Ratana believed that having areas or regions with designated boundaries, like those established for Ngā Koata e Whā, would ultimately make it easier. 'The idea is not to build fences, but to indicate clearly where each area or region begins and ends.' He also raised the issue of the declining use of the Māori language.

> The young people of this Pa do not understand the Maori language. When one speaks to them in Maori, they reply in English. I have always said we should preserve our Maori language. It is plain, the government wants the Maori race to disappear totally. For if your Maoritanga disappears, so also will your mana motuhake . . . and the Treaty of Waitangi.

Southern seat secured
The political opening Ratana had been waiting for came through a by-election, forced by the sudden death of Southern Māori member of Parliament Tuiti

Makitanara. Ratana had expected Harry Holland would be true to his word and endorse a Ratana candidate. Instead, Labour put forward its own representative, Peter McDonald. However, Ratana's southern quarter, Eruera Tirikatene, having campaigned extensively on the Ratana Independent ticket, romped home on 3 August 1932 with 425 votes from a total of 951.

There was great celebration. At last Ratana had a voice in Parliament to raise issues past and present and, in particular, to shake the dust off the Treaty of Waitangi. Despite the Ratana Independent win, the alliance previously discussed with the Labour Party still appeared to be the best option. It had most in common with Māori connections to the land, and the working man or 'the carpenters, the blacksmiths and the shoemakers' mentioned in the prophecies of Tawhiao.

In his maiden speech, Tirikatene would for the first time place Ratana's intentions for the treaty on public record. Ratana, his wife Te Whaea, their family and 57 mōrehu left for Wellington on Tuesday, 20 September, where they were joined by about 200 elders from around the country, including many direct descendants of those who had originally signed the treaty.

The thoughts of many of Ratana's followers turned to an occasion fourteen years earlier in 1919 when Ratana had first visited Parliament House and planted a geranium cutting in the gardens, proclaiming, 'I plant you here today, and some time in the future I will return and pluck from you a flower.' Tirikatene and Paikea, who would be his assistant, met with Ratana for prayer before entering Parliament through the original Parliament House, 'where the mauri [life force] lies'. Previously only the secretaries of Ministers of the Crown had been permitted to enter the debating chamber, so Paikea was recognised as Tirikatene's secretary and interpreter. Tokouru Ratana, who had earned his share of political experience, also moved to Wellington not only to represent his quarter, but to confer with and support Tirikatene and Paikea.

On Thursday, 29 September, in the Address in Reply debate, Tirikatene placed before Parliament for the first time the conditions outlined in the Treaty of Waitangi. In his maiden speech he humbly described himself as 'a new leaf sprouting forth', but confidently stated he had been elected as an 'Independent' specifically to look into winning back the rights of the Māori people. While he stated his platform involved the rights and privileges of the Māori people as embodied in the treaty, there were other matters that needed addressing. He spoke of mana motuhake, Māori fishing rights, Māori lands, electoral laws, pensions and the Maori Returned Soldiers Fund, and he requested that Māori be treated the same as Pākehā when it came to their qualification for an unemployment benefit.

He quickly proved to be a wise and authoritative representative, not only for the Ratana movement, but for Māori generally. Other members of Parliament regularly sought his advice. He expressed his concern that, of the Māori petitions that came before Parliament, few were ever investigated or dealt with. 'These petitions contain most sad but worthy requests . . . from what I understand, the people receiving those petitions on behalf of this House are in no way at all conversant or sympathetic with what the petitions really mean.' While some compensation had been paid to resolve certain issues, many petitions for compensation since 1925 had received nothing. He announced his intention to bring before Parliament a claim from the people of Te Waipounamu.

Tirikatene asked for a thorough investigation into the taking of Māori land under the guise of unpaid rates and taxes. He also approached inequality at the polling booths, and provided evidence that despite spending many years in the school system Māori children who gained qualifications were being denied employment.

Treaty finally tabled

In October 1932 Tirikatene further stated his intentions in Parliament:

> I represent the Ratana policy, the Treaty of Waitangi . . . My platform is the fulfilment of the conditions set out in the Treaty of Waitangi. Without the spilling of one drop of blood the great chiefs of the past handed over their sovereignty to Great Britain in return for an assurance that they and their descendants would have full, exclusive, and undisturbed rights and possession over their lands, forests, and fisheries, or such properties as they owned at that time. It seems sad to think now that the descendants of these chiefs are now penniless.

Tirikatene had taken on the symbolic name Te Omeka, which related to his political constituency of the South Island. Ratana had even said his son Te Omeka was Eruera Tirikatene's 'spiritual guide', claiming it was through him that Tirikatene won his place in Parliament. In November 1932 Tirikatene took Te Omeka to the parliamentary debating chamber to show him the work his father had completed. Within days, Te Omeka passed away after a long illness, at the age of seventeen years.

Two weeks after the death of Te Omeka, on 25 November 1932, Tirikatene walked into Parliament with the petition signed by the majority of the Māori population, requesting that the Treaty of Waitangi be tabled and made part of the laws of the country. The statement read:

> That the Treaty of Waitangi be embodied in the Statute Book of the Dominion of New Zealand, of the Dominions of the British Commonwealth and of the British Government respectively, in order that all may know that the Treaty of

Joe Mick Ratana (Te Omeka) passed away on Armistice Day, 1932. *Uri Whakatupuranga* (Ratana Archives).

Waitangi is operative, also to preserve the ties of brotherhood between Pakeha and Maori for all time.

According to Wellington's *Dominion* newspaper, the copy of the Treaty of Waitangi, and the seven books of signatures asking the General Assembly to make it statutory, weighed in at 16 lb (7.2 kg) when placed on a set of scales.

While it was a momentous occasion, a further fourteen years would pass before the petition was reported on by Parliament's Native Affairs Committee. Nevertheless, a token gesture was made. Land at Waitangi where the treaty had been signed was gifted to the nation in May by Governor-General Lord Bledisloe and Lady Bledisloe. Then the Waitangi National Trust Board Bill was passed, creating a board to manage the land at Waitangi.

Tirikatene said on 8 December 1932:

In acquiring the site on which the Treaty of Waitangi was signed . . . Their Excellencies have, as it were, dispelled the nimbus that has enshrouded not only the property but also the document that was actually signed there. It is in keeping with my policy that the Treaty of Waitangi shall be brought into prominence.

Inspired by Ratana's political progress, and keen to hear the words of encouragement and inspiration from the movement's founder, a greater number than usual turned out at Ratana Pā for the annual Christmas hui. While there were many political and social considerations, Ratana kept the overall focus on Jehovah and Māori unity. There was good reason to celebrate, but that desire was dampened by the great losses he had suffered with the death of his sons Arepa and Omeka in such a short space of time. However, he insisted on seeing the the vision through. He urged the people to 'hold fast and be loyal' and look to Ihoa for refuge. Great hardship was ahead for the world as the nations were 'agitating for war'.

Ratana followers seemed more determined than ever to back Ratana's political plan, signing a new kawenata restating their willingness to have him lead them in the work of the Ture Tangata and the Treaty of Waitangi. A major restructuring was underway to give the movement that Ratana had birthed a more solid framework to tackle the challenges ahead, including a clearer distinction between the spiritual and political work.

The Ture Tangata committee would be responsible for administering affairs

One of the many banners created to commemorate important events in the Ratana faith. Here the lives of Ratana's sons Arepa and Omeka, the beginning and the end, are remembered along with images of Ihu Karaiti above and the Ratana temple below. *Sam Dale, W. G. Blundell collection. ATL PA11-058-03, Alexander Turnbull Library, Wellington.*

at the Pā as well as those relating to the treaty and the political work. A separate committee would deal with all church matters. Ratana would initially oversee both. The reworked committees were to be in place in time for the 1933 Easter hui, which would largely be devoted to matters of a spiritual nature, along with sports and other competitions.

TWELVE

LIGHT FROM THE EAST

We go now to see that this land will be made productive again, and to see that the sea will again provide food for the people. I feel very calm and easy at this time. I am fit this morning. I've got my running shoes on now.
—T. W. Ratana preparing to lift several curses along the Māhia Peninsula, October 1933

Ratana, I greet you as I hear that it is because of love that you are here. I heard you say that you have tried in vain for 14 years to arrange a meeting with Te Rata. I agree, it was not Te Rata who didn't want you to come face to face with him, no it was those people who go around carrying yarns. Ratana, I believe that had you and Te Rata met together regularly, all would be well now . . .
—Apirana Ngata at the funeral of King Te Rata, 6 October 1933

Long live the king
While Ratana had met with strong support in the north and south of the country, there was still resistance from the people in the west where his own tribal affiliations lay, and in the east where Christianity and the kotahitanga movement had taken deep root among Māori from 1836.

The northern tribes were seen as guardians of the birthplace of Christianity, where the Holy Bible was first made available and the gospel preached. It was in the north also that Māori independence was first declared and the Treaty of Waitangi initially signed, and this was seen to relate to Ratana's role as Piri Wiri Tua, the campaigner. The South Island tribes were guardians of the greenstone and gold, the spiritual and economic power or mauri (Te Omeka).

The West Coast tribes (Te Arepa) were seen as guardians of the blood spilt upon Waitara and Parihaka, where the Crown was seen to have provoked civil war through its invasions. This area included Mount Taranaki and the waterfall of the prophets.

The East Coast tribes were viewed as guardians of the first rays of the sun, and associated with Hamuera, the door or gateway, and retained special significance in the Ratana prophetic understanding. Ratana often referred to the East Coast from Wairarapa to Māhia as his 'father and mother' because the people had been eager to accept the Bible and support the independence movement and the Treaty of Waitangi. Christianity had caught on like a fire down this coast after Māori slaves, freed from Northland, brought the gospel to their own people, even before the missionaries had made any impact.

Ratana's supporters continued to travel among the people seeking whakakotahi (to unify or make one), but the Waikato people largely insisted on separate action. Ratana still had the full support of Piupiu Te Wherowhero and her elders, and continued to affirm his support for King Te Rata. It was with great sadness he learned, through a telegram from Te Puea, that Te Rata had died.

When Te Rata's obituary appeared in the newspapers, Ratana could not make up his mind whether to go to the tangi. 'What good will come out of going to see him now that he is dead?' However he was overcome with sorrow and his official party left for Waahi Marae on 6 October 1933. At 2.30 p.m. word came that Apirana Ngata was claiming to be the appropriate person to mourn Te Rata, as he had advised and helped him. Haunui Tawhiao, Te Puea's uncle, said he would let the people decide when Ratana arrived.

Musicians from the Pā led Ratana and his people onto the marae, playing the 'Ratana March'. He then stepped forward and began to farewell Te Rata, but was interrupted by a man named Tutanekai, who asked, 'Who gave you permission to speak first? It is I who should speak first not you . . . You do not have the blood of a rangatira [chief] in your veins.' Ratana replied, 'I am greeting the dead Te Rata, not you the living. It is because of this man lying here that I have come to this place. I am here paying my respects and saying farewell to him. Further it was not you who asked me to come here.'

One of Te Rata's family then called out, 'Carry on, Ratana, there is no one here with the right to stop you. That man who interrupted you is not ours, we know him not. He is from Te Arawa. Speak.' After Ratana, the various orators of the marae welcomed him and his people. Everything went according to marae tradition with one exception, a statement made by Apirana Ngata who said he wanted the position of king to be recognised by all Māori.

> Ratana, I greet you as I hear that it is because of love that you are here. I heard you say that you have tried in vain for 14 years to arrange a meeting with Te

Rata. I agree, it was not Te Rata who didn't want you to come face to face with him, no it was those people who go around carrying yarns. Ratana, I believe that had you and Te Rata met together regularly, all would be well now . . . I know that you are all right, it is [not] your people who spoil things for you, just the people of Waikato . . .

There are many who claim to be able to best lead the Maori people, but they are all the same. However, where the spiritual needs of the people are concerned, that is a matter for you and the people; but the Ture Tangata, leave that to me. Ratana, the people of Waikato are afraid that you might take their Kingitanga from them. It is true, that is why they have been hiding Te Rata from you.

On 9 October at 9 a.m., Koroki Te Rata Mahuta Tawhiao Potatau Te Wherowhero was ordained the fourth Māori king by clergy of the Anglican and Methodist churches. It is said Koroki had little ambition to succeed his father Te Rata, believing he was unfit for the task. Because his people were so poor he doubted they could support another king. The various chiefs gathered at Te Rata's funeral obviously thought otherwise. After the coronation ceremony, Ratana was among the first to speak.

I ask that the Treaty of Waitangi and the mana motuhake be the King's platform. My son [Koroki], this is where your mana lies. This is what your tupuna and your father took to England and so did I. Support the treaty and your position of kingship will be stronger. I have 40,000 people who support it. The treaty was taken into Parliament last year. If you agree to uphold the work for the Treaty of Waitangi, you will have over 60,000 people behind you.

Then came the welcoming of manuhiri (guests). The official party included former prime minister Gordon Coates and Labour leader Harry Holland. After speeches farewelling Te Rata, Holland entered Ratana's tent and shook his hand. 'I wish you good luck, Mr Ratana. I just had to come and see you before I leave. I wish you good luck.' Rain continued to pour throughout the proceedings, and at 2 p.m. King Te Rata's body was lifted from the marae for the journey to Taupiri Mountain for burial. Ratana told the band to go and play 'Ngā Anahera' ('The Angels') when the casket arrived at the grave. At the service on Taupiri Mountain, Harry Holland collapsed. He was rushed to Huntly, but on arrival was found to be dead.

The next day, in saying farewell to King Koroki and his people, Ratana urged the new king not to let his elders lead him astray as they had with his father. He invited him, Piupiu and the elders of Waikato to come to the Christmas hui at Ratana Pā. 'Do not hesitate, Ratana is your Pa.' However, some of the people began accusing Ratana of cursing Harry Holland because he had backed off his original support of Ratana in favour of the Kīngitanga. 'How can I curse him? It was your disloyalty. How many times have I asked for King Rata to come and visit Ratana but who blocked him, who blocked the unity of the people?'

Cancelling curses

In the earlier years (1921–22) Ratana and his two boys had travelled throughout the East Coast, reaching into Ngāti Porou and Tūhoe territory. His grandfather, Te Pakaru Ngahina Ratana, had been an active member of the Kotahitanga movement in the late nineteenth century. Among his allies was Mohi Te Atahikoia, an elder of Pakipaki, 'a keeper and witness to prophecy', who had taken Ratana and his boys under his wing and opened up the way for Ratana in Wairarapa, Heretaunga and Wairoa.

In response to a request from the people of Tairāwhiti, Ratana and a group of 46 departed Ratana Pā on Monday, 16 October 1933 to meet with elders, encourage his followers and clergy in the East Coast region, and battle against the atua Māori (Māori gods or dark spiritual forces) that had a stronghold there. Ratana had high hopes of unity under Ihoa, and the possibility of strong political support, even though he was encroaching into Apirana Ngata's territory.

He visited Wāimarama in Hawke's Bay, where the great *Takitimu* waka, one of the legendary seven that came from Hawaiki, had berthed. Its passengers included a number of powerful tohunga who set up two whare wānanga (schools) for the teaching of the arts and traditional knowledge. Ratana hadn't planned to go any further than Pakipaki, near Hastings, but on finding strong support he decided to make Nukutaurua his ultimate destination. Everywhere he went, he left behind an invitation for the people to attend the Christmas hui.

On 17 October at Tangoio, at the marae named after his sons Arepa and Omeka on the coast above Napier, he mourned his children. In his earlier years Ratana had travelled with them throughout the country claiming the prophecies of the nation. He spoke to his group about Nukutaurua, a lonely spot on the coast along from Māhia township, on the eastern side of the Māhia Peninsula, where it was believed an evil curse was affecting the region. A prophetic song or pao had been written in England in 1924 referring to this place: 'Tohutohu te ringa o Wiremu atu i Ratana ki Nukutaurua' (Let the hand of Wiremu point the way from Ratana to Nukutaurua).

Ratana explained that Nukutaurua was a place of great mana and mauri. He was certain Ihoa would manifest. 'When the time comes it may be in the form of fire, or it may be in some other form. If it is not to be in the form of fire, then the whole world will be set alight.' He expressed again his sense that the world was on the brink of a second Great War.

It's a radiant display when the flowers are in bloom around the Ratana Temple. Te Kooti had prophesied that a 'garden of flowers' would bloom from the Whangaehu, and Ratana often spoke of his followers in these terms.

While 8 November is the time when Ratana faithful recall their founder's visionary encounter with the Wairua Tapu (Holy Spirit), there are also hui at Easter and Christmas. The main gathering today, however, is to celebrate T. W. Ratana's birthday on 25 January. Over three days, mōrehu and guests from across the country remember Ihoa's desire for unity among the Maori people, review that state of the nation and catch up with old friends. There's usually an opportunity to listen to impassioned speakers who might encourage people in their faith or raise awareness about political or social issues, a wide range of sporting and cultural activities and of course music with the seven Ratana brass bands, and those with more contemporary sounds, entertaining.

While the politicians typically show up in strength on 24 January to conjure up support and announce their latest stance on issues relating to Maori, the birthday itself is supposed to be more of a spiritual time, with a church service the main activity. Naturally, any large gathering must also have plenty of food and cups of tea. Behind the scenes, butchers, bakers and kitchen staff busily prepare for the large communal mealtimes in the Kī Kōpū dining room.

At other times of the year there have been visits to Te Rere o Kapuni, the waterfall of the prophets where T. W. Ratana went for inspiration and insight. In 2008 the waterfall where many Ratana faithful had gathered over the years was significantly damaged by flooding. *All photos Ans Westra (1963–64).*

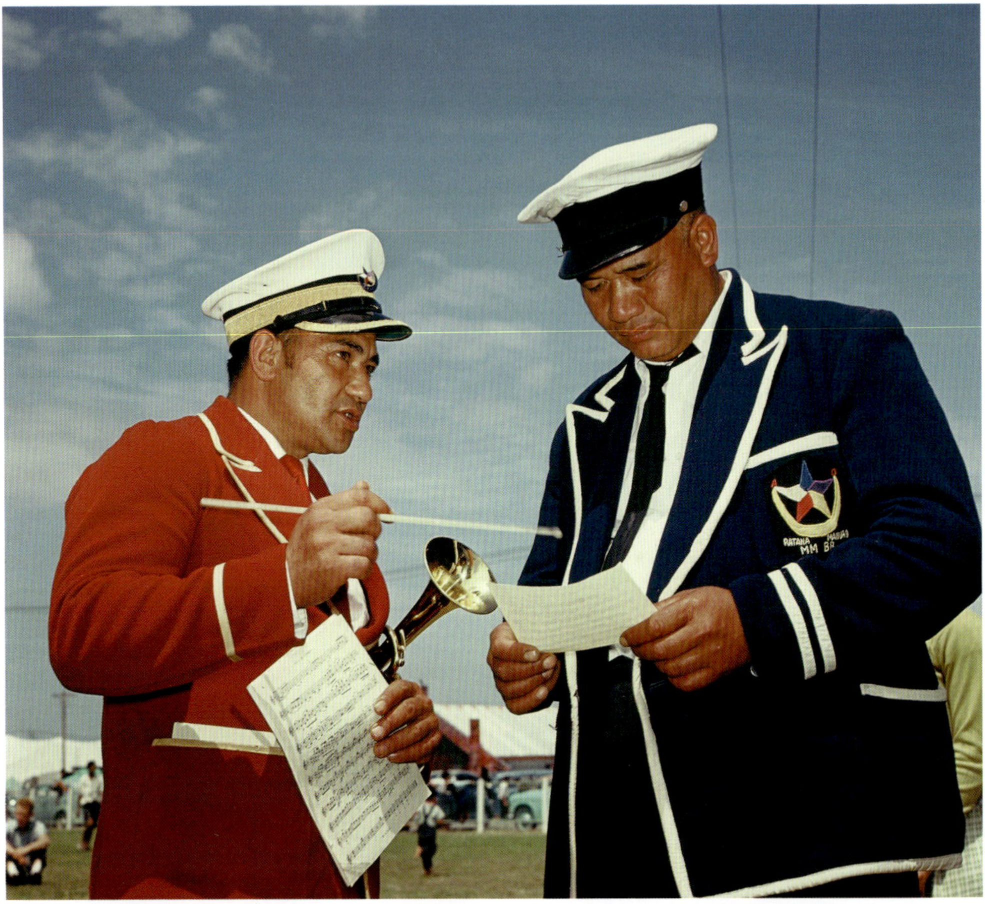
RATANA
MM BR

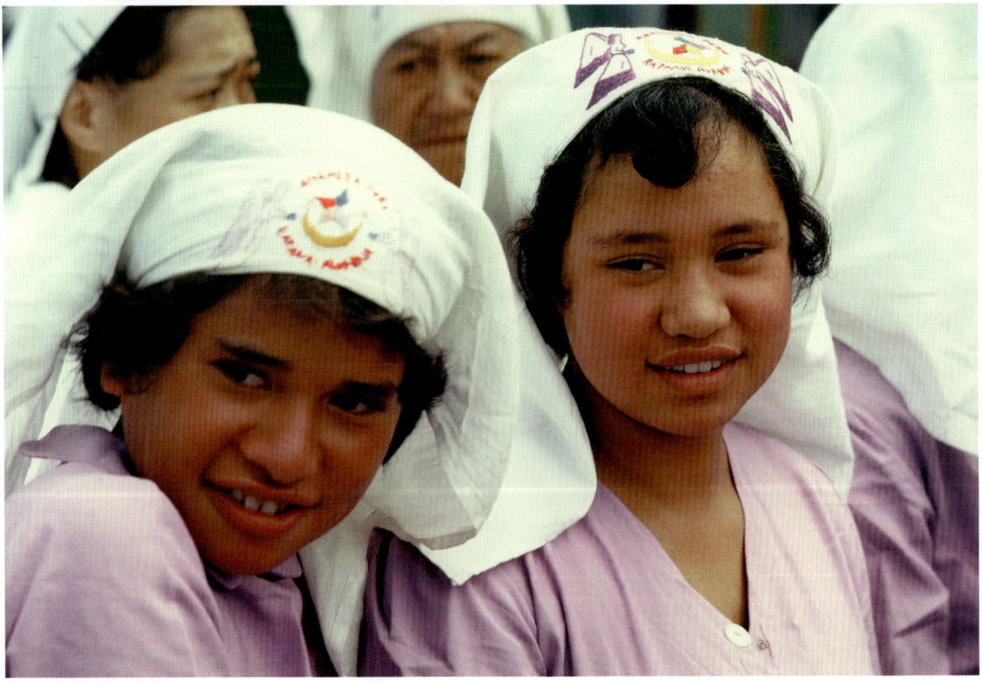

Left: Apotoro Kereama Pene with Andre Mason at Te Rere o Kapuni, Mount Taranaki, 2016. *Photo Beverley Broughton.*

Below: In 2023 the Ratana family elected Sonny Manuao Tamou as tumuaki of the Ratana church and movement at an official hui. A rival group challenged that decision and elected his cousin Andre Mason, son the former tumuaki, as 'people's choice' for leader. Both men are a great-grandsons of T. W. Ratana.

Bottom: (from left to right) Ringatū elder Te Kaihoutu; Che Wilson, spokesperson Whanganui River people; Labour ministers Rino Tirikatene and Adrian Ruarawhe (speaker of the House from 2022); and Perenara Rirunui, National Ratana Band master, at Ratana Pā, 2018. *Newman Collection.*

Mana Wahine. A curious convergence of events culminated in the commissioning of Paula Newman to produce a visionary painting a year ahead of the resignation and final speech for prime minister Jacinda Ardern at Ratana Pā on 24 January 2023 and the death the following day of Māori activist and matriarch Titewhai Harawira. *Artist Paula (Novak) Newman ©, Jackie Seward Collection.*

Ratana church buildings with their distinctive twin towers have borrowed from the mother temple at Ratana Pa in creating a Ratana architecture. These include buildings at Raetahi (above), Te Kao in the Far North (top left) and Ahipara at the southern end of Ninety Mile Beach in the Far North. There were similar structures at Mangamuka in the Hokianga, Paparore near Awanui and Te Hapua in Northland. *Raetahi by Ans Westra; Te Kao by Jim Henderson; Ahipara by Dr Deidre Brown.*

Top: The Ratana whetū marama flag (right) flies high alongside the banners of Maori independence as foreshore and seabed marchers gather at Parliament grounds protesting 'yet another act of confiscation' in 2004. *New Zealand Herald (www.photopix.co.nz).*

Above left: The official opening of the Ratana Archives Centre in the restored former Ratana Post Office was supposed to have been opened by Prime Minister Helen Clark on 23 January 2004, but after official speeches at the Pa she was whisked away by Ratana elders to the dining room. Members of Uri Whakatupuranga (New Generation Archive Trust) were horrified as they had arranged media coverage and key people were waiting, including librarians, archivists and representatives from government departments. In a last-minute effort they co-opted the mayors of Marton (Bob Buchanan) and Wanganui (Chas Poynter, centre) and former member of Parliament John Tamihere to cut the ribbon so the world could see what they had achieved after many years of tireless effort restoring Ratana history including photographs and documents from around the country. The two mayors are flanked by Ratana Archives Centre members Arahi (far left) and Puawai Hagger. *Uri Whakatupuranga (Ratana Archives).*

Above right: Ratana Archives Centre researcher and webmaster Arahi Hagger fills in some missing links for guests inquiring about family members who were involved in Ratana's mission. *Uri Whakatupuranga (Ratana Archives).*

Top: Members of the Ratana Youth Organisation Inc., outside the newly opened Ratana Archives Centre. *Uri Whakatupuranga (Ratana Archives).*

Bottom: Young people from Auckland are presented with certificates of achievement at Ratana Pa as part of efforts by Tumuaki Harerangi Meihana to reinvigorate the organisation's youth movement. *Uri Whakatupuranga (Ratana Archives).*

T. W. Ratana depicted among some of the more powerful symbols of his ministry, including the Bible and the Treaty of Waitangi, the two whales that appeared in 1918, the whetū marama tohu (symbol) of the Ratana movement, the Ratana Temple, the rainbow, Mount Taranaki and Te Rere o Kapuni, the waterfall of the prophets. *Paula (Novak) Newman. All rights reserved.* ©

Tiaki Omana (Jack Ormond) welcomed Ratana to Opoutama Marae on the morning of 19 October, saying his presence brought great comfort. Watene Kara welcomed Ratana with the words 'te pua o te tawa' (the blooming tawa blossom, a highly prized perfume). 'All I want to know is, why have you come here? Secondly, our seafood all along this coast disappeared many years ago; we want that you should restore our seafood along these beaches.'

Patu Te Rito explained the history of the house named Ruawharo that stood on his marae.

> [He] was one of the chiefs of *Takitimu* canoe. Our ancestor Hina-tamure was one who practised witchcraft. So we see now why the house was named Ruawharo . . . but you are here now. We want you to go and finish it all off. Whatever you want, just let us know. But please do not ask that we should sign up. Putting signatures to paper is a practice belonging to the Pakeha; the way of our people is different, our word is our bond. Although we do not sign [your kawenata], in our hearts we pray that the work you do will succeed.

He passed the mana of the location into Ratana's hands and seemed eager to know when he would go to Nukutaurua. Ratana changed the subject to football (rugby) and the eagerness of the locals to play the visiting Ratana team. 'Look at all the young people I brought with me. They come from all parts of the land and are emblematic of kotahitanga, for they represent the Tairawhiti, the Taihauauru, the Tai Tokerau, the Waipounamu and Whare Kauri.'

Concerning the song, which contained the prophecies about the lands being in the hand of Ratana, he said: 'Truly, this and all the prophecies are here in the palm of my hand. Our old people were not meant to see the fulfilment of those sayings.' Addressing Patu, he declared:

> There is only one way for us to be sure of survival and justice, and that is through the ratification of the Treaty of Waitangi. That is why I have been calling for our people to unite under Ihoa, and under the angels. That is the only way, if we want to succeed. The saying goes – 'Ma te rino ano te rino e kuru, e hara i te mea ma Ihoa' . . . You say that you, the Tairawhiti, must work to be united as one. That is good. When you do this, let me know. You talk about our young people engaging in friendly games of football. Good. I leave that for you to organise and arrange . . . but on Saturday I will have a programme ready for us.

Ratana then extended an invitation to Patu to come to Ratana Pā and bring Tiaki Omana with him. Ratana regarded Omana as a son, and noted that he had a 'similar wairua' to himself, saying he could see his people truly lived in faith, hope and love.

East Coast tapu

That night, in the house known as Ruawharo, Ratana thanked God and asked for peace among his followers as they prepared to visit the places that the locals believed were under a great curse. He asked for Ihoa to destroy the 'hurtful and evil powers' that were the result of the misuse of the gifts and powers given the 'ancestors of old'. He asked for divine help in 'annihilating the evils of tohungaism' so that Ihoa's glory should reign among the people.

Ratana concluded: 'We go now to see that this land will be made productive again, and to see that the sea will again provide food for the people. I feel very calm and easy at this time. I am fit this morning. I've got my running shoes on now.'

On Saturday morning, 21 October, the Ratana party, now consisting of 160 people travelling in four lorries and eight cars, stopped at Kaiuku, which Ratana and his son Omeka had visited in the early days of his mission. He wanted to see if the legendary 'whale' made an appearance. The local kaumātua said a whale was believed to be the keeper of the evils that existed there. Parea, an elder of the Mormon Church, and Waihirere, president of the Ringatū Church, explained it had last been seen during the time of the local prophet and tohunga Te Piwa. It had come to Nukutaurua in 1894, when all kaimoana disappeared from the area between Māhia, Kaiuku and Opoutama. Parea, however, thought the taniwha (water monster) was actually a mangō poropu (type of shark) common in the area. Just as he said this, the group observed a shark swimming just beyond the breakers.

It was at the invitation of the local families and tribes, living in poverty because their lands had been confiscated, leaving them without a natural source of food, that Ratana came. The fishing was good further up the coast on both sides, however in their territory there was nothing. They were convinced the tapu had to be lifted.

Ratana told his group he had brought them for the purposes of stamping out 'the evils' that existed there so it would be safer for coming generations. He prayed to lift the tapu and told everyone they were now free to go anywhere without being afraid. Just then they saw a whale spouting offshore. The group became quite excited, but Ratana asked them to 'contain themselves', and keep joy and praise to Ihoa in their hearts. The local people were extremely grateful that the evils had been taken away, and thanked Ratana over and over again.

Back at Opoutama there was discussion of Ratana's kaupapa, in particular the prophecy regarding Nukutaurua, and what had been said between Ratana and Tiaki Omana. Patu Te Rito asked why he should sign to support the treaty: 'No one can truly claim that the treaty is wrong, or that the treaty is dead. But it can truthfully be said that the treaty is being dishonoured by the government. If it was God who ordained that Queen Victoria draw up the treaty, then I say the treaty will never die.'

Te Rito said those who sit in Parliament seemed to give no thought to this treasure. He was frustrated that attempts to redress grievances seemed to get nowhere and argued that what was needed were representatives who could not be bought with money. He agreed a mōrehu should be chosen to represent the East Coast, at which point Ratana revealed that Tiaki Omana had agreed to accept the nomination.

Ratana and his group left Opoutama for Manutūkē on Wednesday, 25 October. 'I have been asked to go stamp out certain tapu in this area. Let me tell you, Patu, there is one coming after me who will baptise you all with the Holy Spirit and with fire. The Son of God said this also.' Hori Te Awarau agreed with Ratana's treaty work, but objected to him trying to stamp out the tapu. 'No man can do this. All who have tried have met with the same fate – death.' The source of the tapu was a lemon tree that had allegedly been 'bewitched' by a certain tohunga. When they arrived, Ratana sent a young apostle, Manakore Tamihana, to follow after him and pick the lemons when he had finished praying.

> I ask, oh Ihoa that your power and glory be planted here, and that of your Faithful Angels. I ask that by your power the evils that are here be totally destroyed. Make this place safe for children and the people of this area. Oh Ihoa, you hear the voice of this stream that flows through this area; grant all that is evil will be carried away by these waters to disappear in the depths of the ocean for ever, and grant only that which is good will remain . . .

The next day, Ratana and his troupe began the long journey home, calling in at Waihirere, Wharite and Pakipaki. At Pakipaki, 600 people witnessed a strange sign in the sky on Saturday 28 October, as a white and blue light appeared to travel from the direction of the Ratana Pā towards Nukutaurua. Patu Te Rito claimed this was what the ancestors had called a rehita, a white lunar rainbow, believing the angels were inside it. During Te Kooti's time it was thought a rehita was a sign that the way ahead was clear.

THIRTEEN

A PREMATURE AFFAIR

Here I am, your servant, explaining the sayings, knowledge and other precious things revealed to me by the One who sent me; may you all be cleansed, to be as white as snow and as sinless as a dove. The prophecies of this land, of Potatau, Tawhiao, Tohu, Whiti, and others, are all here in the palm of my hand. The wa [time] already ordained that you should come here Koroki, that is why . . . I persevered for so long. I do not blame Waikato for taking so long to make up their minds, for what has happened in the past was meant to be. The right time for this to happen has finally come.

—T. W. Ratana to King Koroki at Ratana Pā on 28 January 1934 after gifting him with a ring, a carved walking stick and a feather cloak

Yes new things are coming and you have all now seen the new symbols printed on our money and currency, they are Maori symbols belonging to you. This is an indicator that today you are coming into partnership control of the country. Yet I tell you, not until the names Matua, Tama, Wairua Tapu and the Holy Angels are upon the currency of Samuel's time, and then Jehovah will have glory throughout the entire world.

—T. W. Ratana, opening the memorial archway in front of Ratana temple in July 1935

The final sacrifice

By Christmas Eve 1933, 700 people had arrived at Ratana Pā by train, car and truck for the annual Christmas hui. One group had even made the 600-mile trip by bicycle from Mangamuka in the Hokianga to join the festivities.

King Koroki couldn't make it, but sent word that he would come at Easter.

Tirikatene had made a big impression in Parliament, and those who turned up for the Christmas 1933 celebrations at Ratana Pā were also impressed when he brought with him Labour leader Peter Fraser.
Uri Whakatupuranga (Ratana Archives).

The honoured guest ended up being deputy leader of the Labour Party, Peter Fraser, who arrived with Eruera Tirikatene and made it clear that if his party became government he would not forget the Māori people.

'We wish there were three more Maori Members of Parliament like Tirikatene . . . When the Labour Party becomes the government, one of the first things it will do, will be to attend to Maori Policy in a fair and acceptable manner.' He prayed that the Spirit of God would work among the people of Ātiawa, Waikato and Maniapoto as it had among the Ngāti Apa so that they, too, would unite under this kotahitanga. That pleased Ratana. 'Mr Fraser knows, unlike most of our people, that the Holy Spirit is the power that can influence our people to unite as one.'

On Christmas Day the people continued to get involved in all manner of discussions, but mostly they wanted to know the next stage of Ratana's plan. Te Kore Mahuta Tawhiao, a son of Tawhiao and brother of the late Te Rata, arrived by train accompanied by mōrehu elder Hori Tana, saying he had came out of respect and aroha and was sad the people had persuaded Koroki not to come. Chief Patu Te Rito, who had spoken so eloquently on Ratana's visit to the East Coast in October, also made his first visit to Ratana Pā and spoke his mind.

> For you are the root of what has grown, and is still growing, among us, the Maori people. That is why we are all here. We have come to hear what you have to say . . . I suggested to you when you visited the Tairawhiti, that a kawenata be drawn up asking Ihoa to help us complete our work. Your answer at that time was Ko ta te rino i tukituki ai, ma te rino ano hei hanga, thus we will have to 'use the law to make the law sit up and take notice'.

He said many were willing to enter a kotahitanga, but some were pulling out. 'Kings and treaties go together. What about our king [Koroki], where or what is his turangawaewae? Is it this treaty that we talk so much about?' Ratana welcomed his guests to 'the day on which we celebrate the birth of The Christ', and thanked Te Rito for bringing his concerns about the treaty. 'When the time and season is right, the treaty will speak out,' said Ratana, who had hoped to explain his strategy to all Māori representatives including Koroki and the Waikato people. He wasn't interested in waiting for April for a possible visit, so he extended an invitation for the new king to come for the January hui.

By the time the train arrived on the morning of 25 January, about 5800 people were waiting to greet Koroki and his entourage. Haunui Tawhiao said the people from the Waikato were at Ratana for three reasons: for the love of the people, the laws of the land and how they were affecting the people, and the need for kotahitanga. 'The greatest of these is for the love of the people.' Another Waikato elder, Tonga Awhikau, made it clear he was there to follow behind the 'stern of the waka' that Koroki leads, to show his support for the kaupapa laid down by his ancestors and to see without doubt that 40,000 mōrehu would be placed at the king's disposal for a tūrangawaewae.

Tuarau Waranui addressed Ratana. 'I heard you say the king will remain as king, and the prophet will remain as a prophet. I say therefore, now that the king has come here before the prophet, let us finish the job.' Tuwhakaririka acknowledged the welcome. 'This man Koroki stands firm on the kaupapa of absolute mana motuhake as laid down and observed by his forebears at the very beginning.'

After prayers on Sunday, 28 January, Ratana welcomed Koroki into 'the house spoken of by Tawhiao'. He again quoted the prophecy of a national church and political structure for the broken and discarded people, which would have a hīnau pole through the centre. 'Maaku ano e hanga tooku whare, ko nga poupou o roto he mahoe, he papate, ko te tahuhu he hinau.' He then asked:

> Who or what is that hinau? It is you! . . . I dearly wished to shake the hand of your father Te Rata, but the wa decided otherwise. Your tupuna (Tawhiao) said, 'The people of this land may all be scattered to the Milky Way, but I have other friends; they are there and there and will give me support. It will be during the time of my mokopuna that the blessing and saving of our people will become known.'

Ratana then displayed three taonga: a ring, a carved walking stick and a feather cloak. 'Koroki, my son, I give to you these taonga in the hope that they will serve as a reminder to you in days to come of your meeting with me, and of your coming into this temple today.' He continued: 'The king has entered this temple today, and has met here with the Mangai; thus, what we have sought after has been accomplished. Our son has this day been baptised and ordained. Likewise, I also baptise him.' Koroki responded: 'Thank you, Mangai, for these taonga which symbolise and endorse kotahitanga for the people of this land.'

Ratana responded:

> Here I am, your servant, explaining the sayings, knowledge and other precious things revealed to me by the One who sent me; may you all be cleansed, to be as white as snow and as sinless as a dove. The prophecies of this land, of Potatau, Tawhiao, Tohu, Whiti, and others, are all here in the palm of my hand. The wa already ordained that you should come here Koroki, that is why . . . I persevered for so long. I do not blame Waikato for taking so long to make up their minds, for what has happened in the past was meant to be. The right time for this to happen has finally come.

Tawhiao said that the people had come to see and listen and they felt a warmth and joy in their hearts. He commended Ratana for the work being done for the people of the land. 'It is sacred work, and may it always remain so. We all look to you, O Mangai, to show our mokopuna the way and the truth.'

Ratana greeted Tuwhakaririka as his elder. 'Our treasure [the treaty] and our petition are in Wellington awaiting some action. It follows now, that we will await word from the king.' Tuwhakaririka pledged himself to peace and love and to cast all troubles and arguments aside.

Te Kiri Katipa looked at the taonga given to the king, and gave his interpretation.

> The Maori cloak represents Maori sovereignty; the carved walking stick represents spiritual power; and the ring represents a marriage between our people, yours and Waikato. After all that has happened, I am reminded of what Haunui said recently when he quoted these words – 'Ka mahue a Ihipa te Kainga o te He, he Kainga hou te rapua nei' (We have come out of Egypt, the place of evil and sin, and look for a new home). I thoroughly endorse this, and also the promise that we will never do anything to lead the king astray.

When word got back to Waikato of what had transpired at Ratana Pā, Te Puea was furious. She was in no mind to allow rumours of a marriage between Ratana and the King movement to go unchallenged. She had worked hard to ensure Te Rata kept his distance and was incensed that Koroki had accompanied her uncle to the January 1934 celebrations. She was a formidable and controlling woman, and was in many ways the 'power behind the throne', often making

While Ratana never got to have a personal meeting with King Te Rata, his son and successor Koroki did come to Ratana Pā in January 1934. Ratana gave him three symbolic gifts: a ring, a carved walking stick and a Māori feather cloak. Koroki thanked Ratana for the gifts, which he recognised as symbolising kotahitanga for the people of the land. The visit, however, caused a great disturbance in political circles and from Princess Te Puea, who wielded much power behind the throne. Although her cousin Piupiu and senior members of the Kīngitanga Parliament were strong Ratana supporters, Koroki was dissuaded from visiting Ratana again or following through on promises of unity between the two movements. *Uri Whakatupuranga (Ratana Archives)*.

decisions without consulting Koroki, and reprimanding him if his actions conflicted with hers.

According to Te Puea's biographer Michael King, she was determined to make Koroki pay, and during the Treaty of Waitangi anniversary celebrations in the north in February 1934 stayed glued to his side but never uttered a word. Koroki keenly felt her unspoken rebuke and, being vulnerable through his 'natural shyness' and awkwardness at public speaking, was now the one to feel embarrassed.

Back at Ratana Pā where everyone was preparing for Easter, reports came back about various hui in the Waikato where there was quarrelling among members of the 'royal family' after Koroki's visit to Ratana Pā, particularly over the embarrassment and inconvenience it had caused to Te Puea. Much political mileage was made of this by Apirana Ngata.

Taite Te Tomo had asked that an application be made to the government for money for the king and a document prepared, requiring Māori to unite under the king, along with a demand they be given back their mana motuhake. Koroki refused to sign it, and on being asked what he thought of the proposal, simply replied, 'Next week, I will be attending the Easter hui at Ratana.'

Prophecies in Parliament

Tirikatene had kept a close watch on the various members of Parliament, observing their skills, their politics and ethics to see who would make the most amenable allies to help move the Ratana agenda forward. He kept in regular touch with T. W. Ratana, and if issues of importance came up at Bellamy's Bar in Parliament buildings or in the House it was not uncommon for him to drive back to Ratana Pā in his car or even on his old Indian motorcycle.

He reported that Michael Joseph Savage, in particular, had a Christian ethos and after many conversations believed he was the man Ratana had been seeking. At the end of June 1934, Ratana and a large group of faithful followers walked into the empty debating chamber at Parliament House in Wellington. From the Speaker's chair, looking up at the New Zealand Coat of Arms, he exclaimed: 'O Lion, O Tiger, O Crown, you are the emblem of the British Empire. As I stand before you, you are stronger than I. I say to you, let there be sweet fruits for me from you.' He then spoke to the chair: 'I greet you, for upon you sits the person who deals with passing laws which concern me, the Maori people,

T. W. Ratana with younger Ratana band members, around 1934. *Uri Whakatupuranga (Ratana Archives).*

good laws and bad laws.' He addressed the chairs of the members, urging them to do their work well and fairly, and not permit the passage of laws that would hurt the Māori people. If bad laws were passed, he said, 'the root of the tree would wither and die (me pa te titaha) and when the wind comes the tree will be blown away to be consumed by fire until only the ashes remain'.

He spoke in parables, further addressing the debating chamber and then the upper house, warning politicians to take heed. In the Maori Affairs room he sat on the chairman's seat, repeating the admonition to treat the Māori people fairly. He then had the clerk bring before him the documents and claims of the Treaty of Waitangi, which Tirikatene had tabled in Parliament and were yet to be considered. He explained the sacredness of those documents. The party then went to the top of Parliament House, where Ratana prayed out loud: 'O rain, fall upon this Parliament, let water spill upon it, so that what I say may be blessed and carried out.'

Ratana and an entourage of 54 people, including his wives Te Whaea and

Rumours that Ratana Pā had become a hotbed of Japanese sympathisers expecting Emperor Hirohito's fleet to come and liberate the Māori people would have gone into overdrive had it been known publicly that a senior Japanese navy officer had privately visited Ratana in the late 1930s. Ratana had already prophesied the Japanese would join with the Germans for the second Great War, and trade and political relationships with New Zealand were rapidly deteriorating in line with Japan's increasing aggressiveness toward China and other nations. Ratana is seen here with his 'second wife' Iriaka and a Japanese naval captain around 1936.
Uri Whakatupuranga (Ratana Archives).

During his 1934 South Island visit, Ratana officially opened the Arowhenua archway, which led into an empty paddock on the site of Te Maiharoa's old marae, dedicated to those who had died prior to the Treaty of Waitangi, to Māori who had died in the First World War, and to Ratana's sons Arepa, Omeka and Hamuera. *Uri Whakatupuranga (Ratana Archives)*.

Iriaka and his son Hamuera, made a further trip to the South Island in August 1934. He again took with him his covenant to unite all the tribes under Ihoa and have his four quarters represented in Parliament. They were welcomed at Lyttelton by Tirikatene's father, John Driver Tregerthen, a carpenter, boat skipper, wheat farmer and minister of religion, who had been one of the prophet Hipa Te Maiharoa's twelve apostles. They attended a rugby game between North and South Canterbury for the TWR Challenge Cup trophy. Ngāi Tahu added their prize, a greenstone patu.

On arrival at Temuka the brass band played at the railway station and marched the guests and the local welcoming party through the town. Flags from Ratana Pā were taken the following morning to Tuahiwi where Ngāi Tahu chiefs and orators spoke at the hall named Te Hapa o Niu Tireni (the broken promises of New Zealand). This was the building established by Te Maiharoa for the first South Island treaty claims. The band and culture groups performed at the Tuahiwi Picture Hall ahead of a healing service. That night a direct descendant gave Te Maiharoa's covenant and personal records, along with a gun and sword – gifts from Queen Victoria – to Ratana as a sign of support from the people.

Another reason for the journey was to officially open the Arowhenua archway, which led into an empty paddock on the site of Te Maiharoa's old marae, a task Ratana was unable to perform a decade earlier because of disputes between local Māori and the authorities. The Oamaru stone memorial, known as Te Niho Tangata, had been worked on by craftsmen from the North Island and was dedicated to those who had died before the Treaty of Waitangi, to Māori who had died in the First World War and to Ratana's sons Arepa, Omeka and Hamuera.

Ratana also visited Kakaramea on 10 September and the caves at Mawhera in Greymouth where the elders of Arahura, including the principal chief Tuhurua and his ancestors, were buried. This site was considered the gateway from which the local tribe could protect the pounamu (greenstone) from those in the north who sought to pillage it. Ratana also visited Hokitika and other locations important to Māori.

On his return he brought with him greenstone from the Arahura River and gold from the mines in Hokitika, both of which are now strategically placed at the Ratana Temple. The gold was buried beneath the Ratana Temple and the greenstone inlaid at the frontage and dedicated to the time in the future when Māori would regain both their spiritual and economic mana. At Arahura, Ratana made a prophecy that descendants of the lineage of that area would not only enter te ana raiona, 'the den of lions', but take on the role of ministers of the Crown.

Another son sacrificed

Shortly after the South Island tour, Ratana's young son Hamuera, considered by Ratana to be the 'price paid for the work of destroying tohungaism and its evil practices', passed away after a tragically short and painful life.

After speaking to the people on the marae, Ratana went to sit at his son's bedside on 22 October 1934. Hamuera asked, 'What is that I hear?' referring to the noise outside. Ratana replied, 'It is the people,' and asked, 'Tell me, my son, when I go, who will lead them?' Hamuera answered, 'I will.' He then closed his eyes and died.

His death, like that of his older brothers Arepa and Omeka who had passed on within the previous three years, was believed to mark a significant point in Ratana's mission. Hamuera was Ratana's son by his second wife Iriaka, and is remembered in the ancient saying, 'Mai i te pō uriuri, te pō nakonako ki te whai ao ki te ao mārama', or 'out of darkness into light'. He had been given two names, Hamuera Te Ra i Kokiritia, meaning 'the sun that cuts through the dawn', and Hamuera Te Tatau, or 'the doorway, or gatekeeper'.

He was named both for T. W. Ratana's uncle Hamiora Hamuera Te Uruangina, an elder of Ngāti Apa who was one of the financiers behind the 1924 world tour, and for Ria Hamuera or Ria Te Ra i Kokiritia, the close family member who raised Ratana. She had been blessed by King Tawhiao, who had placed his hat upon her head in a sign of anointing. The names and his association with the Eastern Māori region of Ratana's koata – where the sun first rises – are believed to confirm that Hamuera would herald a new dawn for the movement and a future time of spiritual and economic enlightenment for Māori.

October was also the time of the pīpīwharauroa (the shining cuckoo), regarded by the Māori of old as the month for planting kūmara. This was the end of the cold and hungry months of winter, and the beginning of the season of warmth and plentiful food. It is said Hamuera is also represented by Te Puawaitanga, or the blossoming, another sign of the turning seasons when the barren trees bud forth with colour.

In early January 1935 Ratana, when conferring with his representatives in Parliament, again visited the geranium he had planted there in 1919 when he had prophesied: 'Mā te wā, in God's appointed time, I will return to pick it, and its pollen will be blown to the four corners of the world'. This time, he said: 'This is I (Piri Wiri Tua) your father standing here before you, Arepa, Omeka and Hamuera are with me; they are mine to give to you. You must support and use the old kaupapa (our purpose or what we stand for), Father, Son, Holy Spirit and the Faithful Angels and the Mangai.'

Then, on his sixty-second birthday, 25 January 1935, Ratana spoke again about the important part his sons had to play, representing the seasons of his ministry, the four quarters of political influence and the events he had prophesied, including the imminent war and the flood of changes about to affect the nation and the world. From this time on, he made it clear how he wished his work to be completed.

> The glory of heaven is that it is lofty and high, and the glory of the land is that it is so deep down underneath; the glory of kings is to seek materialism (and wealth), but the glory of Jehovah is invisible and hidden. Today Jehovah hides away his children Te Arepa, Te Omeka and Hamuera . . . After Te Arepa and Te Omeka, then came Hamuera, and this child was born from out of sin. Therefore Hamuera is the bearer of sin, and all of these children shall fulfil all prophecy . . .

When Ratana consecrated the Memorial (Hallelujah or Hamuera) Archway at the Ratana Temple gates on 5 July 1935, he stated: 'this treasured memorial now stands revealed, from now on the Spirit will do its work and you shall know its fruits.' The inscription reads: 'Alpha and Omega the beginning and the end of T.W. Ratana's work, the Ratana Church and the Temple and the rights and privileges of the Maori people as embodied in the Treaty of Waitangi ... 40,000 members. Samuel's work is the annihilation of tohungaism.' According to Ratana tradition, the era of Hamuera, the youngest son, is the

Above left: The death of Ratana's primary school-aged son Hamuera was believed to represent the end of the age of tohungaism and the gateway to a new age of enlightenment for Māori. Many believe that gateway opened at the dawn of the new millennium. *Above right:* The archway in front of the Ratana Temple was a memorial to Ratana's three sons, Arepa, Omeka and Hamuera, and specifically symbolises the Hallelujah Gateway or door to a new era for all of Māoridom. Under the archway are (from left): Te Ao Wirihana (who lost his son on the trip to Te Rengarenga Wairua and subsequently raised Ratana's son Raniera), T. W. Ratana, E. T. Tirikatene and Matiu Tane. *Uri Whakatupurangoa (Ratana Archives).*

'full stop' on the works of men and the beginning or doorway (Te Tatau) of the Kōroria Hareruia or 'Glory Hallelujah' era when Ihoa would make his purposes known to the faithful mōrehu.

The world was about to change drastically because it had forgotten 'the Spirit and Jehovah', but the kingdom of the spirit world was intended to be demonstrated on earth through the Māori people. Soon, however, the trumpet would blast and a time of darkness would engulf the world.

> This day is the day . . . where scripture says: 'Leave the wheat and the weeds to grow together until the day of harvest' . . . Arepa, Omeka and Hamuera and the faithful angels, they have it now [are responsible for the mission] . . . Time desired that you the Maori nation should unite, for the chance perhaps of his [Hamuera's] timed appearance where he will let the world go, and when this happens you the Maori nation have already united . . .
>
> Yes new things are coming and you have all now seen the new symbols printed on our money and currency, they are Maori symbols belonging to you. This is an indicator that today you are coming into partnership control of the country. Yet I tell you, not until the names Matua, Tama, Wairua Tapu and the Holy Angels are upon the currency of Samuel's time, and then Jehovah will have

glory throughout the entire world. Furthermore, that is the entire fulfilment and outcome you are aiming for. I have already explained to you in 1928 that 'the foreshore is my boundary' and what I have just explained about the time of Hamuera and Jehovah's Kingdom and glory is its real meaning. I wish that these words be pressed deep within your hearts so that when these things . . . come upon you, you will already know and understand and face them without fear or doubt.

Ratana was determined to leave the people with a deep sense that the mission he had begun did not end with him. Over the next year he would compile all his documents and labours for the time when 'Jehovah's Kingdom shall stand upon the face of the earth'. The work would go on, but achieving the many goals ahead would be up to the people. He pleaded with them to put aside their differences for the sake of unity, and seek the healing gifts of Ihoa themselves rather than relying totally on him or the apostles.

He continued to stress that the doorway to a new era would be opened to them, but first a time of fire and great darkness lay ahead. During the opening of the memorial archway Ratana prayed for strength to lead the 40,000 Māori people mentioned on the memorial plaque. 'Though there are others not included here, I pray that you, Jehovah, will gather them in, now and forever.'

FOURTEEN

SIGN OF THE BROKEN WATCH

> I take it upon myself to remedy those wrongs and injustices in a manner as near as possible to that required by the spirit of the Treaty of Waitangi. And so, for your benefit, I tell you, if I am able to remedy the ills you suffer, my soul will not have fear when I finally face God my Maker, as I will have done what was required for you, the Maori people. Listen well, Ratana, only by removing the chains that bind and restrain the Maori people will I be able to say I have accomplished something in this land.
>
> —Michael Joseph Savage confirming his commitment to Ratana at Parliament, 22 April 1936

Promises for the future

Ratana had been 'tilling the soil' of the nation to prepare for the full political impact of his movement for three years; during his marae tours of 1933 and 1934 he had faced followers and detractors with a convincing kaupapa, and enthusiasm for his mission seemed stronger than ever.

A report in the Christchurch *Sun* stated the Ratana Church had nearly 40,000 adherents from a total Māori population of 74,000, and there were now 134 apostles licensed to conduct marriage, 245 'faith healing' apostles, 658 lay readers, 1028 sisters and 110 wardens. It was on the back of strong Ratana support that New Zealand's first Labour Government, with its 'Labour has a plan' strategy, came to power in 1935 promising to make New Zealand the centre of a new socialist state to inspire the world.

Existing member of Parliament Eruera Tirikatene held his seat with a majority of 43 votes, and Ratana's eldest son Tokouru, who had stood on two

Above: T. W. Ratana around 1935, wearing his trademark hat and coat. *Sam Dale, W. G. Blundell Collection, ATL PA11-058-04, Alexander Turnbull Library, Wellington.*

Above left: Ratana's son Tokouru gave him his second seat in Parliament in 1935. *Henderson Collection.*

Left: Michael Joseph Savage, with his ethical approach to politics and his platform of 'Christian socialism', seemed an ideal partner for Ratana to complete his 'body' through the election of four young men who would put the interests of all Māori ahead of tribal or personal goals. *Newman Collection.*

previous occasions, scraped home 38 votes ahead of sitting member Taite Te Tomo. Both stood as Ratana Independent, and Labour once again put forward its own candidates in opposition. Tokouru, a gentle and humble man who suffered from bouts of illness, continued to work alongside Tirikatene. While an informal agreement was in place for Ratana members to vote with Labour, Tirikatene felt it was time to make things official. It was too easy for the government to ignore one or two members standing on their own, and virtually impossible for an 'independent' to push legislation through the House.

Tirikatene and Tokouru Ratana signed the 'candidate's pledge', becoming members of the Labour Party. Their ultimate loyalty however would be to T. W. Ratana, with whom they had signed a much deeper and spiritual covenant. One of their first goals was to shake up the Māori section of the Labour Party by establishing committees to ensure they remained in touch with the people and their needs.

The government under Michael (Mickey) Joseph Savage was determined to eliminate the growing barrier between the haves and have-nots and drag the country and its emaciated economy into a new, more prosperous era. Ever since he had entered politics in 1911, Savage had railed against unfair distribution of wealth. He wanted increased pensions and a free health system. He quickly established the 40-hour working week, paid a Christmas bonus to the unemployed and the poor, and established a programme of state housing. Within three years he had drawn up the basis for New Zealand's social security system, describing it as 'applied Christianity'.

Tirikatene arranged a meeting between Ratana and Savage to cement the new relationship, hoping to achieve 'solidarity and acceptance' of the Ratana approach to Māori problems. The historic meeting in Parliament buildings took place on 22 April 1936 in room 13, just below the House of Representatives. Present were Ngā Koata e Whā, with Ratana's secretary Paraire Paikea acting as interpreter. Ratana wasted no time in reminding Savage of the promises made by the late Harry Holland to help the Māori people and to fulfil certain obligations. Now, he said, that role fell to Savage.

This put Savage in an awkward position. He and his deputy, Peter Fraser, were friends with Princess Te Puea, who was lobbying them on behalf of the Kīngitanga movement. Nevertheless, he was an honourable man and Ratana was prepared to trust him. In a symbolic act Ratana set out a series of objects: 'I place in your hands these gifts as a memento of our meeting today as well as a symbol of our unity under the law of the land.' First he placed before Savage a potato with three hua feathers stuck in it.

> The first of my gifts are these three huia feathers and their waka. These feathers are emblematic of the heritage of the Maori in this land. The huia was a native bird. When a person is seen wearing this feather, it signifies that person is Maori. As it happens, this bird is now extinct, having been destroyed by the weasels and other preying animals introduced by the Pakeha.

He explained the waka carrying the feathers was a potato. 'We had no land left in which to plant these foods.' He next produced a greenstone tiki. 'This represents the power, richness and nobility of the Maori people which I place in your hands. Yes, greenstone represents the power and authority of the Maori people which in this day and age has been lost to them through European laws.'

Ratana then handed Savage a broken gold watch and chain that had belonged to his grandfather, Te Ratana.

> Te Ratana was loyal to Governor Grey and to Premier Seddon of New Zealand. I am his descendant who now professes loyalty to the government of this time, your time. As it happens, this te wati koura [gold watch] has no glass. My ancestor had no money to replace the glass, and it so happens I haven't any money either to replace the glass. I give these objects into your hands.

He also presented an emblem of the Ratana movement, he tohu o te māramatanga. 'This badge represents the Ratana people, the 40,000 people of my organisation. I hand this over to your safe keeping and care, that you may be their father in justice in the physical works.' Ratana added, 'My boys are here with you, attending to their duties. If you should need more of them in your work, let me know and I will provide you with the same.' He concluded: 'May you never forget your responsibilities to the Maori people, for when you forget this, your government will fall.'

Savage welcomed Ratana to his 'marae', thanking him for the gifts and the explanation of their significance.

> Don't think I've fenced it off with barbed wire so that you will be unable to enter to see me. You are welcome to come direct to me at any time. I know the treaty is precious to you and your people. I agree, the wrongs and injustices you suffer were brought about by man. It follows that I am a man, thus I take it upon myself to remedy those wrongs and injustices in a manner as near as possible to that required by the spirit of the Treaty of Waitangi. And so, for your benefit, I tell you, if I am able to remedy the ills you suffer, my soul will not have fear when I finally face God my Maker, as I will have done what was required for you, the Maori people. Listen well, Ratana, only by removing the chains that bind and restrain the Maori people will I be able to say I have accomplished something in this land.

If Savage would fix the problems relating to Māori land by introducing new laws and help save the Māori people, he would earn the right to wear the huia feather, the sign of the ariki, the paramount chief of Māoridom. He would become the father of his Māori people. It was through this historic meeting that an informal alliance was confirmed between the mōrehu throughout New Zealand and the Labour Party. In May, Ratana declared himself and his family, 20 adults in all, to be Labour Party members, as did another 200 adults at the Pā.

Symbols of commitment. At the historic meeting in Parliament buildings on 22 April 1936 cementing the original alliance with Labour, T. W. Ratana placed four symbolic objects before Prime Minister Michael Joseph Savage to remind him of his obligations to the Māori people. He presented a potato with huia feathers in it, symbolic of Māori loss of land and chiefly rights; a greenstone tiki representing power and authority lost through European laws, a gold watch with a broken glass face that had belonged to his grandfather, representing the legal mechanisms that had deprived the people of financial ability to thrive. He also presented a whetū mārama badge for the 40,000 people he represented, which he placed in Savage's care that he may be 'their father in justice in the physical works'. *Painting by Dick Frizzell.*

A shaky union

Later in 1936, at the first conference of the newly formed New Zealand Labour Party Organising Committee, Tirikatene was elected president, Paikea became secretary and Tokouru Ratana became an executive member. A conference was held in Wellington in October. Many recommendations were made with a strong focus on the Treaty of Waitangi and the legislation that had been passed by previous governments, which had rendered Māori destitute. The 220 Maori Labour Party delegates attending sought a wide range of actions relating to the financial, social, physical and moral welfare of Māori.

Existing members of Parliament and Labour Party executives were astonished at the organising power of the new members and what they had

Ratana and the men he chose to represent his body, the four political quarters, celebrating the completion of the Manuao (Man-o'-war) administration complex, often referred to as the Parliament of Ihoa. At back, from left: Paraire Karaka Paikea and Tiaki Omana. Front, from left: Haami Tokouru Ratana, T. W. Ratana and Eruera Tihema Te Aika Tirikatene. *Sam Dale, W. G. Blundell Collection, ATL PA11-058-02, Alexander Turnbull Library, Wellington.*

The opening to the Manuao on 11 September 1938, which also became known as Te Āka or the Ark, a place of shelter for the massive changes that Ratana had predicted were ahead for the Māori people. He also referred to this building as the 'last chance', referring to his frequent urging for the tribes to unite as one under Ihoa o ngā Mano. *William Hall-Raine, Te Papa Tongarewa Museum of New Zealand.*

T. W. Ratana and members of the Kotahitanga executive in front of the Orakeinui homestead at Ratana Pā, celebrating the completion of the Manuao, 11 September 1938. Back row, from right to left: Tema Heemi, Adon Hui, Nikora Te Mete (Smith), Koro Fisher, Lofty Hohaia, Patema Tupe, Tawake Raroa, Te (Tete) Taiaroa, Pani Kahotea. Centre row, from right to left: Clement Tamati, Tangipere Makere, Hori Maika, Pango Puketohe, John Aperahama, Maki (Mark) Mete Keepa, Wira Grey, Kingi Topia, Patu Koroneho, Olie Nathan, Bill Waitai. Front row, from right to left: Bob Tamou, Kaponga Erueti, T. W. Ratana, Takawaenga Hohaia, Boggie Tuwha and Waipa Karena. *William Hall-Raine, Te Papa Tongarewa Museum of New Zealand.*

unleashed. The Maori Organising Committee had during its first year in operation formed over 160 committees and boosted membership to a total of 9000, brought in over £1000 to Labour's coffers and run the most successful conference of Māori Labour supporters yet. However, those efforts were quickly undermined to prevent future Māori committees being top heavy with Ratana members. The replacement Labour Maori Advisory Committee was restructured to include a majority of Europeans.

Tirikatene was in demand for official celebrations and ceremonies in 1937, including the Waitangi Day celebrations in the Bay of Islands on 6 February. Ratana directed him to drive from Ratana Pā to Waitangi with Rangi Mitchell, of Wairoa. 'Take your piupiu, rapaki and taiaha,' said Ratana as he presented him a kākahu kiwi (kiwi-feather cloak) for the occasion. 'The Wairua Tapu will guide you, and give you knowledge and wisdom. When they arrived there was some confusion: 'Who will do the wero [challenge] to the Governor-General?' Apirana Ngata looked around and pointed to Tirikatene. 'How about you?' 'Yes, that's what I've come for,' said Tirikatene.

His daughter Whetu Tirikatene-Sullivan was later informed by her father's contemporaries that a photo of his performance of the wero that day was the pattern used on the one-shilling coin.

Tirikatene was also among the contingent from the New Zealand Army that formed a guard of honour at the coronation of King George VI in London in May that year. Ratana told him he was representing the Māori people, and that 'if this wasn't going to be the king who would remain loyal and honour the treaty, then blood must be spilled in the king's courtyard'. Tirikatene would then be responsible for uplifting the mauri from the Crown, and bringing it back home.

The story is told that Tirikatene, fair-skinned but obviously of ethnic origin – unusual among the Royal Guard – was hit on the side of the head when an object was thrown from the crowd. Being a trained soldier he instinctively reached for his sabre but cut his hand. It was only when his blood began dripping onto the paving, and he closed his fist to stem the flow, that he recalled Ratana's prophetic words.

While it seemed logical that all Ratana candidates should again contest the forthcoming elections, the National Executive rejected Paikea and Tiaki Omana in favour of their own candidates. Both stood as Ratana Independents, with Paikea finally taking the Northern Māori seat he had contested in 1928, 1931 and 1935. He defeated the incumbent Tau Henare by 2011 votes, entering Parliament as a Labour minister. Paikea, an ordained Methodist minister, had been one of the first registered to take marriages and funerals within the Ratana movement. He had been Ratana's secretary, editor of the *Whetu Marama*, and in 1936 was secretary of the Maori Advisory Council.

Tokouru was returned in Western Māori with an increased majority of 4267 and Tirikatene in the south had a majority of 485. The Eastern Māori seat was retained by Ngata, largely because Labour had stood not one but three candidates against him. Omana had done extremely well to gain 2126 votes; if Labour had put forward only one candidate it could have easily achieved its goal of displacing Ngata. Instead it embarrassed itself and the Ratana movement. By 1938 Ratana candidates held three out of the four Māori seats, and by 1941 Paikea was appointed to the executive council representing the Māori race.

Prophecy on the Mount

At times it was perfectly clear what Ratana's intentions were, as he spoke forthrightly about immediate needs or challenges; at other times he was more cryptic and spoke in parables or riddles, requiring the listener to refer to the old Māori prophecies, the history of the nation or more often the pages of the Bible, for understanding.

Frequently, the key to unravelling his words was to be found in the deeper truths conveyed in Ihoa's dealings with the twelve tribes of Israel and the life and parables of Jesus Christ. One of the names given to Ratana Pā is Hiruhārama Hou, or the New Jerusalem (the Promised Land). As you turn off the main highway between Palmerston North and Whanganui towards the tiny village there is a dip in the road, known as Te Moana Whero, or the Red Sea. In other words, you have to go through the Red Sea to get to the Promised Land.

There are two houses flanking the main road into the Pā. The one on the left is Ringa Poto (the short hand or exhaustive action) where Te Arepa used to live, and the farm there is called Maunga Hinai, or Mount Sinai. The house on the right as you go into the Pā is called Ringa Kaha (the hand of strength or persistence), where Te Omeka lived. The farm there is known as Puke Marama, or the Mount of Transfiguration.

The hill as you head down into the first gully from the turn off into Ratana Pā is known as Maunga Oriwa, or the Mount of Olives. On 11 November 1936, Ratana was speaking to the mōrehu about the Kotahitanga land scheme, its history since 1928 and the mortgage problems it had struggled with, when he began to prophesy:

> Kua rongo, a, kua mohio hoki koutou ki te kupu e mea ana 'Kua aua atu te po, kua tata te ao', he ra kei te takahuri mai e kite ai koutou e rua nga tawa, nga pourewa e tu ai ki runga o Maunga Oriwa, hei taua wa hoki koutou kite ai i tetahi wahine e kake ake ana i te Roopu Reipa, ka tu hoki ko ia hei Pirimia, hei taua wa hoki koutou mohio ai kua tae kei nga kuaha, ehara i te mea kua tata, Engari, kua tae …
>
> You have all heard and are familiar with the word that says: 'Night time has passed, the new break of dawn draws near', there is a day unfolding when you will see two towers standing on the Mount of Olives, and at that time you will see a woman rising up from the Labour Party who will become prime minister, and then you will know you are at the doorway, not nearing it, but actually at the doorway …

It is certainly curious that today Spark and Vodafone (renamed One NZ in early 2023) cell phone towers stand in that field, and that in 2005 Helen Clark became New Zealand's first elected woman prime minister in 1999. Others suggest the tohu may have referred to the rise of Clark's successor, Jacinda Ardern, as Labour leader. In 2017 Ardern became New Zealand's fortieth prime minister. She resigned two years into her second term, giving her final speech at Ratana Pā on 24 January 2023.

FIFTEEN

THE PARLIAMENT OF IHOA

Ships have only one captain but with your Manuao there are two captains. Look for yourselves, there is Piri Wiri Tua at one wheel, and the Mangai at the other. Yes, two captains, both smoking their pipes and waving goodbye to those who are left behind and missed the boat. Piri Wiri Tua controls the Ture Tangata, and he is waiting, and looking out for the enemy. The Mangai controls the Ture Wairua, and will fire the guns and shoot the enemy. My friends, this is spiritual talk.

—T. W. Ratana, opening the Manuao building or Te Āka (The Ark) at Ratana Pā, 11 September 1938

There is a day unfolding when you will reach the doorway of the year 2000, verily, there will be thousands and thousands of Japanese people [Asians] who will come to these shores to seek after your revelation for themselves, therefore you should hold fast to your footstool, and hold firmly to your revelation, your crown of glory, it will only be through sheer laziness and neglect this revelation will be lost to you all.

—T. W. Ratana, prophecy, 29 May 1939

All the canoes together

Ratana had begun to talk about a new centre for the physical side of his work, where important issues relating to the unity of Māoridom and ongoing claims under the Treaty of Waitangi could be debated, and the supporting documentation he had gathered about land grievances displayed.

This new 'secular' centre would free Ratana Pā to focus more on the

spiritual side, for example establishing a Bible college to train up new apostles. Among the priorities of this new centre would be fundraising to support both the spiritual work and the ongoing research into outstanding treaty claims. It would also be a learning environment to assist Pākehā in particular with their acceptance of, and integration with, Māori.

On 22 February 1933, during an afternoon sleep, Ratana had experienced a vivid dream. As the people gathered around for the customary kōrero (talk), he explained what he had seen.

> As I walked I saw a ship there, sitting on top of a hill all white in colour, with its two funnels so prominent. I thought to myself, what is that ship doing there? I felt that I wanted to go there, and at that same time I heard a roaring sound behind me. On turning around I saw a great flood rushing towards me and covering the land mass as it did so. Then I saw people running and seeking a place of refuge. I called and beckoned to them to hurry towards the island nearby. By now I had reached the safety of the ship by climbing a ladder to get aboard. I heard another roar, and on looking down I saw the floodwaters pounding against the side of the ship. When I looked up towards the bridge I saw Te Whaea standing there. I asked her, how they were, and she answered that all were well. Again I heard the roar of water, then I woke up, and at that time the rain was falling heavily.

It was to be another four years before Ratana moved to establish a second centre. Because of his relationship with the people in the Hauraki region, and the longstanding friendship with Tupu Taingakawa, Ratana turned to relatives including Nikora Te Mete (Nick Smith) at Te Poi near Matamata. He had already dedicated the Ratana Temple, representing his spiritual works, as a tribute to his son Arepa. Here at Te Poi, in view of the Kaimai Ranges, he would establish Te Omeka Pā, representing the physical works or the Ture Tangata, as a tribute to his son Omeka.

Left and facing page: Ratana had hoped to have a 'secular' base closer to the people in the Waikato where issues relating to the Treaty of Waitangi could be discussed, freeing Ratana Pā to focus on the spiritual issues. While Te Omeka Pā near Matamata was officially opened in 1937, issues over land ownership soon saw the focus back on Ratana Pā. *Uri Whakatupuranga (Ratana Archives).*

During a sermon on 21 September 1937 he explained his reasoning for two separate buildings. 'In ancient times there were two exalted places, Jerusalem and Zion. Today we have Ratana Pā and Te Omeka Pa; thus shall it be the role of Zion to maintain and to beautify the New Jerusalem which cometh down from out of heaven.' He quoted from Isaiah, 'Put on thy strength, O Zion, put on thy beautiful garments, O Jerusalem', explaining that Hiruhārama Hou would uphold the spiritual works, while Omeka Pā would depict the strength of Hīona (Zion) as an economic or material platform.

The building, funded by donations and built by voluntary labour from within the Ratana movement, featured two halls, an office, kitchen and bakehouse, and was completed late in 1937. Soon after the official opening however, infighting and disagreement surfaced over the ownership of the land Omeka Pā had been built on, and how the centre would function. This turned Ratana's attention back to his home base. He had learned a lot about design and construction over the past few years and could see there was a great need to integrate the various buildings at his own marae. He would take what he had learned at Omeka Pā as a prototype for the much grander complex at Ratana Pā, effectively bringing the physical and spiritual works together.

A series of buildings had evolved haphazardly over time to meet the needs of the community. The double-gabled Ki Kopu cooking facility had a boiler that was activated when the farm's traction engine was driven alongside and connected to the pipes, sending steam to the cooking bins. The bins themselves were made of wood and the lids covered with sacking. Heavy weights were placed on top to reduce leakage. All water came from an artesian well.

While walking around the village with his advisers Ratana looked at the ageing facilities and began drawing in the dirt with a stick. He turned to Wira Grey: 'E Wira, he kamura koe. Wira, you are a carpenter. Make this. Take all those halls and put them together. This will be our Manuao, our man-o'-war.' Wira looked closely at the markings and after some thought returned with a canvas tarpaulin and translated Ratana's ideas ahead of developing building plans. The first stage of redevelopment, Ki Kopu, the cooking and dining facilities, was opened on 6 February 1938.

Ratana used the occasion to collect what he called the unfinished work, specifically the Treaty of Waitangi petition that now lay gathering dust in Parliament. He would parcel up copies of all the petitions and documents relating to the treaty and bury them under the foundation stone of the Manuao. He called back the mauri of what had been tabled in Parliament, uplifting the responsibility for the work he had given the government to do, and placed it back with his own movement. An inverted whetū mārama marks the spot where the documents are buried.

> Oh Ihoa, we place . . . our petition, before you and your government, as your Parliament has now been established on your Sacred Mountain; and because the Treaty of Waitangi is also your treasure given to us, we pray that it be returned to your own Parliament which has been established here, that it may be finally ratified. We ask all matters concerning the spiritual works and the physical works be brought back here to your Parliament for discussion and final decision . . . Oh Ihoa, you are the Author, the Judge and the Law.

He again described the Manuao as 'the Parliament of Ihoa', and prayed the entire complex would have 'an enduring spirit' and the children would grow up to be strong and know God's power on the earth. He declared he had 'branded' the 40,000 people chosen by God and sealed their names in the Holy Bible. 'This covenant is closed, and there will be nobody taken out of it from this day on.' He said the new building would be a shelter from the storms that were coming. The rest of the complex was officially opened on Sunday 11 September 1938. An estimated 5000 people turned out for the official opening, officiated over by the Minister of Lands, Frank Langstone.

Ratana referred to Te Manuao as Koha Mutunga, the 'last chance' or parting gift, to bring the people together in that elusive unity he had untiringly promoted throughout his ministry. It now included four halls: Rangimarie (Heavenly Peace), Whare Marama (House of Light), Piki Te Kaha (Seek Strength) and Ki Kopu, the dining hall. To these were added a kitchen, boiler house, butchery, storerooms, the church office Te Aroha, a base for the kātipa or Ratana police force, offices for the *Whetu Marama* newspaper and a post office.

As well as being an administrative base for the movement and a communal centre for the small township, with facilities for large gatherings throughout the year, the Manuao, like the Ratana Temple built a decade earlier, was rich in symbolism. A prominent collage above the entrance of the building features the seven canoes of the 'Great Migration' alongside Abel Tasman's *Heemskerck* and Captain Cook's *Endeavour*. The pillars holding up the veranda represent the captains and boats that travelled across the great oceans, along with the name of each waka or ship, and the whetū mārama symbols of the Ratana movement.

Ratana had already extended the term mōrehu beyond the dispossessed stragglers of his own people, to anyone who could get behind his vision for the country. This inclusive fleet is perhaps the strongest outward indication that the unity Ratana sought extended not only to Māori but all tribes who had made New Zealand their home, regardless of race. Also on the front of the Manuao are illuminated portraits of Ratana, Te Whaea, Arepa and Omeka, and representations of the Trinity and the Faithful Angels.

Originally, the whole building was green with pink trim as it was built during the time of Piri Wiri Tua. Later, it was painted green and gold – green representing greenstone or spiritual power and the gold, financial or economic power. However, gold can and does also represent the māramatanga and enlightenment when it is depicted in the points of the whetū mārama or the colour of the crescent moon.

In his speech on the evening of the opening on 11 September 1938, Ratana explained the significance of the complex.

> Many of you Morehu ask, 'Why have these waka been brought together on this Manuao?' Let me tell you, they are lifeboats of this Manuao; should the Manuao capsize all you have to do is jump aboard your own waka or lifeboat. But do not jump aboard the lifeboat of others, it would be wrong; further if you do this, the lifeboat will become overloaded and will capsize and sink. You know the function of a lifeboat, it is to save lives should a ship capsize, or . . . be wrecked by a storm or gale. Therefore it is up to you to persuade your people to come on to your own waka, and so finally end up on the Manuao. Look for yourselves, there is Aotea, Tainui, Kurahaupo, Tokomaru, Takitimu, Te Arawa and Mataatua. Further along you see the ships of Captain Cook and Tasman.

He said he had greeted many people in their own Māori language which they had not understood. 'It appears they must have come here on Captain Cook's waka, for they do not know the Maori language.' He then turned his attention to education, explaining that while it was important to send children to school, they should not look at 'high' education as the most important thing of all. 'Let knowledge of A.E.I.O.U., the Maori language, and A.B.C.D., the Pakeha language, be your aim. The Maori language is dying out, and you know it is through the Maori language that the Treaty of Waitangi is best known.'

Then he returned to the analogy of the 'great ship' that he had dreamed of in 1933 which had now been built in their midst.

Ships have only one captain but with your Manuao there are two captains. Look for yourselves, there is Piri Wiri Tua at one wheel, and the Mangai at the other. Yes, two captains, both smoking their pipes and waving goodbye to those who are left behind and missed the boat. Piri Wiri Tua controls the Ture Tangata, and he is waiting, and looking out for the enemy. The Mangai controls the Ture Wairua, and will fire the guns and shoot the enemy. My friends, this is spiritual talk.

Māori mana

The Ratana movement carried with it the hope of the majority of Māori and a much deeper legacy that could be traced back through the old prophets and T. W. Ratana's family line, to the latter half of the nineteenth century when both his grandfather and father had taken on secretarial roles in the various Kotahitanga movements. It was not surprising to tribal elders around the country that the name Ratana would again come to prominence in the early years of the twentieth century.

Ratana believed he was building on the legacy of the United Confederation of Tribes, which in 1835 declared the independence of the Māori nation. Members of the Confederation, a core of tribal chiefs who met to consider trading arrangements and to choose a Māori flag so that New Zealand-built ships could enter international ports, were among the first to sign the Treaty of Waitangi.

There was an understanding that they would continue to meet to consider how the partnership with the Crown and the New Zealand Government would be worked out. However, movements that sought to unite tribes, achieve representation for Māori and provide a forum for grievances based on the conditions of the treaty, were sidelined by a succession of governments. Ratana helped keep the flame of Māori unity burning in the hearts of the people. While he had initially pushed for a separate Māori government he eventually amended his approach to achieving partnership through parliamentary representation, nevertheless his immovable agenda was to have the Treaty of Waitangi embraced as part of the constitution.

A partnership between the Ratana and Kīngitanga movements was the great hope of both Tupu Taingakawa and Methodist missioner the Reverend A. J. Seamer, who saw the immense possibilities of a Christian-based, nationwide Māori movement. Reweti Te Whena and Tupu Taingakawa, who were both constitutional lawyers, had long discussions about the way forward and believed the Declaration of Independence gave Māori the right to form their own Parliament. Ratana, however, saw the declaration more as a stepping stone and the Treaty of Waitangi, which replaced it, as a licence for Māori to act independently in partnership with the Crown.

T. W. Ratana and Te Urumanao (Te Whaea), the patriarch and matriarch of the Ratana family, gather with their extended whānau at the wedding of a relative in the Manuao at Ratana Pā in 1938. *William Hall-Raine, Te Papa Tongarewa Museum of New Zealand.*

He had taken on twin roles to fulfil his vision: tumuaki, head of the Ratana Church or defender of the faith, and perehitini (president) of the Ratana movement. But his influence was much wider. It was clear from those who became signatories to various petitions and covenants that people from all tribes and denominations had given him authority to speak for them, and that Ratana sustained the hope that ultimately there would be a united body. After the failed attempt to get the Crown to honour its agreement with Māori, the tone of his work began to change. It was clear neither the New Zealand Government nor the ultimate treaty partner were interested. He would have to restructure his movement along more efficient lines, creating a religious and political body that could no longer be dismissed as insignificant.

Ratana had divided the country into four quarters, stating his body would become whole when he had won all Māori parliamentary seats. Through powerful biblical-based symbolism and spiritual gifts of healing and prophecy he would continue to unfold for the people a hope much greater than that of mere political representation. He would, like the British Crown before him, set forth a system where church and state operated side by side. Unlike the British, though, it would not be the political side that would end up dominating. If all was well with the spiritual, only then would the physical be put right.

Ratana would start at the beginning and map out a plan to the end, leaving the 'doorway' open for the people to walk into the future. This was the Arepa, Omeka, Piri Wiri Tua and Hamuera model: the north, south, east and west of the plan to take over the Māori seats of physical government and set up the signposts to draw all mōrehu or faithful believers into the Parliament of Ihoa.

Ratana, in his final years, began restructuring his movement and gathering together all his kawenata into a final form that would help guide the people into the future. *Uri Whakatupuranga (Ratana Archives).*

Fixed on the future

Finally, when Ratana's goal was in sight, his health began to fail him. He had three members in Parliament, and the Treaty of Waitangi petition with 45,000 signatures had been tabled and was waiting to be actioned. Through various restructuring processes Ratana Pā was being geared to become a place where spiritual and political issues affecting all Māoridom could be worked out.

Te Rere o Kapuni, beside Mount Taranaki, had been a place of solace and inspiration from the earliest days of Ratana's ministry. This was the waterfall where the prophet Titokowaru – who had helped Te Whiti and Tohu plough the land – had blessed 'special' children who had the gift of second sight (matakite) or were to be raised as tohunga. Ratana had renamed the waterfall Kapuni (spiritual gathering place) and rededicated it to Ihoa o ngā Mano; his followers believed the angels were present in great number whenever there was a gathering of the faithful, and at the waterfall revelation would come to give guidance or insight.

He made two final visits up to Te Rere o Kapuni. The first, on 20 January 1939, was to dedicate the key points from all his covenants, the treaty and his petition. Before a great crowd of followers he symbolically baptised them, dedicating them to a future time. He saw everything around him was failing, but not futile. He knew the world war was imminent and there would be darkness for a time. He said that after the war the Holy Spirit would go throughout the world seeking after pure hearts.

Present for the occasion were hundreds of mōrehu and all the church and Ture Tangata administrators, Ngā Koata e Whā, secretaries, editors of the *Whetu Marama*, and the brass bands.

When Bishop Nakada's daughter-in-law Daisy finally made her promised visit from Japan to Ratana Pā in 1986, the only member of the world tour party left alive was Ratana's daughter Maata (Te Reo). Both women had been married in the symbolic double wedding linking the two peoples in 1924. *Uri Whakatupuranga (Ratana Archives).*

> I establish my church upon this rock [foundation] and all of its laws and policies are to be sealed upon this rock so that it may never be shaken from this day forward or hereafter. In the past the church had been established with all of its policies upon the onepu [shifting sands]; this day the Ture Wairua and the Ture Tangata have been secured upon this rock even unto heaven. The Treaty of Waitangi has been established and baptised by this waterfall whose water flows from the snows that Jehovah has provided and given upon this mountain.

He prayed that the renewed covenant, which mapped out the way forward for the church and the movement, would be sealed. 'I have come to support the words of the covenant of 1939. I place this covenant to be baptised by this waterfall.' Then he heard a voice speak from out of the waterfall, saying that on this day it was fulfilled.

> You must all know that when the whole world is lost and in complete and total darkness it will be at this mountain you will find the life force for all the treasures and prophecies of this nation that have been placed here in the palm of your hand. There is a new experience coming that will fulfil the Treaty of Waitangi. If the nation had united as one it would have already been fulfilled and established upon this unshakeable rock.

From the hui on 25 January 1939, Ratana began to refer to the Manuao complex as Te Āka, or the Ark. The first covenant between God and man occurred after the great flood of antiquity, when eight people escaped in the Ark of Noah to

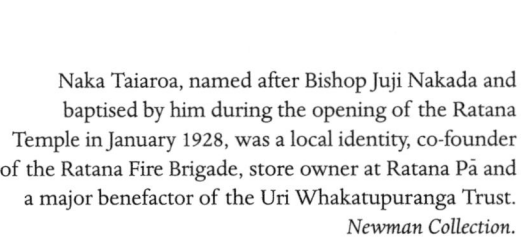

Naka Taiaroa, named after Bishop Juji Nakada and baptised by him during the opening of the Ratana Temple in January 1928, was a local identity, co-founder of the Ratana Fire Brigade, store owner at Ratana Pā and a major benefactor of the Uri Whakatupuranga Trust. *Newman Collection.*

populate the new world. The sign that the earth would no longer be destroyed by flood was the rainbow, another prominent Ratana symbol. Noah began building the Ark 120 years before the 'the fountains of the great deep' and the 'windows of heaven' unleashed the 40 days and nights deluge. Likewise, Te Manuao was seen as a safe haven, a place to escape the rising tide of worldly worries and the massive changes that Ratana warned lay ahead. This building would be a place where they could gather together in unity and seek the light. That light would not only be the māramatanga of spiritual enlightenment, but of learning and understanding. He also referred to the Manuao as a wānanga, a national college or university.

However, the principal architect of this highly symbolic and yet practical structure knew his health was failing him. There was much work to be done to ensure the people understood his intentions, so Ratana moved into the front office, or lounge, at the marae end of the Manuao office block.

Asian revival foretold

On his second visit to Te Rere o Kapuni on Waitangi Day, 6 February 1939, Ratana was physically carried up the mountain by Eruera Tirikatene, where he lamented that the mōrehu and the Kōmiti Hāhi Matua had focused more on the messenger than the message. He was just 'a fingerpost pointing the way'. Whetu Tirakatene-Sullivan heard directly from her father the words that were spoken to him by Ratana: 'The morehu have made a tin god of me and the Holy Spirit power has been taken from me. I'm sad the morehu have not seen it as clearly as they should have.'

Regardless, elaborate prophecies relating to the future, including the role of the Treaty of Waitangi, continued to be spoken, including a claim the Ratana movement would enter a new era after the year 2000 (Te Rua Mano). Among the signs of the times would be an influx of Asian people, particularly from

Japan, seeking the māramatanga. These, and similar statements on the Ratana marae and in the temple over the ensuing months, pointed to the fulfilment of things promised during the time Ratana had spent with Bishop Juji Nakada in 1924 and 1927.

Ratana had left Bishop Nakada 'a gift', the same blessing of the 'divine light and enlightenment' that had been granted the Māori people under the 'star of the south'. He had seen the Japanese as another iwi mōrehu (nation of survivors), and believed they shared similar bloodlines. Nakada and Ratana had agreed that the sign of the rising sun on the Japanese flag was actually a sign of the 'rising Son' or the new dawn which would herald the return of Christ, and as such was embraced on the Ratana flag, the front of the temple, on the bonnet of Ratana's daughter Te Reo Hura from 1924, and the Ratana Youth Movement logo from 1983.

It was said that if the mōrehu, who were inheritors of the Ratana legacy, did not step forward and point the way or share the 'divine light', strangers would come to Ratana Pā and learn for themselves. Japanese minister in training, Haeretika Kito, had lived at Ratana Pā ahead of Bishop Nakada's arrival to open the Ratana Temple. A number of babies were baptised by Nakada at the temple opening, including Naka Taiaroa, elder, store owner, significant property owner at Ratana Pā and patron of the Uri Whakatupuranga Ratana Archive Trust.

In the temple at midnight on 29 May 1939 Ratana again very specifically spoke of the Asian influence that would affect New Zealand.

> There is a day unfolding when you will reach the doorway of the year two thousand, verily, there will be thousands and thousands of Japanese people [Asians] who will come to these shores to seek after your revelation for themselves, therefore you should hold fast to your footstool, and hold firmly to your revelation, your crown of glory, it will only be through sheer laziness and neglect this revelation will be lost to you all.

The presence of Ratana and his troupe in Japan in 1924 had clearly made an impression on many Japanese people, and correspondence continued between members of Bishop Nakada's music school and members of the touring party for many years. In these letters they often mentioned Ratana's special day of 8 November, which coincided with an important blossom festival. Among others, Machiko Aoyagi, head of Japanese studies at Tokyo University, lived at Ratana Pā in the early 1980s researching the Ratana-Japanese connection. She helped co-ordinate a visit by Bishop Nakada's daughter-in-law Asa (Daisy), who had been married in the symbolic ceremony by Ratana and Bishop Nakada in 1924. An earlier reunion was cancelled, and when she eventually made the journey in 1986 all the tour members – with the exception of Ratana's daughter Te Reo Hura, who was also married in that ceremony – had passed away.

Daisy closed her speech in the temple by singing 'Mā te Mārie' (Peace and Righteousness), the 'national anthem' of the Ratana movement, in Māori and Japanese, seeking the protection of the Holy Trinity and the angels and guidance in truth and righteousness from the throne of Ihoa. Many wondered just how far ahead in time Ratana was able to look when they saw the huge influx of Asian people into New Zealand from the year 2000. A group of six Japanese Catholic bishops met and exchanged gifts with Ratana elders in 2007, and Prime Minister Helen Clark signed open trade relationship agreements with China and Japan in 2008. In 2022 New Zealand celebrated 70 years of diplomatic relations with Japan, New Zealand's fourth largest trading partner and source of foreign investment and fifth largest source of tourists.

Leaving a legacy

In June 1939, in a further effort to tidy up his affairs and show the way forward for the church and movement, Ratana rolled existing committees into a single body to handle the political and economic side of the work, including treaty issues. He had already appointed his son Tokouru as president for the social, political and economic side. According to a report in *Whetu Marama*, responsibility for the spiritual side was to have been vested in Patu Koroneho, a kaumātua from Waikato, who would step in as 'defender of the faith while Ratana retained the role of 'spiritual advisor'.

> It was at this time that I, the *Whetu Marama*, heard Te Mangai explaining to the morehu of his intentions to resign from his position as Defender of the Faith regarding the law, that being the removal of his name from the Register, but will continue to be paramount spiritual adviser according to the Spirit. Also at the same time, I, the *Whetu Marama*, also heard Te Mangai saying that he will also be resigning from the President position of the Federation . . . That is why I, the *Whetu Marama*, herein wish to explain to every morehu that Te Mangai has appointed [Patu] Koroneho as Defender of the Faith for the Church in accordance with the law, and Haami Tokouru Ratana as President of the Federation . . .

Ratana had also been training up Homai Tamaiparea, the son of Iwiora Tamaiparea, the Anglican clergyman married to his sister, Puhi o Aotea, who had confirmed Arepa and Omeka. Homai had been appointed as chairman of the newly formed church executive and was believed to be another potential successor to lead the church in spiritual matters.

SIXTEEN

PASSING OF THE PROPHET

Oh, Jehovah, the Father. Oh, Lord Jesus Christ. The tree whose seeds I planted in the four corners of the land has grown. Come now, and rule over all the people, so that the tree may bring forth the spirit of righteousness for the body and for the soul.

—T. W. Ratana, 16 September 1939

Farewell, my friend. For your way was not an easy one to walk but you had intentions to run off because people like you who are prophets can see things coming before they reach us. You see the fire burning on the other side, this is why I said . . . your body is a different body unlike the body of others because your body is the body of a prophet.

—Sir Apirana Ngata at Ratana's funeral, 1939

Tidying up the legacy

As the winter of 1939 drew to a close, the German army encroached deeper into the territories of surrounding nations, making a second global war inevitable. At Ratana Pā the gardens were blossoming, the shining cuckoo could be heard heralding the spring and the time for kūmara planting; but in the small lounge at the end of the Manuao, political visionary and Māori prophet T. W. Ratana felt his strength ebbing away.

Members of the church committee, his family and the political candidates representing his four quarters knew these were his last days. At least two people remained with him at all times to witness his last words. He called his family and his inner circle Ngā Koata e Whā, and their wives, to make a statement for their

Ratana's health was rapidly failing him, his demeanour had changed drastically and he had lost a lot of weight in the last year of his life. He was concerned the people had set him up as a 'tin god', and in his final 'Christian kawenata' urged them to return to faith in Christ and not to change the 'values and beliefs' or the symbolism he had embedded into the buildings at Ratana Pā. *Henderson Collection.*

future guidance. They called in a secretary Te One Motu to make a permanent record of his kaupapa, or foundation of faith.

Among his words, couched in prayer, he said:

Oh, Jehovah, the Father. Oh, Lord Jesus Christ. The tree whose seeds I planted in the four corners of the land has grown. Come now, and rule over all the people, so that the tree may bring forth the spirit of righteousness for the body and for the soul. The body that covers my soul is worn out. Thus, I confess to all my many pitiful complaints, which I have scattered at the feet of my Lord Jesus and of the people. Unburden me of all my sins, wrongdoings and ills. Undo the chains which bind the angry protests to my body and to my soul.

He said the old ways had passed, and wanted all things to be renewed.

I bend to the will of the one Jehovah and his Son, Jesus Christ, in whom the darkness is as nothing and the dawn is at hand. It is now the world of light. The world of spiritual enlightenment, let it live on. Let it last forever in the time that stretches before me, that no word of instruction or of inducement be passed over, but that all of it be fulfilled. I write my name to this as my final message to the upcoming generation and to the great body of faithful followers of God, Te Morehu. This is what I have chosen as the foundation of conversion to the Christian faith, that they may receive God's blessings through the love of the Lord, our Saviour, Jesus Christ. Amen.

After reciting the Lord's Prayer, Ratana sent another secretary, O. H. Nathan, for his personal stamp that he had used on his covenants, and then he rested. On Sunday, 17 September 1939 at 9 p.m. Ratana stated before the four quarters, the church council and family members: 'Toko, light the torch. I am leaving the spiritual and material works to you. The European and the Maori sides of the work are in your care.' The next day at 3 a.m. he gave his last message in the church office: 'I do not desire that anyone should finish my work, other than Tokouru and the family.'

Ratana the miracle worker and passionate advocate for the unification of the Māori people, the one who broadcast the word of God to the Māori people and anyone else who would listen, took his final breath at 10 a.m. on Monday 18 September 1939, aged 66.

Among those at Ratana's bedside when he died were Mura Kawana, whose husband Joe was a grandson of prophetess Mere Rikiriki, his longtime friend Reverend Seamer, and Sister Irene Hobbs who had recently been reappointed by the Methodist Church to serve another term at Ratana Pā. It was Sister Hobbs who washed and prepared Ratana's body for burial. At his last breath, the kuia or older women who gathered outside began wailing and rocking in grief, mourning the passing of their beloved leader.

Paraire Paikea announced to the nation over the radio the passing of the great man. Ratana's body lay in state on the veranda of the family homestead where he had so often addressed and inspired his people and performed healings. A large crowd, including the Prime Minister Michael Joseph Savage, several members of Parliament, and about 3000 faithful gathered for the tangi, which lasted a week. Reverend A. J. Seamer was invited by the family to address the people:

> He was called by many a great saint; by others he was classed as a great sinner. Which was he? From one point of view he was a very great saint, but if he were to stand by my side now, he would say he had been a great sinner. The outcome of his work depends upon us who follow him, particularly those who have wandered far from his teachings. His work will succeed only where it is built on truth.

His old nemesis, Sir Apirana Ngata, made a gracious speech to commemorate the passing of the man he had often criticised and challenged in the public arena, and whose koata would ultimately unseat him in Eastern Māori:

> Farewell and go to the many and go unto the powerful, go and return to your ancestors. Farewell the man that trampled the nation bringing you even into my own region Ngati Porou where you trampled my head and disturbed the

Above and facing page: Tahupotiki Wiremu Ratana, the healer, prophet and political visionary, who had received his vision to unite the Māori people under Ihoa o ngā Mano at the close of the First World War, passed away just as the German Air Force moved in to bomb Warsaw at the outset of the Second World War in September 1939. Thousands, including leaders from across Māoridom, and from all political parties and faiths, came to Ratana Pā to mourn the passing of the man who gave his people hope and faith and raised the Treaty of Waitangi from the dust of obscurity. *Uri Whakatupuranga (Ratana Archives).*

courtyards of Ngati Porou. What for? What were your intentions? It was to bind and unite people. Your body is a special one, a different one, unlike other people's bodies; and this is the reason why I have come here today to pay you respects.

In the days when Maori were secure in being Maori it was easier for us to understand the Maori heart. Again, another reason why I pay respects to you. Farewell the man that was responsible for creating and developing his own systems right in the middle of the time of the Pakeha. You were responsible for creating your own systems and pathway which you spread and shared throughout the country. Therefore, farewell the one who dealt with the issues of the body, and the grievances of the land.

This is I, the stubborn one who has come here today. Farewell the one who reached out into the depth of all things, the one who was determined to see the nation united and now I come here to honour you; farewell because you have left behind a legacy. Now at this moment as you have gone the fires also burn but for me I cannot see that far. Farewell, leave behind your legacy for others to maintain and care for, or manipulate and destroy . . .

Therefore farewell, my friend. For your way was not an easy one to walk but you had intentions to run off because people like you who are prophets can see things coming before they reach us. You see the fire burning on the other side, this is why I said earlier your body is a different body unlike the body of others because your body is the body of a prophet.

In the small Piki Te Ora church, the Reverend Seamer conducted a short service before Ratana was carried in his casket ahead of a procession that moved

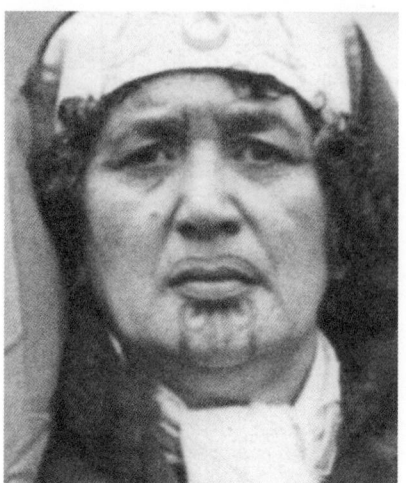

Ratana's faithful partner, 'Te Whaea' Urumanao – the mother of all – passed away within months of her husband. She was buried next to him in front of the Ratana Temple. *Uri Whakatupuranga (Ratana Archives).*

across the marae to the temple where a Ratana apostle performed the last rites. T. W. Ratana was buried in a large stone tomb in front of the temple on 24 September. He was survived by both wives, three daughters Maata, Piki Te Ora and Winnie (Rawinia), and three sons Tokouru, Raniera and Matiu. Within seven months of his death his wife Te Urumanao (Te Whaea) passed away on 26 April 1940 and was buried next to him.

As Ratana's spirit passed on to be with his Creator, Germany moved in to bomb Warsaw and bring the world into the second great global conflict of the twentieth century. New Zealand made its declaration of support for Britain a week after it declared war. At the time of his death, 100 years after the signing of the Treaty of Waitangi, the followers of T. W. Ratana had grown to become New Zealand's largest and most influential Māori religious community.

Memories of a child

Whetu Tirikatene-Sullivan, who was raised at Ratana Pā, was seven years old when she heard the news. She was with her grandmother in the South Island when she learned that the man, who had selected her name and prophesied she would enter politics, had died. She had loved her regular conversations with the prophet and to her it seemed he was her best friend. 'I shed tears for hours. I was inconsolable.' She said Ratana took every opportunity to personally teach his tamariki nohinohi, the little children of Ratana Pā.

> He used to engage with me and ask me what I had learned at Sunday School and I was very pleased to report to him. He would make it more meaningful and suggest that rather than just learning about Jesus and talking with him in prayer we should be like him as well . . . All the children were familiar with the

Wairua Tapu, although we did not altogether comprehend this. Ratana had made it clear the Holy Spirit was the gift of Jesus to his apostles and to all the people who invited him into their lives. I asked my father and he agreed.

In her exchanges with Ratana it had been made clear that it was in relationship with Jesus Christ that she could talk to or approach God. Tirikatene-Sullivan had learned the Lord's Prayer off by heart and won a small mounted likeness of Jesus at the Ratana Sunday School for her efforts.

At the next opportunity, when I saw the Mangai sitting in the sun on his veranda, I couldn't wait to say it to him. He said I should say it every night because it was the prayer that Jesus taught his apostles. Furthermore he said he never missed saying it every night before he went to sleep. My father told me Ratana often said it when he would meet with his four koata after the evening services, and they would all join in.

Tirikatene-Sullivan recalls the often told story of when her father was asked to recite the Lord's Prayer at one of the early gatherings, and did so in English.

Above left: Reweti Te Whena, a senior member of the Kīngitanga Parliament who accompanied Ratana on the 1924 world tour, was placed in a caretaker role after the prophet's death, while various committees debated the way forward. *Uri Whakatupuranga (Ratana Archives).* *Above right:* Tini Whetu Marama Tirikatene-Sullivan was raised at Ratana Pā and given her name by T. W. Ratana, who prophesied she would enter politics. *Tirikatene-Sullivan Collection.*

Soon Ratana realised the man couldn't speak Māori at all.

> Ratana said 'E taku tamaiti, homai to ringaringa?' and as he grasped my father's hand, he said, 'Nau, to tatou reo' and he then instantaneously spoke Maori. When he used to relate this event to us, my mother affirmed it, pointing out that she knew it was his voice that she heard as he walked home in the early hours of the morning, and she was amazed to hear him speaking in Maori. She said he did not utter a word of English, and the Maori flowed out of him for the next seven days. That is the only event of its kind imparted by Ratana that I have heard from first-hand witnesses.

September 18 remains a red letter day on the Ratana calendar. Each year, a memorial and thanksgiving service is held and the people reflect on his mission, his accomplishments and the state of the movement he founded. At this time, the events of 8 November 1918 are recalled, when Ratana was anointed by the Holy Spirit to begin a journey that would startle the nation, as he worked to restore Māoridom to faith in one God and heal the minds, souls and bodies of thousands of people. It is also an occasion when Tawhiao's prophecy is brought to mind: 'Kia tupato ki te tekau ma waru o nga ra, ko Hepetema te Marama, tau ariki te tau, he tau tuku whakarerere ki a Ihoa', which means '[Take note] the 18th day of September will be a month, a year [when you will be reminded] of a first born of one high born, a year [when you will be reminded] of sacrifice to Ihoa.'

According to church tradition, this prophecy reminds the people of the great sacrifices made in order that the Kupu or Word of God be preached and understood. As the *Whetu Marama* reported:

> It reminds us too of the sacrifices made during Christ's lifetime, culminating in the crucifixion on Calvary, the extreme pain and sacrifices of the apostles of old, the whakamatautauranga (testing) endured by T. W. Ratana immediately after November 8, 1918 [and] the torment, hard work, worry and sacrifices . . . endured during his lifetime, eventually culminating in his death on September 18, 1939.

In his final words before departing this life Ratana reinforced his intention that Ratana Pā should stand 'in the likeness of the House of Israel' as a testimony to biblical truth and the intent of his mission. 'Let not its values and beliefs be destroyed by man, or by modern learning, or by the Devil!'

SEVENTEEN

DRAWN AND QUARTERED

Control had been taken from the Maori MPs and the Maori people and vested totally in the Native Department. The committees became a mere shell of what they had been. A further move by Maori to contribute more effectively through the political system had been denied.

—Ralph Ngatata Love, in his 'Policies of Frustration' thesis, describing Māori concerns at having numerous proposals for advancing the Māori nation shut down by the Labour Party

This [Treaty] deals with rights and privileges of Maori as British subjects. Where do our rights and privileges come from as a British subject? From the Magna Carta. Likewise, the Treaty of Waitangi gave certain rights to the Maori people, the indigenous people of this country, as British subjects . . . My policy was then and still is to stand for the rights and privileges of the whole Maori race, as embodied in the Treaty of Waitangi.

—Eruera Tirikatene, speaking to the Waitangi Day Act 1960, a small step along the way to having the Treaty of Waitangi officially recognised

Performing under pressure

Ratana's passing seemed like a mortal blow to his followers; without a natural successor to pick up his vision and drive through to the other side, the movement he founded soon became distracted. Reweti Te Whena, an elder who had accompanied Ratana on the world tours, was placed in a caretaker role while various committees debated the way forward.

Before her death, Ratana's wife Te Whaea ensured her son Tokouru was appointed both president of the movement and defender of the faith. This

Left: Tapihana Paikea took over the Northern Māori seat on the death of his father Paraire Paikea in 1943. *Right:* Matiu Ratana took over the Western Māori seat, succeeding his older brother Tokouru who died in October 1944. *Uri Whakatupuranga (Ratana Archives).*

seemed in conflict with the emerging plan to separate responsibility for the Ture Wairua and Ture Tangata sides of the organisation. While Ratana had previously held both roles, it had been a great burden to him. He delegated at every opportunity and had been training others to take leadership roles. Tokouru had been more comfortable dealing with treaty and social issues, and even in Parliament his voice was rarely heard. During the time of his greatest responsibility he was facing the darkest days of his ongoing illness.

Within a short time there were heated debates over what Ratana may or may not have intended, and passionate exchanges over his theology, in particular the wording of his final 'Christian kaupapa'. The restructuring remained incomplete, leaving concerns about accountability and uncertainties about how church and state assets would be administered. Disputes flared over whether to take a political or spiritual direction, and then there was the question of who actually owned the assets at the Pā.

Issues relating to the treaty and Māori grievances were increasingly put aside, while the 'fire' Ratana had predicted was spreading around the world. Tokouru was grateful that Eruera Tirikatene was able to stand in the gap, particularly in matters of the Ture Tangata. He had become an impressive speaker on the marae and exhibited charismatic leadership qualities that many believed had been inherited from Ratana. He had been fully briefed by Ratana about spiritual and political matters and his policies for the future.

Complicating the political platform was the death of Michael Joseph Savage, who had struck the historic alliance with Ratana. He had promised Ratana that he would look after the interests of the Māori people by addressing their grievances in relation to the Treaty of Waitangi. In 1937 he had travelled to Britain for the coronation of King George VI, and made headlines for his repeated

Left: Tiaki Omana (Jack Ormond) finally captured the Eastern Māori seat in 1943 from Sir Apirana Ngata, completing T. W. Ratana's four quarters prophecy. *Right:* After the death of Matiu Ratana in 1949, his widow Iriaka Ratana became the first Māori woman in Parliament. *Henderson Collection.*

criticism of Britain's failure to take a stand against the growing militarism in Japan, Italy and Germany. Shortly after his social security bill was introduced he had been diagnosed with cancer, but delayed treatment so he could participate in the forthcoming election where he increased Labour's vote from 46 to 56 per cent. His condition worsened until it was too late for treatment. Following Savage's death on 27 March 1940 at the age of 68, the leadership of the Labour Party fell to his deputy, Peter Fraser.

Unlike Pākehā, Māori were not conscripted into the armed forces. Initially, there was low enlistment, particularly in districts where there had been a high confiscation of land following the New Zealand Wars. It is estimated only a quarter of the Māori workforce were registered for social welfare purposes, and without a Māori electoral roll it was difficult to identify eligible men. Without the firm guidance and input of their great mentor and leader, the Ratana members of Parliament became divided over some issues. Paikea, who had been elected member for Northern Māori in 1938, began to lean towards Apirana Ngata, who urged him to put treaty issues aside and focus on getting Māori people behind the war effort.

Paikea broke ranks with the other Ratana members by independently lobbying Labour members of Parliament at a meeting in Auckland at the end of 1940, when he was supposed to be at Ratana Pā discussing who would be the best candidate on the Executive Council representing the Māori race. With the backing of the Auckland members, he ultimately became the first Māori to hold ministerial rank in a Labour Government, as minister in charge of the Māori war effort in the War Cabinet. One of his challenges was getting the full support of Princess Te Puea and King Koroki in the Waikato. Tirikatene threw his energy into fundraising, while Tokouru Ratana, uncomfortable with the

Above left: Eruera Tirikatene remained a driving force behind the Ratana politicians, with his daughter Whetu in later years acting in a secretarial capacity. *Uri Whakatupuranga (Ratana Archives).* *Above right:* When Iriaka Ratana stepped into politics, the role of tumuaki of the Ratana Church went to Ratana's sister Puhi o Aotea, seen here with Henare Edmonds, the church vice president in 1962. *Henderson Collection.*

idea of conscripting Māori into the forces, preferred to work on drumming up recruits for the Home Guard.

Meanwhile, in June 1942 the three Ratana members outlined an organisational framework to handle recruitment and war-related activities through the pan-tribal Maori War Effort Organisation (MWEO), which they believed might facilitate Māori unity and development even after the war. Under Paikea's guidance the MWEO became the main adviser on Māori activities.

With support from Māori committees across the country, Paikea made several strong representations to government that the MWEO be retained. His final submission to Prime Minister Fraser in April 1943 asserted the organisation was the greatest thing that had happened to the Māori people since the signing of the Treaty of Waitangi. If it was allowed to continue as a refocused body it could contribute significantly to the 'future prosperity, development and happiness' of the people, and play a worthwhile and practical part in rehabilitation of the soldiers as they returned from war. To remove government support from the organisation, he said, would 'endanger the whole structure and the successful development' of Māori.

However the government opposed the move, believing the MWEO had served its purpose. Within three days of making his statement to the War Cabinet, Paikea was dead. Moves were quickly being made to curb any further growth of the widespread body of Māori councils; Fraser took control before handing the reins to Tirikatene to wind things down.

A full house

Labour was returned to power in the 1943 elections with Tirikatene and Tokouru Ratana holding their seats. The Northern Māori seat previously held by Paikea was retained by his son Tapihana Paraire Paikea. Tiaki Omana finally captured Eastern Māori from Sir Apirana Ngata, giving Ratana its fourth seat in Parliament. The election result was seen as fulfilment of prophecy: Ratana finally had Ngā Koata e Whā in Parliament; his body was complete. Their vote was now essential for Labour to retain a working majority.

The promises began again: equality between Māori and Europeans, better housing and schools, free medical and maternity care, old-age pensions and other social-security benefits for Māori. There would be extensions to agricultural and technical training, finance for the prompt settlement of land grievances, and rehabilitation and training for Māori returned servicemen. One of the policy points stated: 'a complete settlement of the Maori claims will be immediately resumed with a view to an early and complete settlement'.

However, there was ongoing frustration with the Native Department and its handling of Māori welfare and related issues, largely viewed through Pākehā eyes. A call for a thorough investigation of Māori concerns was all but ignored. The Ratana members called a nationwide conference of Māori leaders, including the MWEO, to champion ongoing independence in their own administration. Prime Minister Peter Fraser, in addressing the October 1944 gathering, opposed the theme, saying the Native Department was able to meet all Māori needs.

Over 400 delegates voted to keep the MWEO in some form, to extend the number of Māori seats in line with the growth of the Māori population, and to have the government address Māori social, health, education and land confiscation issues. Nothing came of it. A week after the conference, T. W. Ratana's oldest son Haami Tokouru Ratana, president of the Ratana Church, passed away at the age of fifty years.

Tokouru had been returned to his seat for Western Māori with a strong majority, less than a year previously. He had been ill for months, and frequently in hospital. He died at Ratana Pā and was survived by his third wife and several children. He was succeeded as president of the Ratana Church by his younger brother Matiu. However, Matiu was required to seek the official Labour nomination along with fourteen other candidates. He ultimately won selection and the by-election, affirming the Ratana stronghold across all the Māori seats.

In 1932 Ratana had taken the Treaty of Waitangi to Parliament and asked for it to be written into the laws of the nation. His request was ignored for thirteen years, until Tirikatene raised a motion to have it considered alongside petitions from the Maori Affairs Committee and the formal investigations of the 1926 Royal Commission. On 25 October 1945 the select committee reported to the

House on petitions seeking statutory recognition of the Treaty of Waitangi, including those compiled by T. W. Ratana and others. Together there were a total of 47,471 signatures representing 75 per cent of the Māori population, which was at the time 63,670.

Cabinet recommended that the Treaty of Waitangi be published 'as a sacred re-affirmation of the agreement' between the two peoples, and copies should be hung in 'all schools throughout the Dominion and in all Maori meeting-places'. At least there was some official, albeit token, recognition of the treaty, and at the same time several land claims from Taranaki, Waikato, the Bay of Plenty and the South Island were brought before Parliament, and 'a full and final settlement' reached. Proposals that other land grievances be resolved, along with appropriate rehabilitation of Māori soldiers, were sidelined.

The old patterns of compromise continued; the promised new deal didn't eventuate. Māori members of Parliament and those who still clung to the structure of the MWEO were seriously concerned about the future of Māori policy and the role of the Native Department. Tirikatene, along with his secretary and long-time associate Ralph Love, put together the framework for the Maori Social and Economic Advancement Bill, based on the 'Ratana experiment' of self-sufficient communities. They recommended that health and welfare liaison officers be appointed to encourage people to take greater responsibility for themselves, with resources and training available to help Māori work their remaining land along with a Māori apprenticeship scheme to train up young people in a range of trades. Hundreds of intersecting organisations

In front of the 'Lion's Den', 1936. The first meeting of Labour's Maori Policy and Advisory Council, the extensive national network of influential Māori leaders from across the country that Ratana and his koata regularly consulted on matters affecting the people. The natural extension of this council, comprising politically active individuals and many direct descendants of the original members, continued through until 1999 when the Labour Party deregistered the 4000-strong Māramatanga affiliate, claiming they had not paid their fees. In the front row, E. T. Tirikatene sits between Prime Minister Michael Joseph Savage (far right) and his deputy Peter Fraser, with Paraire Paikea (on his left). *Tirikatene-Sullivan Collection.*

representing Māori interests would ensure local and regional accountability reporting back to government. In later years the wide-ranging proposal was often attributed to Sir Apirana Ngata, however he was no longer in Parliament.

Regardless, the largely Ratana-inspired bill was hijacked by the Native Affairs Minister, Rex Mason, who brought it under the control of his department and transformed it from a pan-tribal proposal, placing it in the hands of tribal committees. Tirikatene's liaison officers became Māori welfare officers, and specific proposals for Māori leadership were axed. The Act – ironically passed on 1 April 1946 – rather than bringing Māori together with a common goal, diffused the growing political momentum by creating an atmosphere of intertribal competition and dependence on the government, something that was anathema to Ratana thinking.

According to Ralph Ngatata Love in his Victoria University thesis 'Policies of Frustration', the changes were a clever way of absorbing MWEO personnel into department ranks and a compromise that only served to increase Māori frustration with bureaucracy.

> This effectively destroyed the incentive and initiative of a large measure of self determination which had been built up by Maori across the country building networks and co-operating during the time of the MWEO. Control had been taken from the Maori MPs and the Maori people and vested totally in the Native Department. The committees became a mere shell of what they had been. A further move by Maori to contribute more effectively through the political system had been denied.

The 1946 general election was the first time the Ratana members contested the four Māori seats together. Once again, attempts were made within the Labour Party to unseat them as they positioned non-Ratana members to displace Omana and Paikea. Only intervention by Prime Minister Peter Fraser prevented this. Omana was under challenge from his nemesis Ngata, who wanted to regain his old territory. Tirikatene planned the strategy and the campaigns for all koata, urging Ratana members to recall the prophecies of their founder and vote accordingly. All were returned, three with increased majorities.

However, reluctance to allow any level of Māori control to be put into Māori hands brought things to a head with the Ratana members, who began to seriously reconsider their Labour loyalties. They were forced to remind the Labour Caucus that they currently held the balance of power, and then asked whether Labour was fulfilling its obligations to Māori or simply 'giving them crumbs from the Pakeha's table'? Caucus was stunned at this reaction, but nothing changed.

Between 1946 and 1949 National and Labour held 38 seats each with only

From left: Paraire Paikea, Ormond Wilson MP, Eruera Tirikatene and Gisborne MP Reg Keeling addressing a gathering at Ratana Pā. *Uri Whakatupuranga (Ratana Archives).*

Matiu Rata (third from left) was sworn in to the Northern Māori seat in 1963, following a long involvement in the union movement and with Ratana youth. Puti Tipene (Steve) Watene, a Mormon who had full Ratana backing, took Eastern Māori. At left are elder statesman E. T. Tirikatene (Southern Māori) and Iriaka Ratana (Western Māori). Watene died from a heart attack in Parliament buildings in June 1967 while opposing the Maori Affairs Amendment Bill, which sought to further alienate Māori land. *Tirikatene-Sullivan Collection.*

the four Ratana members keeping the government in power. They had failed to gain any control over Māori affairs, although their efforts in Parliament meant Māori could now apply for unemployment benefits and housing finance. More money was available for Māori health and education. There was a Māori secret ballot, and the term 'Maori' was substituted for 'Native' in all matters relating to Māori affairs. Another Act further shifted the distinctions between European and Māori, enabling Māori to buy beer, for example.

Leadership loss

The tragedy of war had seen many Māori lives lost on foreign ground, but at home there was also great sadness and loss when key figures in the Ratana movement who had been attending to the political and spiritual battle passed on. Paraire Paikea and Tokouru Ratana had died within eighteen months of each other and, in May 1949, Matiu Ratana was seriously injured in a car accident. He died unexpectedly after a bone-graft operation a month ahead of the general elections.

Labour stepped in once more in an attempt to undermine the Ratana alliance. There were twelve nominations for Matiu's seat, and the Maori Advisory Council was completely bypassed when the National Executive chose John Grace, the Māori secretary to the Prime Minister. Matiu's widow Iriaka stepped into the fray, threatening to stand as a Ratana Independent. The Labour Party was reminded that Ratana had 2000 supporters in Western Māori, and that breaking the koata could result in the loss of votes in other regions. They quickly reconsidered.

Iriaka became the first Māori woman to represent her people in Parliament, breaking a long-standing tribal tradition that women did not take leadership roles. Her nomination was strongly opposed by Princess Te Puea, who explained to a meeting of 1500 Māori leaders: 'I did not want a woman to belittle men. It is the tradition of the Tainui canoe . . . a woman must not jump into the front before the men.' This seemed to contradict Te Puea's own unofficial but nonetheless controlling influence over kings Te Rata and Koroki.

In the 1950 elections all Ratana seats were retained and, while Labour ultimately lost to National, Iriaka still polled more votes than any other candidate. The one-time member of the 1924 world tour concert party had married Matiu Ratana in 1940 and run a dairy farm at Whangaehu with her family when her husband had been away at Parliament. She decided to retain only the political side of the role, leaving the associated responsibility (head of the Ratana Church) to Ratana's sister Puhi o Aotea Ratahi.

Ratana Pā had come a long way from the shantytown that emerged in 1919 at the dawn of Ratana's healing ministry, but its evolution had not been easy. The outward focus of the movement, and the relative poverty of those who lived

Top: Former Ratana apostle Koro Wetere (left) and Paraone (Brown) Rewiti (right), conductor of the Tauranga Ratana band, join existing members of Parliament Matiu Rata and Whetu Tirikatene-Sullivan in Parliament in 1969. *Right:* The last koata to come from a strong Ratana background: Paraone (Brown) Rewiti with Whetu Tirikatene-Sullivan, Matiu Rata and Koro Wetere. Rata quit Labour to form the Mana Motuhake Party in 1979. *Tirikatene-Sullivan Collection.*

there, meant that the tiny township failed to keep pace with demands from the thousands of visitors who expanded it into a tent city several times a year.

T. W. Ratana, in his strategy to get certain politicians behind his plans for the Māori nation, had tested their integrity by making requests for assistance to bring electricity and a water supply to the Pā, and to shift the old railway station so that elderly people didn't have to walk across the lines. None of their promises came to pass, and a decade after his death those attempting to keep his movement alive were struggling with many of the same issues.

His proposed restructuring remained incomplete, and there were uncertainties about how 'church and state' assets would be administered and managed. Land title ownership for Ngāti Apa (the Ratana family tribe) and mōrehu, including section development, remained controversial. Part of the problem was that people who lived at Ratana Pā had no security of tenure. As a result, upkeep and plans for maintenance of homes and facilities were put on hold, and at one point Ratana Pā was under threat of being closed down.

Many of the houses were overcrowded and dilapidated, with earth floors, and there were no cooking or washing facilities. Some who recall those days deny reports of problems with disease, saying even the dirt-floor homes were well kept. In March 1954 the Pā again received strong criticism, this time from Marton magistrate, S. S. Preston S. M., who described it as 'a blot on the New Zealand landscape and a law unto itself'. As Eruera Tirikatene pointed out, the publicity was unfair. Through Iriaka's earlier intervention, living conditions had improved. There was now a water supply and a school subsidised by the government, and the people had finally been able to apply for assistance to build good houses, even though very few had done so.

Iriaka invited Ernie Corbett, the National Government's Minister of Maori Affairs, to visit the settlement, where he discovered what others had been trying to explain for some years. The land belonged to the members of the Ratana family, and the people living there did not feel they had sufficient security to invest further in their homes or Pā facilities, but feared they would be forced to leave unless conditions improved.

The solution meant the area – including land and roads – came under the control of the Rangitikei County Council, and Ratana Pā became a county township. The land originally owned by the Ratana family was put into a trust. New sewerage and water systems were completed; from 1963 the old houses at Ratana Pā were rapidly replaced and many of the signs of the transitional period 40 years previously were disappearing.

The Ratana foursome – Tirikatene, Paikea, Omana and Iriaka Ratana – while serving in Opposition, had no chance to make any major changes until they were all returned to power in 1957. They enthusiastically campaigned for 'full equality and rights for Maori and Pakeha and the progressive development of both races' and were returned with increased majorities. However, Prime Minister Walter Nash retained the Maori Affairs portfolio, giving Tirikatene what was to become a 'token' role as 'associate minister'.

Regardless, the Ratana politicians set about delivering a comprehensive Maori Affairs Policy paper for Cabinet, including proposals consistently raised by T. W. Ratana. The submissions related to Māori welfare, land claims, housing and education, with supporting evidence of how little had been done for the race so far. They reiterated their request that Waitangi Day be made a public holiday. After receiving his copy of the paper being circulated, Nash was livid. He informed Tirikatene that the portfolio of Maori Affairs was no concern of his, he had no legal right to submit such a paper, and then refused to put the matter on the Cabinet agenda.

It was a severe blow to have their well-researched views rejected so vehemently, and so soon after the election. Māori leaders from throughout the country expressed their disappointment that Tirikatene hadn't been given the full Maori Affairs portfolio and demanded to know exactly what the government's Māori policy would be, as there was now a clear conflict with its election

During the 1960s many homes at Ratana Pā were found to be in a derelict condition and had to be bulldozed. Part of the problem arose from the fact that the Ratana family owned the land, and those living in the village had no guarantee of tenure and were reluctant to invest in improvements. *Henderson Collection.*

promises. The Maori Policy Committee continued to find proposals that they were directly opposed to being presented to Parliament. Again they debated whether to leave the Labour Party and start all over again.

At the annual conference of the Labour Party, the comments of Tirikatene, who was retiring as president after 22 years, were placed on record ahead of the Annual Report. A unanimous request for action on Māori policy issues was passed and Nash was approached again. He said he would consider the submissions and 'if necessary' consult with Māori. There was no evidence of progress and this was bluntly reflected in a brief statement from the Māori members at the forty-fourth annual conference of the Labour Party:

> It must be obvious to all that the frustration of constantly repeating requests for an enquiry into matters of paramount importance to the Maori race has come to a stage where the practicable effectiveness of this Committee is completely nullified, and to say that its requests have been ignored is putting the matter very bluntly to the organisation which publicly states that the Maori adherents will remain loyal to it . . . loyalty is a matter of degree and while any group can be loyal to a principle, apathy towards receiving that loyalty brings its own inevitable reward and this regrettably is where we are at today.

Firm assurances had been given by the prime minister that Waitangi Day would be officially recognised but Tirikatene, concerned this was simply more bluster, warned a private member's bill would be presented if action wasn't forthcoming. The Waitangi Day Act was eventually passed in 1960.

In addressing the Waitangi Bill, Tirikatene said:

> I rise in gratitude at the passing of this Waitangi Day Bill which commemorates the signing of the treaty 120 years ago . . . down through the generations the document, in the mind of Maoridom, has come to be looked upon as one of the most sacred possessions . . . Even in the early days the Maoris based most sacred reliance on the document which Europeans had referred to as being 'not worth the paper it was written on' . . . On behalf of those Maori elders who have passed on beyond the soft veil into Spiritland and whose last words were 'Te Tiriti o Waitangi, taku turangawaewae – the Treaty of Waitangi, my foothold' – I rise in this House and take full responsibility in supporting this Waitangi Day Bill . . .
>
> This [Treaty] deals with rights and privileges of Maori as British subjects. Where do our rights and privileges come from as a British subject? From the Magna Carta. Likewise, the Treaty of Waitangi gave certain rights to the Maori people, the indigenous people of this country, as British subjects . . . My policy was then and still is to stand for the rights and privileges of the whole Maori race, as embodied in the Treaty of Waitangi. From the time I came into this House in 1932 until this day I have been a very proud man indeed to have helped rectify these wrongs . . . From the time I entered this House I have not lost sight of the Treaty of Waitangi.

Iriaka Ratana spoke of the decades of determined lobbying by various chiefs and the Ratana movement to have the treaty recognised, and the various actions and Acts of Parliament that had undermined its legal status and the faith of the Māori people in Parliament and the role of Britain.

> Over the years the Maori people were led to believe that the treaty had legal force, but as certain legislation was brought down they came to understand . . . that the treaty was just a piece of paper, but the Bill now before us would be to me a mark of the trust which the Maori has in Her Majesty the Queen.

Although the day was flagged 'as a national day of thanksgiving in commemoration of the signing of the Treaty of Waitangi', the Act was another compromise with no provision for a public holiday. Pressure from Māori increased and in 1963 a National Government passed the Waitangi Day Amendment Act. However Waitangi Day simply replaced Auckland Anniversary Day for those

A model of the new-look Manuao held by Tahupotiki 'Mooch' Motu and Whaimatua Anaru (Sam) Andrews, with the real thing under construction in the background.
Uri Whakatupuranga (Ratana Archives).

in Northland, serving only to associate the day with the north. Queen Elizabeth II was at Waitangi in February 1963 for the 123rd anniversary of the signing of the treaty, and gave a solemn assurance to renew the pledges and to assure Māori that the obligations entered into 'go far deeper than any legal provision in any formal document'. She said:

> Whatever may have happened in the past, whatever the future may bring, it remains the sacred duty of the Crown today, as in 1840, to stand by the spirit of the Treaty of Waitangi and to ensure that the trust of the Maori people is never betrayed . . . European and Maori can go forward together in confident partnership to make New Zealand a modern and prosperous nation, at the same time showing understanding and tolerance of each other's distinctive culture and customs . . . After the treaty had been signed and witnessed on that historic February day, Captain Hobson spoke these challenging and prophetic words: 'He iwi kotahi tatou – We are all one people'.

Certainly all the right words of conciliation were being spoken. At last the country was giving some credence to the historical significance of the treaty. There was a national day of commemoration and Queen Elizabeth, representing the British signatories, had affirmed everything Māori could have wished for.

The Labour Government was again defeated in the 1960 election, however all Ratana members were re-elected. At the forty-fifth annual conference of the Labour Party in 1961 the Maori Policy Committee Report stated 'any organisation reaps its just reward in direct relation to the work effort and real energy put into its work . . . we stand before you with an indictment that for years the acceptance of the Maori Policy Committee Report has been but empty gestures'.

In Opposition after 1960, the Ratana members could only express their hopes, views and hostility towards government policies on Māori affairs. Their voice became a thin whisper to which the Europeans who formed the policies affecting Māori gave only courteous attention. With no Māori members in government, according to Ralph Love, policies on Māori affairs lacked any Māori contributions or feeling and became based largely on Pākehā considerations.

Urban drifters

New Zealand was a nation in the midst of significant social and political change, and Māori in particular were forced by those changes to move more rapidly into the towns and cities to work and live alongside the rest of the population. This presented a real test for promises of equal opportunity. Intermarriage had weakened tribal affiliations, with Māori now more prepared to act independently of tribal allegiance. Their increasing visibility drew wider public attention to the plight of Māori as a poorer sector of the community and to education, employment, health and housing needs.

Māori still lagged behind Pākehā in many respects. By 1951, 32 per cent were still living in shacks and overcrowded houses, and only 30 per cent of Māori children aged between thirteen and seventeen years attended secondary school. The population increase also meant that remaining Māori land could not support larger families as much of it was in small, scattered holdings, or marginal and expensive to develop. Multiple ownership meant it was difficult for Māori farmers to get government development loans, which further spurred the migration to the cities. Like the rest of the population Māori also experienced a post-war baby boom resulting in half their number being under fifteen years of age by 1961. Following the Second World War, 25 per cent of Māori had moved away from rural areas and villages to the towns and cities for employment; by the mid-1970s this escalated to 75 per cent.

Iriaka Ratana described the move as 'a migration as adventurous as that from Hawaiki to Aotearoa . . . from the stone age to the atomic age'. She pleaded with Pākehā 'for tolerance and understanding' during this great task of adjustment, urging them to accept Māori on their merits rather than judging the many by the failures of the few.

The growing restlessness among youth – including the escalating crime rate among Māori – saw the Ratana movement step into another period of social action, with the formation of the Ratana Youth Movement in 1953. Under the auspices of Puhi o Aotea, thousands of mōrehu from across the country began attending youth rallies. Between 1956 and 1970 their numbers were swelled by young people from non-Ratana churches and communities.

The gatherings were designed to help young people 'understand the principles of the church, to promote and encourage leadership, foster and maintain Maori

Right and facing page: The main administration building of the Manuao was partially condemned in the early 1960s. Fundraising for reconstruction continued for two decades. Here is the centre point of the building in 1963 and again in 2007. *Uri Whakatupuranga (Ratana Archives) and Newman Collection.*

language, cultural activities, arts and crafts' and to educate young people 'in the appreciation of dress and of good conduct'. There were mass brass band performances, pop concerts, marching teams, youth clubs, choirs, sports teams, Māori cultural groups, leadership forums, nightly talent quests, dances and a prizegiving.

Speakers addressing the youth gatherings, which often attracted up to 10,000 people, included Māori elders, Christian ministers, government ministers and department officials. It was inclusive, encouraging and inspiring. The opening prayers from the 1967 gathering in Whangārei, for example, thanked the Trinity and the Holy Angels for giving courage and strength to guide the people through the many perils and problems of the world. It asked Ihoa to 'minister to the sick and needy and bereaved and bless the elderly and those in need of Ihoa's spiritual and healing hand'. It sought courage and blessing for the Queen and the royal household, the Māori Queen and her household, the leaders of the nation, Christian churches and all those observing Easter when '[Ihoa's] only begotten Son rose from the dead'.

Unfortunately, these huge gatherings didn't always manage to cover costs, leaving the Ratana movement to pick up the deficit. The 'official' Ratana Youth Movement was wound up in 1970, which allegedly had an 'immediate impact' on Māori youth across the country who had come to rely on the network of friends and supporters to lift their spirits and keep them focused on higher goals. Many youth leaders began putting their energy into politics, social concerns or joining the ministry through the Ratana Church, however many also became involved in gangs. The figures show the level of violence and drug and alcohol abuse increased dramatically around the country in the following years.

Tribunal for treaty

In 1960 Eruera Tirikatene had put forward a proposal to make Waitangi Day a national public holiday. The proposal had languished for over a decade, until Matiu Rata introduced a Waitangi Day private member's bill in 1971, but the new Labour Government, under Norman Kirk, preferred to have it known as New Zealand Day.

Rata, one of a new breed of leaders arising from within the Ratana movement, former chairman of the Auckland branch of the Ratana Church and a registered apostle, stated the day was to be neither 'a symbolic nor religious occasion' but a day for each New Zealander to enjoy as they saw fit, and the forerunner of an effort to achieve a 'full sense of nationhood'. Rata's Treaty of Waitangi Bill – introduced into the House in November 1974 – was finally passed into law in 1975, just as the 3000-strong Māori land march fronted by Dame Whina Cooper, reached Parliament grounds in Wellington.

Rata said the law change was intended to observe and confirm the principles of the Treaty of Waitangi and determine claims about certain matters inconsistent with those principles:

> While the Treaty can be regarded as the possession by the whole of our nation, of an instrument of mutuality that has endured for the past 134 years, to the Maori people it is a charter that should protect their rights. The Bill is primarily aimed at satisfying honour. It will also give physical and lawful sustenance to the long-held view that the spirit of the Treaty more than warrants our country's continued support.

The name Waitangi Day was restored in 1976, but with little effort to resolve outstanding Māori issues it was not surprising National had to deal with major protests over land confiscation at Bastion Point and Raglan during its term of office. The Waitangi Tribunal, eventually convened in 1977, could only investigate grievances that had happened since 1975. From 1985, however, under David Lange, Labour changed the law, allowing it to hear claims dating back to 1840.

The tribunal can order witnesses to come before it, order material or documents to be produced and actively search out material to help it decide on a claim. It can examine any claim that Māori have been prejudiced by laws and regulations or by acts, omissions, policies or practices of the Crown that are inconsistent with the Treaty of Waitangi. The tribunal publishes its findings in an official report to the minister of Māori Affairs, and may recommend to the government what can be done to compensate or to remove the harm suffered.

Icons of faith restored

While residents at Ratana Pā now had a renewed sense of ownership of their own homes and their place in the community, the central buildings that symbolised the true aims and mana of the movement had been seriously neglected. In the 25 years following T. W. Ratana's death the old Ratana family residence required intense work and the pride of the Pā, the Ratana Temple, also needed urgent attention.

Work had begun as early as 1941 when Puhi o Aotea unveiled and blessed the cornerstone ahead of major painting and refurbishment. She was also preparing plans to rebuild the Manuao, after parts of it were condemned by the authorities in 1962. Following her death in April 1966, Ratana's daughter Maata (Te Reo) took on the role of tumuaki and began returning Ratana Pā to the original form laid out by her father.

Stage one of the Manuao restoration was undertaken with voluntary effort, and a trust was formed to raise funds and manage the construction. A decade later, further development was required after health authorities again refused to allow the dormitories to be used. Late in 1974, it was agreed to launch the second stage of the project, also championed by Te Reo, at a cost of around $600,000. They already had $300,000, and fundraising tours by the five major Ratana bands from April 1979 covered the balance.

Under the foundation stone, alongside the box of treaty petitions placed there by her father 30 years previously, Maata added her own documents, the signatures from those who had agreed to the Manuao restoration and contributed to its completion. By November 1982 the Manuao had been rebuilt and paid for in full, at which time Te Reo turned her attention to further restoration of the temple, an undertaking that took much of the decade.

EIGHTEEN

BEYOND THE CLOUDS

You have all heard and are familiar with the word that says: 'Night time has passed, the new break of dawn draws near', there is a day unfolding when you will see two towers standing on the Mount of Olives, and at that time you will see a woman rising up from the Labour Party who will become prime minister, and then you will know you are at the doorway, not nearing it, but actually at the doorway . . .

—T. W. Ratana, 11 November 1936

His skilful use of symbols and his religious and political insights were perfectly attuned to the needs of the Maori. Most of the major changes in the social and political world of the 20th century Maori had their origins in the work and energy of Ratana and his followers.

—*New Zealand Yesterdays*, Hamish Keith, 1984

Challenge of a new dawn
T. W. Ratana broke through protocol and superstition and, in insisting on the Māori right to full participation in the affairs of the nation, built a pan-tribal structure that would affirm individual responsibility and destiny, urging all people to work together for the future greatness of the country.

Despite the historic meeting between himself and Labour leader Michael Joseph Savage, which set the tone for the Labour alliance, there was no written contract. Nothing was ever signed; the relationship was based on faith and trust. As long as Labour was seen to be looking out for the interests of Māori the agreement would remain intact.

Ratana's loyal base of followers kept Labour in power for two terms; the petition he took around the world and finally delivered to Parliament asking for the Treaty of Waitangi to be enshrined in law was finally addressed 37 years after his death, and over time long-standing grievances were finally being resolved. Around $1.5 billion in settlements had been made between 1975 and 2008 although a relativity clause ensures individual settlements remain relative to the total value of all Treaty of Waitangi settlements.

By 2021 there were over 90 settlements valued at around $2.5 billion plus land, assets and other considerations. For those seeking perspective, the total was around 1–3 per cent of the present value of total land confiscations and about the same as the Department of Corrections budget for 2020/21. The likelihood was, taking into account relativity payments and other outstanding settlements, including Ngāpuhi, the figure could reach $4–5 billion.

Whetu Tirikatene-Sullivan, New Zealand's longest serving woman politician, remained in Parliament for over 30 years serving the wider interests of Māori under the original Ratana mandate. She refused to be stood down by the patriarchal protocols that forbade women the opportunity to speak on a marae. If she had something to say, she simply said it, as was the case at Te Tii Marae on Waitangi Day 1973. She has spoken on three major marae, including Ratana, Tūrangawaewae at Ngāruawāhia and Waitangi. She also stepped forward uninvited, because she knew she had the heritage and mana, to welcome the people to Parliament during the seabed and foreshore march in April 2004.
Tirikatene-Sullivan Collection.

Rino Tirikatene, 'the Christian crusader', challenged by the Kōmiti Hāhi Matua for not focusing enough on Ratana, is seen here at the opening of Te Māramatanga Marae at his Johnsonville home. *Tirikatene-Sullivan Collection.*

It was always Ratana's great disappointment that the appearance of full national support was given, but when it came to the crunch, cracks and divisions appeared. Often it was the King movement, Apirana Ngata, or divisions among his own people that made it impossible for Māori to move ahead with one voice. Regardless, he continued to represent the essence of Māori democracy by continually consulting the people and equipping them with a vision of unity that continues to reach into our own time.

Today, the pan-tribal Ratana Church and movement maintains a relatively low profile, but can quickly summon a strong political will. The various political parties tend to launch their annual programmes at Ratana Pā during the January birthday celebrations. The Ratana vote is typically cast where there is strongest backing for Māori aspirations. The emergence of the Māori Party (later known as Te Paati Māori) has been a major beneficiary of that support, particularly since its alliance with the Labour Party. Ratana adherents remain somewhat fluid, referencing the broader political spectrum that supports the greenstone and gold (spiritual and physical) aspirations and alliances foretold by prophetic and political visionary, T. W. Ratana. There's also a much closer relationship with the King movement. Māori Queen, Dame Te Atairangikāhu, was a regular at Ratana Pā, and since her death in August 2006 her eldest son and successor King Tuheitia Paki has been at every January celebration. Ratana and Kīngitanga both have a strong pro-Christian heritage, and together represent the largest block of potential Māori voters in the country.

The Ratana church continues to have the largest Māori membership, followed by the Catholics and Anglicans. Today, most mainstream churches have established Māori ministries that often show greater mutual respect across denominational boundaries than their Pākehā counterparts. In recent decades, the divisions between the denominations and Ratana have largely disappeared and tensions over points of theology, other than the perennial one over whether Ratana was man or a divine emissary, seem relatively tame compared to the issues of Ratana's day.

New Zealand Census outcomes for both 2013 and 2018 were botched for several reasons including poor coverage and an attempt to prioritise digital forms. This skewed the numbers, including the lowest yet Māori representation (68 per cent), with concerns the 2023 result may be even less representative.

The 2006 census showed the Ratana Church, after a period of decline, went through a strong growth curve, up 5388 on the 2001 period with 50,565 people claiming membership. In 2013 the number was 52,947. From 2018 Ratana, Ringatū and Pai Mārire were removed from 'Māori Christian' into Māori religions and beliefs categories, which totalled 62,634. It was estimated Ratana numbers had dropped to around 43,821 in New Zealand and around 10,000 in Australia. A high percentage of members were children or youth and those in the 35–60 age group; geographically, Northland, Hawke's Bay, Manawatū-Whanganui, Bay of Plenty and Gisborne (in that order) had the strongest number of adherents. Māori religions were being rapidly superseded by Hinduism (123,534, 100 per cent growth on 2006), Islam (61,455), Jesus Christ of Latter Day Saints (54,123) and Buddhism (52,779). In the 2018 census half the population (48.2 per cent) ticked 'no religion'. All Christian denominations combined still made up the bulk of believers.

In 2023 Ratana had 130 parishes in Aotearoa New Zealand, serviced by 80 registered marriage celebrants and 30 unregistered apostles. Many Ratana families attend traditional and more charismatic Christian churches as well as maintaining loyalty to the Ratana vision. When joined with those who look to Ratana for political guidance, the broader historic loyalty of mōrehu could be far greater than statistics indicate.

Transition movement

Jim McLeod Henderson, the author of *Ratana: The Man, the Church, the Political Movement* (1963, 1972) who began his researches into the movement in the 1940s, continued to believe Ratana had an important role in bringing the nation together. He said the emergence of a new society can best be understood by seeing where the old one came from: 'That's what Tahupotiki Wiremu Ratana gave his people – a vision of the future. The Ratana movement is supra-tribal, an example for our nation-builders. It is a part of our national tapestry bearing all colours, unions, associations, religions and races. Kotahi-tanga [unity in diversity] need not be exclusively Maori.'

Henderson leans on a broader sociological context of 'collective

Above left: Jim McLeod Henderson in 2001, author of *Ratana: the Man, the church, the Political Movement*, who first began researching the Ratana phenomenon in the 1940s. *Newman Collection*. *Centre*: Maata dedicated her time as tumuaki to restoring the church buildings to the way they were when her father was alive. She was a follower of the teachings of Jesus Christ, and encouraged the Ratana Church to embrace all Christian denominations and welcome all religions. *Uri Whakatupuranga (Ratana Archives)*. *Above right*: Harerangi Meihana (Harry Mason, d. 2022), grandson of T. W. Ratana, was president of the Ratana movement, or 'servant of man', and the seventh tumuaki, or spiritual leader, of the church and 'servant of God'. The tumuaki consults on important issues with advisers and the committee of apostles and elders known as the Kōmiti Hāhi Matua, the National Head Office of the Ratana Church. *Uri Whakatupuranga (Ratana Archives)*.

behaviour' to explain what occurs when tribal communities are confronted by the influences of chaos and change.

> I studied the way these [changes] occur. First there is popular tension which creates strains throughout society, until it becomes unbearable and fractures and divisions occur in the social structure. Then a leader arises with a new message and things are put straight. This leader has opposition and there is tension, and this leader either succeeds or is replaced by another, but society is reformed at a new level, with a new belief system. It's a cyclical thing. I believe Ratana was called into being by the social circumstances of the people. The fact there were prophecies about such a person certainly helped.

Ralph Ngatata Love, in his Victoria University thesis, contends that the emergence of Māori prophetic leaders occurred at times when feelings of deprivation and frustration destroyed confidence in the traditional organisations and leaders, causing many Māori groups to seek an individual as a symbol and means of fulfilment. He suggests the success of the Ratana movement was based on its ability to meet the 'social and psychological needs' of Māori groups.

The ability of Ratana and his right-hand man Eruera Tirikatene to identify with and innovate within different Māori and Pākehā groups, and in a Christian and traditional Māori capacity, was the key to that success. They were able to use the myths and culture of traditional Māori society while also pursuing objectives in European society. One of their greatest assets was their high level of energy, which enabled them to maintain late hours and to keep heavy working schedules.

> During the early periods, when planning policy and concepts was important, discussions between Ratana and Tirikatene would continue regularly through the night until the early hours of the next morning. While campaigning for the church or political reasons they would undertake extensive travelling throughout New Zealand and maintain extreme workloads without visible signs of exhaustion. They managed to maintain composure under conditions of extreme stress. Ratana was continually pressed on to provide healing and spiritual guidance . . . he portrayed serenity, a coolness, both under the pressure of the sick and during times of public outcry against his work and rejection by authorities in New Zealand and Great Britain.

A further asset, Love suggests, was their capability to project the image of mental attainment even though they were not scholars in the formal sense, as were Ngata, Pomare and Buck; 'they were able to convey the impression of possessing a wide range of knowledge and a powerful mind'.

While he was all these things, Ratana refuses to be pigeonholed or defined within some academic straightjacket; he's gone before we tighten the straps. If we try to narrow his theology to a formula, there is so much that won't fit, including his prophecies and his work as a spiritual healer. If we attempt to dismiss his movement as a cargo cult, fuelled by collective behaviourism, or see it as an adjustment or transition movement, then we have to ask why, over a hundred years after his vision, is it still so vital? We can no more pin Ratana down with intellectual labels than we can the prophets of Israel.

Challenging the old gods

Ratana was the ultimate networker. He connected with influential people and fostered and maintained those contacts. He took the time to listen to people, he travelled regularly to every marae, shared his wide-ranging knowledge of what had occurred in the past, and overlaid this with his vision for the future.

When he brought his Christian revelation to the people he followed it through with action: when he prayed, people got healed; when he said he would lift the tapu, it was done; and when he said he would take their grievances to Parliament and if necessary to England, he persisted. When it didn't work out he always went back to the people to check they were still with him, so no one could legitimately say that he was speaking or acting out of turn.

He introduced a new set of tohu (symbols) – including badges, colours, uniforms and flags – which related to the Holy Trinity, the angels, the Crown, and elements borrowed from Israel and the Bible. He named periods of his ministry, the four quarters of the country and various buildings and monuments after his children and his own different roles as change agent, weaving a complex tapestry of meaning into just about everything he did and said.

When engaged in healing or being moved by the Spirit, Ratana was Te Māngai, a mouthpiece of God; in his political persona he might be Piri Wiri Tua, the Treaty campaigner; at other times he was just plain old Bill Ratana. For many it must have seemed that he was struggling with a multiple personality disorder, but those who listened closely and understood how he operated knew the difference. However, that didn't help with the many misunderstandings that arose during and after his lifetime.

The first signs of division appeared soon after the Ratana Church was formed in 1925, with discord between those who kept a simple Christian faith and those who believed Ratana as Te Māngai had brought a new revelation or replacement theology that in many ways superseded Christianity. Those who asserted 'a new revelation' often accused those who maintained a faith in Ihu Karaiti or Jesus Christ as being 'deceived by intellectualism', labelling them mātauranga (trying to be clever) or 'ungrateful turncoats'. During this period many Ratana Christians, saddened by the stance of this often volatile group, went back to their old churches.

Others claimed their own special revelation and set up in opposition to Ratana. From 1937 a number of Ratana apostles began mixing what Ratana had taught with ancient Māori religion. Those who held to the faith and accepted Jehovah were 'the wheat' and those who relapsed were referred to as tūmatakuru or 'thorns and thistles'.

Eruera Tirikatene, who had been well versed in Ratana's spiritual and political kaupapa, on many occasions tried to keep a balance in theological debates, and removed photos of T. W. Ratana and statues of angels placed in the temple by overzealous believers. Initially there was a framed painting of Jesus Christ in the temple but after Ratana requested this be brought to him on his deathbed, it was frequently replaced with his own image until the 1960s.

In 1933 Ratana urged the people not to confuse his physical being with the spiritual presence that at times spoke through him. 'Truly, oh morehu, the Mangai is really a Spirit, in actual fact the Son. Know you then, the difference between the Mangai and I. The Mangai is Spirit, I who stand here before you am but a human being.' In his fading years, he tried again to clarify.

You sit here together, and you are of one voice calling to the Father, Son, Holy Spirit, the Faithful Angels and the Mangai. You do not see the Holy Trinity and the Faithful Angels, but if you had faith as small even as a mustard seed you would see, and you would hear and understand; I do not mean that you will see with your eyes and hear with your ears, but with the eyes and ears of your hearts. I will give you a Mangai which none of your adversaries will be able to withstand or contradict. I am going, and I will give you a Mangai. Where is this Mangai? When will this Mangai come? You are not able to answer this. It is not my body that you see here before you, but it is the words that come out of my mouth; you are listening to the Holy Trinity and the Faithful Angels when I mention them, but you do not see them.

Still the people remained uncertain, and they were determined to elevate Ratana. Much of the dissent centred around the covenant signed only days before his death, which appeared to be in the form of a repentance and a desire for the church to return to using the name of Jesus Christ. Shortly after the death of the prophet, Tokouru and Tirikatene engaged in long debates with the people about the theology of the church, in particular the role of Te Māngai. Along with many others, including Ratana's daughter Maata and his sister Te Raupo, they believed Ratana had always acted, preached and healed in the name of Jesus.

Tokouru eventually called the apostles together at a special sitting of the Ratana synod (Hui Whakapūmau) to clarify the issues but the Kōmiti Hāhi Matua, the ruling committee, rejected their proposals. After Tokouru's death the church stayed in a kind of spiritual limbo, recalling the founder's miraculous legacy rather than devising any forward-looking agenda. The open and free debates on theology and issues affecting the Ratana Church, once a hallmark of the major gatherings at Ratana Pā, became more rigidly controlled by a group of elders who felt they were protecting the movement from outside influence.

The annual celebrations were increasingly political and social occasions and, once the speeches were over, the focus was more on sports, cultural events and socialising than spiritual encouragement. Information about Ratana's life and his legacy became increasingly difficult to obtain, particularly for outsiders. There were too many variables, vested interests and conflicting opinions. Consequently, volumes of information, much of it still untranslated from te reo Māori (the Māori language), diaries, photographs and other official records were locked away, or became scattered around the country as various families left Ratana Pā. The translation of Ratana's teachings into English slowed to a trickle, and frustration set in among the new generation, keen to know more.

From 1954 some of the editors of the *Whetu Marama* and private recorders of church history began stating that 'on January 25, 1873 the Son of Man was reborn on the earth in the form of T. W. Ratana' using the term 'Te Tama o Te Tangata'. The divisions were further exacerbated by those who favoured dropping the Christian-based Ratana Creed for the 'Blue Book', which contains hymns, the order of service and the basic belief system used by the apostles. This book underwent many changes as the Kōmiti Hāhi Matua in particular reviewed the theology. It is only available in Māori and makes little mention of the role of the Bible or Christ.

Third generation

In 1967, three women leaders met outside their official capacities for the first time. Ratana's daughter Te Reo Hura had just become tumuaki of the Ratana Church and movement; Dame Te Atairangikaahu was the newly appointed queen of the Kīngitanga movement, having just succeeded King Koroki; and Whetu Tirikatene-Sullivan had entered Parliament, succeeding her father as member for Southern Māori. These women must have experienced a sense of destiny in motion when they were gathered for an unveiling at Te Hauke Marae in Hawke's Bay. One of the Ratana apostles commented that each had just stepped in to succeed their fathers in what could only be described as the most influential roles representing Māori.

That was the beginning of a longstanding and close relationship between the women heading the largest Māori organisations in the country. It was also the start of a career in politics for Tirikatene-Sullivan who, along with Iriaka Ratana, Matiu Rata and others, would bring their unswerving dedication to help fulfil much that both the King and Ratana movements had been striving for since their inception.

Up-and-coming young Ratana leaders sensed they were part of something much bigger than their own careers, reinforced with the knowledge that Ratana had prophesied of a time when the next 'generation' would take up the reins of the movement. They may not have had the sanction of the Kōmiti Hāhi Matua, nevertheless their passion drove them on. Ratana secretary and activist Rapine Aperahama lobbied hard to have the Ratana and Kīngitanga movements move into a closer alliance and for the political base of Ratana to move to Te Omeka Pā. Neither happened in his time. Whetu's brother, Rino Tirikatene, the apostle responsible for the Wellington region, had hopes the movement would return to its Christian roots and sensed this was the generation that would make a difference for Māoridom and the nation in general. Rapine, a studious and fluent Māori speaker, had looked long and hard into the writings of those who had gone before him, and often spoke about the generation that would rise and walk in Ratana's footsteps.

Āpotora wairua Kereama Pene, who began researching the mysteries of the Ratana movement back in the early 1980s, continues to believe Ratana's so-called 'third-generation prophecies' are a source of great hope. While there are conflicting interpretations for the sayings, Pene believes Ratana pointed to a generation that would receive the providence of Jehovah, to carry his vision forward.

In 1933 Ratana spoke clearly about a generation in the future:

> The sins of our ancestors and parents have come down through to the third generation. This now is the fourth generation (since the signing of the Treaty of Waitangi) of which these same conditions continue; but the generation after this one will be made pure and free from these conditions whereby the anointing will only dwell.

He spoke again on 25 January 1937 of a generation that would come some time after the war:

> [I]t shall be at the end of this war that the Spirit of anointing will go forth to search and to seek out the residue of mankind more pure than the snow. I would even suggest that you might perhaps be that residue of mankind where the spirit anointed will find you after that great intense darkness living upon the principles of purity. My greatest desire is for all of us to witness that day . . .

The word 'toenga' for 'residue' is synonymous with 'offspring' or 'product' and similar to the word 'mōrehu'. Pene says successive generations have been given the opportunity to unite under Jehovah in honour of Ratana's covenants but failed to follow through. 'We're still dealing with the consequences of this but trying to pass on the freedoms and benefits promised to our own children.'

Increasing voltage

There are some who say Ratana only had the fullness of his spiritual anointing for the three years (1919–21) when there were mass healings at his gatherings. They claim his powers decreased when he began to get involved in politics. Regardless, his healing tours throughout the nation (1921–23) rivalled those of any other New Zealand faith-healer. While fewer healings were reported after 1923, those that did occur were spectacular enough to keep the legend alive.

Ratana had started a fire, and like moths to the flame the people came, hungry to hear his words and be part of the growing sense of something wonderful happening in their midst. Ratana sought to pass on his gift, or anointing, to those who were eager to join his ministry team. He described the power that ran through him as a 'voltage'; it was said some received 50 volts and others 75 or 100 volts. These were the 'spiritual apostles' who, having been 'charged up', were sent around the country.

On 28 January 1928 during an evening whakamoemiti (church service) Ratana was handing out certificates at a special ceremony for the Pou o Te Hāhi (Pillars of the Church). The Ratana Temple had just been opened, and he was commissioning them to go forth and 'cast out demons and to heal the sick', and battle against 'the blackberry and the thorns' of the tohunga mākutu.

> Greetings to you all the Pillars of the Church . . . during the time of Christ he gave his disciples the power and authority to cast out demons, to heal the sick and to do the will of his Father in heaven. During the earlier years of this revelation, I also cast out demons, healed the sick and also the land, but now as I give you all these certificates, I am also giving you the power and authority of 60 volts to also cast out demons, to heal the sick and the land, in glorifying Ihoa o nga Mano and his faithful angels. During the earlier years of this revelation I had 100 volts of power and authority, but the day is coming when this power and authority will be increased to a thousand watts upon you all.

Ratana believed the Holy Spirit power was available to all believers but there was a special measure for the Māori people. Over time the thought 'this may be the generation' has inspired political and spiritual enthusiasm. Some talk of the third generation prophecies, as if the same Spirit that empowered Ratana would again move mightily among the mōrehu at a specific time, while others suggest it is a general principle of inheritance, intended to inspire each succeeding generation to expand his legacy.

Dealing to the doctrine

In 1955, Puhi o Aotea approved a reformulation of the church's doctrines to no longer mention the Māngai in the same phrase as the Holy Trinity. She died in April 1966, and Ratana's daughter Te Reo stepped into the presidential shoes nine months later and attempted to further clear the air about her father's theology.

Te Reo had not been seen at Ratana Pā for many years. She had been helping her husband run a farm, grow potatoes and raise a family while also working as a cook at the Patea hospital. It seemed the old stories of how she had gained her special name had been forgotten. Some thought her name revered Ratana as Te Māngai, and it wasn't until she was entrenched in office that they had a sharp reminder of the movement's Christian tūrangawaewae.

She had only accepted the role because of the name her father had given her under guidance of the Holy Spirit: Te Reo e Hapai a te Himine e Ihu e te Kinginui (The voice that sings the hymn, Jesus the King of Kings).

She had witnessed the first miracle when the needle came out from behind her younger brother's knee, accompanied her father on healing and teaching tours, been a member of the two world tour bands, and was married in the symbolic dual wedding that united Aotearoa with Japan. When Ratana was engaged in a healing meeting or about to lift a curse he would frequently ask her to sing the hymn for which she was named. Te Reo had dedicated her life to following the teachings of Jesus Christ and encouraged the Ratana Church to embrace all Christian denominations and welcome all religions. For this some openly criticised her.

Late in 1977 Te Reo called together those keen to rejuvenate the Ratana newspaper *Te Whetu Marama o Te Kotahitanga*, the longest-running Māori publication in the country. She occasionally reintroduced the names of 'Jesus' and 'the Christ' and was keen to 'bring the church back on track' according to her father's teachings. Te Reo had become fed up with the errant theology that elevated her father to divinity. Rather than attend church at Ratana Pā, she often preferred to remain in Patea with her family and join with others who had a thirst for spiritual knowledge and wanted to know more about her faith in Christ. A number of young people, also frustrated with the lack of clarity from the church executive, began turning to her for advice.

Kereama Pene was among the many who met with her to rebuild an understanding of what Ratana had taught. In those meetings she clearly denied her father had made any claims to being the Son of God. 'She said don't listen to that nonsense. When you speak your words and nothing happens that's your words. But when you speak Ihoa's Word and you see things take shape before your eyes that's a Mangai. This is the Holy Spirit manifesting in power.' Pene says many people who are likely to take on church leadership over the next few years were inspired by Te Reo Hura from 1981 onwards. 'From that time on she withdrew herself from anything to do with the church meetings at Ratana. She said she had given enough to the older tree and would now water the new sapling.'

Meanwhile others within the Ratana ranks continued to quietly campaign to put Christ back in the centre. Among them was Rino Tirikatene, who had been a Ratana minister since 1963 and was in charge of Wellington, Porirua and Hutt parishes. The Ratana executive committee attempted to defrock him for his insistence on using the name Jesus Christ, saying he should preach more of Ratana. In 1984 he was brought before the committee to explain himself. During a six hour 'inquisition' Rino defended his stance, quoting T. W. Ratana and his love for the gospel.

Te Reo, who was 80 years old at the time, said nothing throughout the ordeal. Then, after Rino had made his defence, she clearly stated that his views agreed with those of her father. The charges were dropped. Shortly afterwards, she made a rare statement. She explained that the Holy Spirit had given her father a job to do – to clear the minds of the Māori people of all the ancient powers. 'But I see them all coming back now, as my father said they would. He said the morehu would, like the Israelites, turn to idolatry.'

She said her father made the Ratana marae unique:

> It is not to be like the rest: it was not to be subject to tribal protocol with the fear if you broke the tribal law. It is unique without all the carvings – my father especially wanted this. My father loved the Bible. He loved saying the Lord's Prayer; he loved Jesus. But the old Maoris misused the Bible, so he taught from it although he didn't show it. After all, the old tohunga could recite chapters of it but they abused it.

She explained Pākehā had abused the name Jesus Christ, and her father did not want the Māori people doing the same. 'But it has been brought back. So has the Bible. It is the time. It is good. Really, there is a fight on.' Despite her clarification, the Kōmiti Hāhi Matua ruled on the non-use of Jesus Christ, claiming the name only applied when he walked the earth and his significance since then was as the 'Son' (Te Tama) of the Father.

Since that time, the Christian focus has begun to gain more emphasis as Ratana's teachings are made more accessible in English and Māori. Most mōrehu pray to Tama, the spiritual Son of God, and believe in and revere Ihu Karaiti, the physical Son of God; in effect respecting different roles for the same being.

Ratana tumuaki, Harerangi Meihana, told the author in 2007 that the movement continued to have its share of problems and challenges. He was keen to see young people seeking out spiritual truth in the founder's teachings rather than getting too sidetracked with politics. That, he says, is how the 'third generation' prophecies need to be understood. 'What it means is they would have more opportunity and understanding than our ancestors. There were a lot of things said at the time that the elders couldn't quite grasp.' The main task of the movement's founder was to take Māori away from tohunga and belief in the many gods of the old Māori religions and superstitions, and show them there was only one God, Jehovah.

> He achieved that but he also said he could see a day that they would return to the old ways. His call to the third generation is to make sure the people don't go back to the old ways but a lot of our people are. We even have our own people

now saying there is a Maori god and a Pakeha god. We don't believe that. There is one God.

The most important thing, Meihana says, is that the Ratana faithful be seen as brothers and sisters of all the people in New Zealand. 'I don't like people saying this is a Maori movement. That's not how the founder wanted it – it is for all people and all races and creeds.' In his foreword to the November 2000 special edition of *Te Whetu Marama* put together by the Uri Whakatupuranga (New Generation) research group, Meihana wrote of Ratana's prophecy that the movement would enter 'a new phase' from Te Tau Rua Mano (the year 2000).

In a 2002 information kit, looking to set the framework to revitalise the Ratana youth movement, Meihana talked about a time of consolidation and encouraged the young leaders coming up through the ranks of the church and movement. He said they held the key to Ratana's prophecy that a 'new generation' would emerge and play a pivotal role in the advancement of the organisation. While the nationwide movement is not as influential as it has been in past decades, there was still a sense of loyalty and commitment to be part of the bigger picture of Māori destiny.

Political persuasion
The majority of Ratana members remain staunchly loyal to the longstanding Labour alliance despite clear evidence that, since the death of Savage, the relationship had been shot through with compromise. No Ratana politicians had been in government since MMP (mixed member proportional voting) was introduced in 1996. The restructuring of electoral boundaries and the mass deregistering of Ratana Labour Party members, including longstanding member of Parliament Whetu Tirikatene-Sullivan in 1999, and the passing of the Foreshore and Seabed Act 2004 that placed ownership of the foreshore and seabed in the hands of the Crown, were seen as major blows to the alliance.

Since then, many have watched with interest the rise of the Māori Party, which captured the hearts and votes of many who desired to see the work of Ratana continue in the twenty-first century. Although it had the option to join with Labour, the Māori Party, having won four seats in 2005, could not in all good conscience find common ground. Māori Party co-leader Tariana Turia, in an address to the Māori Party AGM in November 2004, showed her Ratana roots.

> Many of us used to have the face of Michael Joseph Savage in the photo galleries of our homes. And he has a legitimate place in the promise of what he stood for. But we need to look around the walls of our whare and see again,

Māori Party co-leader Tariana Turia has a strong Ratana heritage and in many ways replicated Ratana's success by gaining four Māori seats from the 2005 elections. *Ans Westra*.

what has always been there, the faces of our tupuna, the faces of our future . . . the ancestral lines that connect us, photos of our grandparents, our parents, our mokopuna, our whanau.

She said Māori must find the courage to pursue a better future for all, and highlighted the courage of Tahupotiki Wiremu Ratana, 'who transformed the lives of our people with simple messages of faith, of hope, of belief and trust, that he would stand not only for the Ture Wairua but for the Ture Tangata also.' Giving his support to the Labour Party came with conditions.

> The treaty to be embodied in statute [and] the protection from sale of our lands; no more land confiscation and compensation for land stolen. And did Labour meet their obligations to that agreement? No! It is a long list of broken promises. The work of Piri Wiri Tua must and will continue.

Turia quoted the kuia of Ngāti Apa, Mere Rikiriki: 'He ringa kaha, he ringa poto, kaore e whakahoa. And so it must be that we stand up, without fear or favour, for our rights as tangata whenua [indigenous people] of this land.'

She slammed Labour for its October 2005 criticism of the Draft United Nations Declaration of Rights of Indigenous Peoples (UNDRIP) as being 'unworkable and unacceptable' a decade after the government delegates had accepted the 45 provisions. Around the globe, she said, indigenous communities had signalled their disappointment at New Zealand's action. Despite National's proposal to do away with the Māori seats in Parliament, she saw these as critical to rebuilding and restoring equilibrium.

Meanwhile a string of complaints from the major tribes protesting the Foreshore and Seabed Act had triggered a visit by Professor Rodolfo

Stavenhagen, United Nations Special Rapporteur on the rights and freedoms of indigenous peoples. He launched his investigation into Māori grievances at Parihaka Marae at the end of November 2005, following a ruling by the Committee on the Elimination of Racial Discrimination (CERD) that the Act discriminated against Māori.

Early on in his tour Stavenhagen said New Zealand was one of the unique examples where a nation was founded on an agreement between the original people and the settlers of the colonial scheme. He expressed his concern that Māori were being 'left behind' socially and economically, and believed the Treaty of Waitangi was 'definitely binding' and the principles were valid. He talked of disparities in housing, income, health and life expectancy, saying something was wrong and it was not just to do with ethnicity but political will.

His eventual report recommended entrenching the Treaty of Waitangi and the Bill of Rights Act as part of a New Zealand constitution, and called for the overturning of the Foreshore and Seabed Act. Prime Minister Helen Clark said the report was 'unbalanced' and 'grossly inaccurate'. Deputy Prime Minister Michael Cullen dismissed it, saying it would be widely read, but 'nothing much will happen'. National's Deputy Leader, Gerry Brownlee, said it should be 'tossed in the bin'. Although the report wasn't legally binding, if ignored by the government it would, said Stavenhagen, be contrary to 'the spirit of the United Nations'.

Many Ratana faithful were scratching their heads and wondering about Ratana's 1924 world tour, when he left a copy of the treaty and his 40,000-signature petition with the indigenous people's representative at the League of Nations in Geneva, saying someone with a firm mandate would be back to deal with the unfinished business. Those documents had been passed on to the United Nations. Ahead of his 1925 American tour Ratana made a curious statement: 'Oh Morehu, you know not the reason of my way, for I shall say to you all, there I shall acquire the olive branch.'

The olive branch Ratana spoke of is believed to refer to his search for the 'new world'. Using the typology of Noah, he was looking for evidence the flood was subsiding after the 40 days and nights of rain. Ratana wanted something he could take back to the Māori people and, although he had struck major business deals with Henry Ford and American Express, he turned them down. He also visited New York where the United Nations, the successor to the League of Nations, would be based from 1945. The UN often uses a dove with an olive branch in its mouth as a symbol of its peacekeeping efforts. It was Māori Party co-leader Dr Pita Sharples, Māori Affairs minister outside Cabinet in the National-led government, who flew to New York in 2010 to sign New Zealand up to UNDRIP. Since then successive governments have worked on what compliance might mean, with two significant reports setting the tone: *Matike Mai* ('rise up'), compiled from 250 hui (2012–15); and the subsequent *He Puapua* ('break in the waves' or 'political norms'), commissioned by Cabinet in 2019. The ultimate goal was embedding tino rangatiratanga (Māori sovereignty/independence) and mana motuhake (self-determination) into 'constitutional transformation' by 2040, the 200th anniversary of the signing of the Treaty of Waitangi. Although a Māori parliament was rejected by then Prime Minister Jacinda Ardern, and there was strong pushback against the idea of racial separatism, the declaration's ideas, aspirations and terminology, including co-governance, were by 2024 well entrenched in all documents relating to public engagements with Māori.

According to *Griffith Law Review* (2011, vol. 20, issue 3), the political roots of the UNDRIP can be traced back to lobbying by Haudenosaunee chief Deskaheh and T. W. Ratana, who in 1923 and 1925 respectively sought access to the League of Nations to bring Canada and New Zealand's violation of treaty agreements and rights to the attention of the international community. They were both denied access after interventions by Britain and their own governments, which argued these were domestic matters. Though unsuccessful in their advocacy, Chief Deskaheh and T. W. Ratana provided a pathway for the contemporary global indigenous rights movement.

However, in October 2023 elections when the Labour-Greens were deposed, a new coalition of National, Act and New Zealand First under Prime Minister Christopher Luxon, moved swiftly to reduce the impact of co-governance and public service use of Treaty principles. It began deprioritising Māori names for government departments, 'disestablishing' Te Aka Whai Ora (the Māori Health Authority) and stopping all work on He Puapua as the basis for compliance with UNDRIP. The abrupt turnaround, seen by many as a direct challenge to Māori progress, triggered an immediate pushback, with public protests including the 11 December 2023 defacing of the English language version of the Treaty of Waitangi in *The Signs of a Nation* Te Tiriti o Waitangi exhibition, which had been on display since Te Papa opened in 1998.

A series of hui expressing Māori frustrations were held around the country, a pan-tribal meeting was called by the Māori king, Tūheitia Potatau Te Wherowhero VII, at Ngāruawāhia, ahead of the annual 24 January gathering at Ratana Pā and Waitangi Day commemorations on 6 February. It was a rallying call for iwi leaders to stand together on issues related to Te Tiriti o Waitangi, justice, equality and tino rangatiratanga (self-determination). The new government's efforts to slow the so-called 'Māorification' of Aotearoa had instead become a rallying call for Kotahitanga.

Ratana suggested that, across history, Ihoa had moved strongly in different nations of the world at different times, bringing great blessing to those who honoured their covenant with him, and removing those blessings if that covenant was broken. Ratana historian Ruia Aperahama says that Ratana referred to America as the new world and the United Kingdom as the old world. He believed his trip to the UK signified the end of one covenant and the beginning of another. The inference through several prophecies is that we are now in the century that will see fulfilment of Ratana's promise to the Japanese along with other Asian and Pacific Rim nations, including Aotearoa and te iwi Māori, the Māori people.

Divisions highlighted

There have been disagreements around the core values and direction of the Ratana movement and church ever since its founder died in 1939. Those generational tensions came to a head when a remit supported by 16 of 18 Takiwā (Ratana regions) was tabled at Hui Whakapūmau (the governing committee of the Ratana Church) in 2019, looking to 'respectfully and graciously' relieve the seventh tumuaki of his public responsibilities. The proposal was that Harerangi Meihana, fading in health and capacity, would retain the title of tumuaki with a plan to support that role and bring the movement back on track. The remit sat with the committee for over two years, but the pushback was already in motion.

Ahead of the 24–26 January 2022 celebrations the locks were changed on facilities at Ratana Pā, which had typically been available to the wider movement. While the 'traffic light' system near the end of the COVID pandemic was a factor in the cancellation of the annual event, other challenges to the traditional Ratana kaupapa (the way things are done) were brewing.

The remit became redundant with the passing of Harerangi Meihana in May 2022, as attention now turned in earnest to the succession plan; who would lead the church and movement and in what direction? Would a revitalised movement work alongside other Māori influencers dedicated to the spiritual and physical needs of the people, with Treaty of Waitangi principles underpinning a wider sense of national identity? Would passionate elders and young visionaries (the mōrehu) motivated by Ratana's life and mission lead the movement into the future, or would his family and their descendants ring fence this rich heritage like a monument to the past based around hosting the annual political and social birthday gatherings at Ratana Pā?

Questions concerning who would make those decisions impacting the church and movement, and how, continued to be a source of tension, splitting Ratana families and communities across the country.

Changing of the guard

When Jackie Seward had a waking vision on Waitangi Day 2021 she looked for an artist to capture what she had seen, eventually commissioning Paula

(Novak) Newman to paint her impression of two strong women in a time of change. Paula had painted the icon-filled portrait of T. W. Ratana that appeared in the original *Ratana the Prophet* (and is on the cover of this publication). Neither visionary nor artist knew the significance of the finished work until the January 2023 Ratana commemoration.

Jacinda Ardern, the country's youngest-ever female prime minister, had announced she was exhausted and planned to resign. She gave her final speech during the annual birthday weekend celebrations at Ratana Pā on 24 January 2023, where traditionally politicians make policy announcements relating to Māori.

The prime minister had earned global respect for her compassionate stance in the aftermath of the Christchurch mosque shootings of March 2019, and in how she navigated the country through the COVID crises and the subsequent incendiary Parliament grounds protests in February and March 2022. Her government had overseen major shifts in climate change policy, allocated Matariki (the Māori New Year) as a public holiday, and introduced local Māori history as a compulsory curriculum subject from 2023. She had distinguished herself as a world leader in difficult times.

On the morning of Ratana's official birthday (25 January), as Chris Hipkins officially took the reins as Labour prime minister, it was learned that Far North matriarch and Māori rights advocate Titewhai Te Hoia Hinewhare Harawira had died, aged 90. Titewhai, an outspoken, steel-willed campaigner who descended from Ngāpuhi chiefs, had been a familiar face at Waitangi Day celebrations, where she frequently accompanied prime ministers on to the local marae.

Immediately after the 2023 birthday celebrations the Ratana family and Hui Whakapūmau accounced that 'Sonny' Manuao Te Kohamutunga Tamou, a great-grandson of T. W. Ratana, was to become the eighth tumuaki ('defender of the faith') of Te Haahi Ratana. This was confirmed at Easter. Concurrently, a strong representation of Mōrehu membership from across the country announced their own candidate, Andre Mason, the son of Hererangi Meihana. Andre, who had stood in for his ailing father on official business over several years, had been voted 'people's choice' for tumuaki.

There was talk of a prophecy Ratana had made around 1930, of two tumuaki rising up from among the people after a split that would be caused by 'colonised Pākehā thinking, the love of money and power and the family'. Some thought this referred to strong leaders in Kīngitanga and Ratana working for the betterment of Māori, while others insisted it related to the 2022 / 23 dilemma that allegedly saw some of Ratana's descendants and their supporters at Ratana Pā assuming control over assets and decision-making against the wishes of the broader membership.

Like other church-based organisations in Aotearoa, there were ideological challenges over direction, diminishing membership and whether leadership was meant to be absolute and presidential or an inspirational role that would guide and direct. Regardless, the story that began with two whales beached at Whangaehu in 1918, leading to Ratana's Bible and Treaty mission, ture wairua (spiritual) and ture tangata (physical), was now presented with another paradox. The matter of who had legitimate control over Ratana (able to appoint a legal tumuaki) and issues of asset and land ownership were taken to the Māori Land Court. As if a mirror of what happened after Ratana's death in 1939, his descendants and many at Ratana Pā closed ranks and declared a virtual media blackout.

None of that changes the matters of historical record presented in this book or what might be an appropriate response to Ratana's visionary insights. Ratana used the deep, rich poetic and metaphoric language of the skilled orator and rangatira to inspire, encourage, give direction and weave people together, not divide them. He worked long and hard developing a series of progressive social welfare, development, apprenticeship and land schemes to help model Māori self-sufficiency. The unity he sought extended beyond Māori to all tribes and cultures that had made New Zealand their home. Even during his lifetime that extraordinary legacy remained riven with tension, frustration, jealousies and unfinished business.

A prophetic heritage

The Ratana family farm lay at a pivotal intersection, where the major rivers that formed the ancient tribal boundaries between the Manawatū, Rangitikei, Whanganui and Taranaki districts ran out to sea, where the prophets had said

Cartoonist Tom Scott comments on the political tug of war for votes that test the so-called Labour–Ratana alliance every January. *Cartoon Archives, DCDL-0005184, Alexander Turnbull Library, Wellington.*

an important leader would arise with the dual kaupapa of the Bible and the Treaty of Waitangi.

Ratana essentially means 'lantern', and in many respects he lived up to his name. The beaching of the whales at Whangaehu was taken as a sign of his calling as 'a fisher of men', and the whale oil provided fuel for the lanterns at the family farm as people were drawn like moths to the miraculous events that began unfolding. The lantern was first shone on his own life, and then into the darkness he saw around him. The enlightenment he represented was the logical next step from the Holy Spirit ministry of his aunty Mere Rikiriki, who had first used the term māramatanga.

A series of 'divine' encounters raised Ratana's faith levels. He simply believed he was capable of works that were equal to those of Christ, and through his tremendous faith, acted accordingly with 'signs following', just as the gospels promised. Like Māori for many generations he had seen the outward claims of Christianity, but little evidence of the supernatural powers promised in the scriptures. Though many had responded to the Christian call and joined the various denominations, they were not treated as equals, given the right to move into positions of leadership, or resourced for ministry. This was a cause of much frustration and a major factor in the exodus to the Ratana movement.

While it was clear that extraordinary things occurred during Ratana's lifetime, the lockdown on information after his death achieved two things. It ensured his story was largely forgotten by outsiders; and it inflamed the imagination of those who continued to feel loyalty to the man and the movement. It was clear some of the editors of the *Whetu Marama* exaggerated, changed a few words here and there, or allowed their own belief systems to influence what they wrote. Just as Ratana had allowed some claims to go unchecked, so it was in later generations.

With the world tour diaries and other written eyewitness accounts locked away, and little in the way of open communication to help discern between fact and fiction, the myth of T. W. Ratana often grew larger than life, with many believing he was the new messiah; that he had walked on water, had a stash of gold dust supplied to him by the angels, raised the dead and caused the stars to fall from heaven. Even a little exaggeration can cast a shadow of doubt across everything. Who can know for certain whether the synchronicity and 'co-incidence' that seemed to be everywhere wasn't just good timing or whether a camellia tree said to manifest multiple fruit at the same time simply had misshapen buds? Who can be certain that some of those who were 'healed' didn't revert to the pains of the past, buying new walking sticks or replacing their crutches after subsequent visits to the doctor?

But what about the miracles recorded and dated in the mysterious 'black book', the hundreds of items – including walking sticks, crutches and glasses – donated by those he healed; the letters of testimony and the relief when curses had been lifted from people and places, often in well-documented circumstances? And Ratana certainly made his share of prophecies, some of which are astoundingly accurate.

It is difficult to dismiss a man who plants a geranium cutting from his front garden in the grounds of Parliament House in 1919, saying one day he'll be back to pluck a flower and that the pollen would be blown to the four corners of the country. Years later he returns, just ahead of capturing the first of four political seats, prophesying at the future site of the 'Beehive', that one day honey would come from the mouth of a lion.

On the way to the United Kingdom and Japan, Ratana's ship stopped over in Capetown, South Africa, where he and his party were disturbed at the way indigenous people were being treated. He put on a feast for the dock workers, talked to the locals and prophesied that the black people in South Africa would one day turn the tables on their white 'masters'. It was 70 years later, in 1994, that Nelson Mandela was released from jail, becoming the first black president of South Africa.

Mandela seemed to see similarities between the struggles of the ethnic peoples of both lands when he visited New Zealand in 1995.

> Our two countries have much in common. Both have known the pain of conquest, dispossession and oppression. And both are now blessed to be living through an era whose challenges are those of affirmation, restitution and reconciliation . . . Through genuine negotiations and a partnership founded on integrity, a way will be found to honour past pledges and build a future in which the Maori community shall truly be able to prosper in your land of birth.

A studious political pundit could have seen tensions and increasing militarism in Germany, Italy and Japan; even Michael Joseph Savage was literally savaged by the media when he tried to alert Mother England to the rising threats. Ratana, however, had begun prophesying the impending war and its consequences fifteen years before it happened. He even went so far as make the statement in the Imperial Japanese palace that two lights in the sky would turn the people to dust, but out of the ashes would come an economic giant that would contribute greatly to the prosperity of the Māori people. The other part of the promise that he had made to Bishop Juji Nakada was that the māramatanga, the Bible-based teachings and the Holy Spirit anointing that Ratana had been given, would be shared with the Asian people.

Could he really have been speaking of the terrorist attack on the Twin Towers of the World Trade Center when he stood in the heart of the future financial district of New York on 11 November 1925 and prophesied of the twins of Babylon falling? And how could he have possibly seen a woman prime minister at the head of a Labour Government in New Zealand, or known that in the year 2000 there would be a great increase in the number of Asian people coming here?

To Ratana, these signs of the times pointed to a future 'doorway' on a dawning age of spiritual and economic prosperity for the Māori people, which was conditional on achieving unity under Ihoa. He warned that if the people did not remember their māramatanga and share it with the Asians and others when they came looking for it, that task would pass on to strangers or tauiwi.

Strong Māori aspirations for 'constitutional transformation' by 2040, the two hundredth anniversary of the signing of the Treaty of Waitangi, resonate with Ratana's ultimate goal to see Māori as a united, spiritually healthy and prosperous people, whether or not those who gather under his name lead by example. In accepting the mantle placed on him through his 1918 encounter and the legacy of the Māori prophets before him, Ratana famously said at Ōrakei in 1921: 'Here in my right hand I hold a Bible and in my left hand Te Tiriti o Waitangi. I say first of all, let us ... unite under Ihoa (and) the Bible, and after this, we will take hold of Te Tiriti o Waitangi'. As my (the author's) late father once said, it seems there are too many walking around with the Treaty in one hand and nothing in the other.

BIBLIOGRAPHY

Books

Best, Elsdon, 'Maori Agriculture: The cultivated food plants of the natives of New Zealand', *Journal of the Polynesian Society*, Vol. 40, 1931.
——, *The Maori*, Polynesian Society, 1924.
——, *Tuhoe, Children of the Mist*, Polynesian Society, 1925.
Binney, Judith, *Ancestral Voices*, publication information unknown.
——, *Redemption Songs: A Life of Te Kooti Arikirangi Te Turuki*, Auckland University Press, 1995.
Bolitho, Hector, aka Rongoa Pai, *Ratana: The Maori Miracle Man. The story of his life, the record of his miracles*, Geddis and Blomfield Printers, 1921.
Buick, T. L., *The Treaty of Waitangi: How New Zealand Became a British Colony*, 3rd edition, Thomas Avery, 1936.
Carmichael, Lieut. Col., *Ratana the Healer*, Greymouth Evening Star, 1921.
Chafer, Lewis Sperry, *Systematic Theology*, Dallas Seminary Press, 1976.
Cody J. F., *Man of Two Worlds — a Biography of Sir Maui Pomare*, Reed, 1953.
Colless, Brian and Donovan, Peter, *Religion in New Zealand Society*, Dunmore Press, 1985.
Davidson, A. K. and P. J. Lineham (eds), *Transplanted Christianity*, Dunmore Press, 1985.
de Bres, P. H., 'Maori Religious Movements in Aotearoa' in *Religion in New Zealand Society*, Dunmore Press, 1980.
Elder, John Rawson, *The History of the Presbyterian Church of New Zealand 1840–1940*, Presbyterian Bookroom, c.1940.
Elsmore, Bronwyn, *Like Them That Dream*, Reed, 1985.
——, *Mana From Heaven*, Reed, 1999.
——, *Te Kohititanga Marama, New Moon, New World: The Religion of Matenga Tamati*, Reed, 1998.
Evison, Harry C., *Ngai Tahu Land Rights*, 3rd edition, Ngai Tahu Maori Trust Board, 1987.

Gittos, Murray B., *Mana at Mangungu: A Biography of William White 1794–1875*, self-published, 1982.
Henderson, J. McLeod, *Ratana: The Man, the Church, the Political Movement*, Reed, A.H. & A.W. Reed in association with the Polynesian Society, 1963, 1972 (revised edition).
Keesing, Felix M., *The Changing Maori*, Thomas Avery and Sons, 1928.
Kemp, Rev. Joseph W., *How I was Healed: A New Zealand Miracle: A biographical sketch of Miss Fanny Lammas*, Auckland Tabernacle Book Room, 1923.
King, Michael, *Te Puea: A Biography*, Hodder & Stoughton, 1977, Reed, 2003.
——, *The Penguin History of New Zealand*, Penguin, 2003.
——, (ed.), *Aspects of Maoritanga*, Methuen, 1978.
Lange, Raeburn, *May the People Live: A History of Maori Health Development 1900–1920*, Auckland University Press, 1999.
Laughton, J. G., *From Forest Trail to City Street: The Story of the Presbyterian Church Among the Maori People*, Presbyterian Bookroom, 1961.
Laurenson, G. I., *Three Half Centuries of the Methodist Maori Mission*, Wesley Historical Society, 1972.
Linnell, R. T. V., *Centennial of Kaiwaka. Rautau o Kaiwaka*, 1959.
——, *Methodism and Ratana among Uri-o-Hau Hapu of Ngatiwhatua*, Methodist Church Archives, year unknown.
McCallum, Janet, *Women in the House*, Cape Catley, 1993.
Macdonald, Charlotte, Penfold, Merimeri and Williams, Bridget (eds), *The Book of New Zealand Women*, Bridget Williams Books, 1991.
Marsden, Samuel, *Second New Zealand Journal*, Elder, 1819.
Mikaere, Buddy, *Te Maiharoa and the Promised Land*, Heinemann, 1988.
New Zealand Labour Party Annual Report, 1937.
New Zealand Yearbook 2000, Statistics NZ.
New Zealand Yesterdays, Reader's Digest, 1984.
Nga Akoranga – the four books (Tahi, Rua, Toru, Wha) of teachings and lessons prepared by past secretaries and elders of the church including Whaimatua Anaru (Sam Andrews) and Rapine Aperahama, 1982 and revised 1997.
Orange, Claudia, *The Treaty of Waitangi*, Bridget Williams Books, 1987.
Palmer, John Bruce, 'Parihaka', *New Zealand Encyclopaedia*, 1966.
Pool, Ian, *Te Iwi Maori: New Zealand Population Past, Present and Projected*, Auckland University Press, 1991.
Report on the NZ Labour Party Maori Organising Committee, 1936.
Rice, G. W. (ed.), *The Oxford History of New Zealand*, 2nd edition, Oxford University Press, 1992.
Riley, Murdoch, *Maori Bird Lore*, Viking Sevenseas, 2001.
Roberts, H. V., *New Zealand's Greatest Revival*, privately printed, 1951.
Ryan, P. M., *The Reed Dictionary of Modern Maori*, Reed, 1997.
Sinclair, Karen, *Prophetic Histories: The People of the Maramatanga*, Bridget Williams Books, 2002.
Sinclair, Keith, *A History of New Zealand*, Penguin, 1973.
Stack J. W., *More Maoriland Adventures*, Reed, 1938.
Statistics New Zealand, *New Zealand Now: Maori*, Statistics New Zealand, 1988.

Strong's Exhaustive Concordance of Hebrew and Greek, Baker House, 1983.
The Bible, King James, New International, Living Bible and Amplified versions.
Treasury of Maori Folklore, The Maori Pantheon, A.W. Reed, 1974.
Williams, H. W., *A Dictionary of the Maori Language*, GP Books, 1988.
Wilson, Ormond, *Kororareka and Other Essays*, John McIndoe, 1990.
Worsfold, James, *A History of the Charismatic Movements in New Zealand*, Bradford (Julian Literature Trust), 1974.
Yoneda, Isamu and Nakada, Juji Den, *Biography of Juji Nakada*. Nakada Juji Den Hakko Kai, Tokyo, 1959.
Young, David, *Woven by Water*, Huia Publishers, 1998.

Diaries and unpublished manuscripts

Farley, Fay, thesis on charismatic movements, Melbourne College of Divinity.
Fisher, David, 'The Phenomenon of the Ratana Movement within New Zealand Society', BA (Hons) thesis, Massey University, 1983.
Fountain, Wyn, Briefing notes for the visit of evangelist Derek Prince, 1985.
——, 'The Spirit of the Treaty', unpublished essay, 2005.
Hagger, A.R., 'Sacred Icons: Ratana Movement and Church', 2003, thesis.
Halliday, H. L. J., 'Rev A.J. Seamer and the Attitude of the Methodist Church to the Ratana Movement', unpublished document held by the Methodist Archives, Auckland.
Ireton, Doug, 'A Time to Heal: The Appeal of Smith Wigglesworth in New Zealand 1922–24', BA (Hons) thesis, Massey University, 1984.
Linnell, R. T. V., 'Methodism and Ratana among Uri-o-Hau Hapu of Ngatiwhatua, New Zealand', religious history assignment for Massey University in 1992 filed at the Auckland Methodist Archive.
Love, Ralph Ngatata, 'Policies of Frustration: the Growth of Maori Politics — The Ratana-Labour Era', MA thesis, Victoria Universtiy, 1977.
Pene, Kereama, 'Te Kara o te Maramatanga', Uri Whakatupuranga multimedia presentation and unpublished teaching document.
Ratana, Haami Tokouru, 'World Tour Journal 1924', Ratana Press, 1924.
Ratana Youth Rally souvenir programme, 1967.
Raureti, Moana, 'The Origins of the Ratana Movement', Auckland University thesis, 1978.
Snedden, Patrick, 'Pakeha and the Treaty: Why it's our Treaty too'. Talk at Tairawhiti Polytechnic on Wednesday, 16 June 2004.
Tane, Matiu, 'Te Rongo Pai Hou a T. W. Ratana'. Excerpts from the three volumes of unpublished chronicles of the Ratana movement from diary entries and secretarial accounts. This remains largely untranslated.
Uri Whakatupuranga, the New Generation Trust, provided access to many photographs, news clippings and documents.
Waymouth, Lyn, 'The Bureaucratisation of Genealogy', Department of Maori Studies, University of Auckland, 2003.
Williams, H. W., 'The Ministry of Healing and Ratana and his Work', College House Refresher course, 1921.

Newspaper and magazine articles

Mana Magazine, article on Tariana Turia, April–May 2005.
Mannion, Robert, 'Ratana, Political life of a Church', *New Zealand Herald*, 14 May 1994.
Maxim Institute newsletter, 17 February 2005.
New Zealand Herald archives, including articles by Audrey Young, Pat Baskett, Robert Mannion. The author had full access to archived news clippings while working on the business news desk 1997–98.
Radio New Zealand. The author was given copies of all its archived news clippings while working on a Ratana-related project for National Radio.
Raureti, Moana, 'The Origins of the Ratana Movement', *Te Ao Hou*.
Te Whetu o te Ata, 1920–23.
'The Ratana Movement', *New Zealand Heritage*, pp. 2185–89.
Voyce, Malcolm, 'Maori Healers in New Zealand: The Tohunga. Suppression Act 1907', *Oceania*, 1999, Vol. 60, pp. 99–123.
Wanganui Chronicle and *Wanganui Herald* archives at the Whanganui District Library and Whanganui Regional Museum.
Westra, Ans, 'T. W. Ratana and The Ratana Church', *Te Ao Hou*, March 1963 (article and photographs).
Whetu Marama o Te Kotahitanga, the official newspaper of the Ratana movement (issues from 1924 onwards). Editors: Ihaka Te Tai, 1924–27; Paraire Paikea, 1928–37, Matui Tane, 1931–38. Other interim editors included Pita Moko, Wharangi Tukotahi, Mete Keepa (1928).
Williams, W. L., 'East Coast (N.Z.) Historical Records', *Poverty Bay Herald*, Gisborne, 1932.

Websites and online resources

Ballara, Angela, 'Ratana, Tahupotiki Wiremu 1873–1939'; 'The life of Rahui'; 'Pepene Eketone, Te Atahikoia, Mohi; 'Te Wherowhero, Piupiu 1886/1887–1937'; 'Koroki Te Rata Mahuta Tawhiao Potatau Te Wherowhero'; 'Haami Tokouru 1894–1944'; 'Tirikatene, Eruera Tihema Te Aika 1895–1967'; 'Iriaka Ratana'; 'Te Waharoa, Tupu Atanatiu Taingakawa 1844/1845?–1929', *Dictionary of New Zealand Biography*, http://www.dnzb.govt.nz/
Ballara, Angela and Keith Cairns, 'Te Potangaroa, Paora', *Dictionary of New Zealand Biography*, www.dnzb.govt.nz
Constitutional Parliament: http://www.constitutional.parliament.govt.nz/
Gustafson, Barry, 'Savage, Michael Joseph 1872–1940'. *Dictionary of New Zealand Biography*, www.dnzb.govt.nz
Hansard, Parliamentary debates: http://www.clerk.parliament.govt.nz/hansard/Hansard.aspx
Hooker, Garry, 'Paikea, Tapihana Paraire, 1920–1963', *Dictionary of New Zealand Biography*, www.dnzb.govt.nz
Indigenous New Zealand: http://www.indigenousnewzealand.com/
Jones, Rhys Griffith, in 'Rongoa Maori in Primary Health Care', http://www.teora.maori.nz, thesis, 2000.

Mormon research: *The Salt Lake City Messenger*, Issue No. 39, July 1978, also http://www.xmission.com/~country/reason/black_1.htm
Nakada, Bishop Juji research: http://www.scvjcc.org/believe/memberchurches.
New Zealand elections website: http://www.elections.org.nz
Ngati Apa iwi website: http://www.ngatiapa.iwi.nz
Orange, Claudia, 'Mawhete, Rangiputangatahi 1880–1961', *Dictionary of New Zealand Biography*, http://www.dnzb.govt.nz
Parekowhai, Cushla, 'Omana, Tiaki 1891–1970', *Dictionary of New Zealand Biography*, http://www.dnzb.govt.nz
Ratana Archive Centre website: www.tehaahiratana.co.nz
Star and crescent moon: http://www.womanastronomer.com/crescent_moon_&_star.htm
Te Ao Hou — The New World, http://teaohou.natlib.govt.nz
Te Ara Encyclopaedia of New Zealand, http://www.teara.govt.nz
Te Puni Kokiri / Ministry of Maori Development. *Post-election briefing 1996*, http://www.tpk.govt.nz (March 1998).
The Electronic Telegraph (www.telegraph.co.uk). 'Republican rumblings at start of royal tour by Robert Hardman in Wellington', Friday 3 November 1995 World News.
Tribal whakapapa: http://maaori.com/whakapapa/examples.htm
Waetford, Aroha M. 'Ratahi, Puhi o Aotea, 1898/1899?–1966', *Dictionary of New Zealand Biography*, http://www.dnzb.govt.nz
Waitangi Tribunal, http://www.waitangi-tribunal.govt.nz

Personal interviews

Arahi and Puawai Hagger, discussions, checking resources, interviews.
Email, personal interviews and information provided by at least ten mōrehu whose parents, grandparents or close relatives were associated with the Ratana movement, including Marama Best and Lydia Faithful.
Harerangi Meihana (Harry Mason), Ratana Church and movement tumuaki, personal interviews and phone calls.
Jemaima O'Brien (née Munn), granddaughter of T. W. Ratana's daughter Maata and her constant companion in her latter years.
Kereama Pene, interviews and conversations over 35 years.
Mihi Rurawhe, daughter of Iriaka Ratana, interview and discussions.
Mina Paikea, granddaughter of Paraire Paikea, Ratana's secretary, friend and member of the original four quarters.
Naka Taiaroa, the largest property owner at Ratana Pā who was baptised by Bishop Juji Nakada in 1927.
Reo Munn and Bella Hura, granddaughters of T. W. Ratana and daughters of Te Reo (Maata).
Ruia (Harerua or Hallelulah) Aperahama, son of former Ratana secretary Robbie (Rapine) Abraham, personal interviews, translations from Māori, cultural advice.

Tapihana Shelford (Dobson), former youth secretary for T. W. Hura.
Wayne Johnson, legal counsel and adviser to tumuaki Harerangi Meihana, personal interviews and personal phone calls.
Whetu Tirikatene-Sullivan, interviews and resource material supplied from her own writings and notes dictated from her father.
Wyn Fountain, Auckland businessman and author.

Photographs and photographers
The majority of historical images were kindly provided by the Uri Whakatupuranga Trust, which gathered material for the Ratana Archives from family and church members over many years. Thanks in particular to Kereama Pene, Ruia Aperahama, and Arahi and Puawai Hagger. J. M. McLeod Henderson provided selections from his own personal archive. William Hall-Raine took photos during the 1920s and 1930s, as did various photographers for Tesla Studios, including Frank J. Denton. There are also images from the Blundell Collection, including those taken by Sam Dale. Ans Westra captured images of people and events at Ratana Pā in 1963, 1964, in the 1970s and 1980s and most recently in 2005, and supplied a wide selection of her wonderful shots for this book. Photographs were also collected from the Alexander Turnbull Library, Wellington, and Te Papa Tongarewa Museum of New Zealand. The Morrin Museum provided access to historical images. Whetu Tirikatene-Sullivan delved into her personal collection and borrowed images from friends. The *New Zealand Herald* allowed access to the foreshore and seabed march photograph (www.presspix.co.nz). Athalie (McCalman) Price supplied the image of the 1955 Ratana rugby team. Dave Grantham provided three wonderful slides taken by his father T. E. Grantham in 1937. Deidre Brown provided an image of the Ahipara church. The author provided shots from his collection taken in 1986, 2002, 2006 and 2007.

INDEX

Akaroa 65
Allen, Lady 92
Allen, Sir James 91, 93–4, 99
America 87
Anaru, Whaimatua (Sam Andrews) 226
Andrew, Walter 90, 94–6
Aotea 197
Aoyagi, Machiko 203
Aperahama, John 190
Aperahama, Rapine 238–9
Arahura River 180
Archer, N. E. 96
Ardern, Jacinda 192, 247, 249
Arizona 116
Arnold, Lord 93
Arohanui Pā 123
Arowhenua 16, 64–65, 179
Auckland Town Hall 62
Averill, Archbishop 112, 122
Awahou 24
Awahuri 24
Awarua, Te Poi 28
Awhikau, Tonga 174

Baker, Te Urumanao Ngapaki 26
Baker, Ngauta Urumanao, *see* Ratana, Te Urumanao
Baldwin, Stanley 93
Bank of the Kotahitanga 78–9, 97. 99, 105, 107
Banks Peninsula 50
Bastion Point 230
Batley Marae 62
Bay of Islands 14, 76, 86

Bay of Plenty 18, 218
Belfast 95
Belgium 92
Bennett, Reverend F. 109–10
Berlin 97
Bledisloe, Lady 162
Bledisloe, Lord 162
Bolitho, Hector 41, 45, 57, 59, 60, 63
Britain 92, 210, 214–5, 225
Broughton-Paratene family 50
Brownlee, Gerry 245
Buck, Sir Peter 13, 18, 80, 86, 115, 235
Buller, Walter 17
Bulls 24
Burma 90

Calgary 116, 118
California 116
Canada 98, 116, 118
Cape Runaway 20
Cape Town 88, 248
Carmichael, Lieutenant-Colonel 70
Carroll, Sir James 136
Chambers, Oswald 101
Chatham Islands 47–8
Cheyenne 116
China 101, 178
Christchurch Press 64
Christchurch Sun 184
Churchwood, Timi Hahiwutu 106
Clark, Helen 192, 204, 246
Coates, J. G. (Gordon) 50, 79, 121–2, 154, 167
Columbus, Ohio 116

Cook, Captain James 197
Cook Strait 50
Cooper, Dame Whina 229, 230
Corbett, Ernie 223
Cornford, Charles 34
COVID 248
Cullen, Michael 246

Dannevirke 107
Dansey, Major 90
Denham, Lord 93
Derby, Lord 86
Deskaheh, Chief 98, 247
Durban 88

Edinburgh 68, 95
Edmonds, Henare 216
Edward, Prince of Wales (later Edward VIII) 90, 94–6
Edward VII, King 86
Egypt 99
Eketone, Pepene 79, 92
Eketone, Te Aorangi O. 106
Elder, John Rawson 53, 56
Elizabeth II, Queen 226
Elsmore, Bronwyn 10, 144
England 29, 48–9, 76–9, 86–7, 89, 91–2, 94–7, 100, 105, 142, 145–6, 154, 236, 246, 248
Erueti, Kaponga 190

Featherston, Dr Isaac 17
Fergusson, Sir Charles 108
Fisher, Koro 190
Ford, Henry 117, 245
France 29, 79, 92–3
Fraser, Peter 173, 186, 215–8

Gallipoli 29
General, Levi, *see* Deskakeh, Chief
Geneva 38, 96–8
George V, King 77–9, 84, 86–7, 90, 93, 98
George VI, King 191, 214
Germany 92, 97, 210, 215
Ghent, Mrs 70
Gibraltar 99
Gittos, William 120
Goddard, Mr 90
Gordon, Governor Arthur 77
Grace, John 221
Great Barrier Island 62

Greece 99
Gregory, Kerikeri (Fred) 64
Grey, Governor George 187
Grey, Wira 190, 195
Greymouth 180
Greymouth Evening Star 70
Groveland Park 95

Haddon, Reverend Robert Tahupotiki 48, 69, 109
Hammond, Reverend T. G. 24
Hampstead Conservatoire 95
Hamuera, Ria 24–5, 180–1
Harawira, Titewhai Te Hoia Hinewhare 249
Hastings 168
Haudenosaunee 98
Hauraki 145, 194
Hawaiki 32, 168, 227
Hawera 70
Hawira, Huitahi 106
Hawke's Bay 45, 50, 61, 86, 146, 154, 168, 238
He Puapua 247
Heemi, Tema 190
Hekenui, Mariana 106
Helena Victoria, Princess 92
Helensville 62, 71
Henare, Tau 190
Henderson, Jim McLeod 43, 68, 71, 109, 114, 123, 125, 234–5
Herangi, Te Puea 156
Hetet, Rangimarie 119
Hetet, Tuheka 119
Hina-tamure 169
Hipkins, Chris 249
Hiroa, Te Rangi, *see* Buck, Sir Peter
Hirohito, Emperor 103, 178
Hobbs, Sister Irene 207
Hobson, Captain William 226
Hohaia, Lofty 190
Hohaia, Takawenga 190
Hokianga 172
Hokitika 180
Hokowhitu a Tū Māori Pioneers 29
Holland, Harry 137, 154, 158–60, 167–8, 186
Hopkins, Chris 249
Hui, Adon 190
Huiarei, Mihara 'Bess' 155
Huntly 75, 167
Hutoia Marae 144
Hyde Park 92

Imperial Palace (Tokyo) 103
Indiana 116
Ireland 95
Italy 99, 215

Jackson, Mrs 44–5
Japan 79, 84, 91, 97, 99, 101, 105, 107–8, 119, 126, 131, 178, 201, 203, 204, 215,
Jellicoe, Viscount 93
Johnsonville 233

Kahotea, Pani 190
Kai Iwi School 24
Kaikohe 63
Kaimai Ranges 194
Kaipara Harbour 62, 120
Kaipara, Eruera Pairama 'Ted' 106
Kaitaia 125
Kaiuku 170
Kakaramea 180
Kansas City 116
Kara, Watene 169
Karaka, Mita 78
Karena, Waipa 190
Kashiwagi 101, 126
Kati Kati 20
Katipa, Te Kiri 175
Kauangaroa Marae 40
Kawaitika 22
Kawana, Joe 207
Kawana, Mura 207
Kawiti, Te Ruki 16
Keeling, Reg 220
Keepa, Mete 142
Keith, Hamish 231
Kemp, Reverend Joseph 53, 60, 68
Kenana, Rua 20, 123
Ki Kōpū 67, 195–6
Kimihana 20
King Country 20, 45, 157
King, Michael 176
Kingi, Ranginui 141
Kīngitanga Parliament, *see* Māori Parliament
Kirk, Norman 229
Kito, Haeretika 100–1, 107, 203
Kiwi, Akuhata (Hata) 18
Kōmiti Hāhi Matua 114, 123, 202, 233, 235, 237–8, 242
Korea 101
Koria, Te Ihipera 24

Koroki, King 167, 172–7, 215, 221, 238
Koroneho, Patu 190, 204
Kotahitanga Bank, *see* Bank of the Kotahitanga
Kowhai, Wiremu 24
Kurahaupo 21, 23, 197
Kurasawa, Mr 100
Kusama, Siko 97, 99

Lake Taupō 158
Lammas, Fannie 53, 58–61, 65, 87, 117
Lange, David 230
Larkin, Charles (Tareha Te Awe Awe) 23
Laurenson, G. I. 113
Little Barrier Island 62–3
London 79, 85, 87, 89, 90, 92, 97, 100
London Evening Standard 95
Lord Jellicoe 64
Louise, Princess 94
Love, Ralph Ngatata 213, 218–9, 227, 234–5
Luxon, Christopher 247
Lyttelton 64, 179

Maata (1840s healer) 21
Māhia Peninsula 142, 165–6, 168, 170
Mahuta, King 86
Mahuta, Tumate 147
Maika, Hori 190
Makere, Tangipere 190
Makitanara, Tuiti 148–50, 152, 155, 160
Manaia 154
Manawatū 21, 23, 61, 246
Mandela, Nelson 251–2
Mangakahia Valley 18
Mangamahu 19
Mangamuka 172
Manhattan 115, 117
Maniapoto 145, 173
Manutūkē 171
Māori Land Court 260
Māori Parliament 23, 28–9, 64, 77, 79, 86, 176
Māori Party (Te Paati Māori) 233, 244
Marlborough 65
Marsden, Samuel 14, 76
Marseilles 99, 105
Marton 40, 123
Mary, Queen 90
Mason, Andre 249
Mason, Harry, *see* Meihana, Harerangi
Mason, Rex 219

INDEX

Massey, William 35
Masterton 83, 139, 141–2
Mataatua 197
Matamata 123, 194–5
Matariki 249
Matike Mai 247
Mawhera 180
McDonald, Peter 160
McDonald, Ramsay 90
Mechanics Bay 62
Meihana, Harerangi (Harry Mason) 235, 243–4, 248
Messina 99
Mete Keepa, Maki (Mark) 190
Metropole Hotel 97
Missouri 116
Moerua, Tahiopiripi 106
Mohaka 50
Moko, Pita Te Turuki Tamara (Peter) 34, 37, 64–6, 75, 79, 80, 90, 92–3, 95–9, 106, 116, 122, 147–8, 154–5
Moko, Waiora P. 106
Moriori 47–8
Mormon Tabernacle 117
Morrinsville 57
Motu, Tahupotiki 'Mooch' 226
Motu, Te One 206
Motueka 65
Mount Hikurangi 7
Mount Ruapehu 19
Munro, Reverend Piri 71–2, 109

Nakada, Asa (Daisy) 102, 204
Nakada, Bishop Juji 100–3, 107, 126–8, 130–2, 201–4, 252
Nakada, Ugo 102
Napier 19, 154, 168
Nash, Walter 223–4
Nathan, O. H. (Olie) 190, 207
Native Land Court 86
Nelson 58, 60–1, 65, 87
Newman, Paula (Novak) 248
New Plymouth 70
New York 116–7, 248
New Zealand Census (2006) 234
Ngā Rauru 23, 25, 106
Ngā Tau e Waru, *see* Te Oreore Marae
Nga Wairiki 23
Ngahina family 21
Ngāi Tahu 64, 158, 179

Ngapaki, Te Urumanao, *see* Ratana, Te Urumanao
Ngāpuhi 16, 76–7, 85
Ngāruawāhia 75, 150, 233
Ngata, Sir Āpirana 13, 18, 75, 86, 122–3, 125, 148, 150, 153–4, 165–6, 168, 176, 190–1, 205, 207, 215
Ngataierua, Te Kere 19–21
Ngāti Apa 19–21, 23, 39, 40, 106, 111, 173, 180, 244
Ngāti Hine 23, 25
Ngāti Kahungunu 106, 141, 144, 146
Ngāti Mahuta 156
Ngāti Maniapoto 106, 121
Ngāti Porou 168, 207, 209
Ngāti Raukawa 20, 23, 106
Ngāti Ruanui 23
Ngāti Te Rangitepaia 21
Ngāti Tūwharetoa 106
Ngāti Whātua 62–3, 106, 120
North Island 47, 70, 86, 112, 180
Northland 46, 120, 142, 166, 226
Nukutaurua 142, 168–71

Oamaru 180
Oihi Bay 76
Okuma, T. 99
Ōmaha 62
Omana, Tiaki (Jack Ormond) 169–71, 189, 191, 215, 217, 219, 223
Ontario 116
Ōnuku Marae 65
Opoutama 170–1
Ōrākei 62–3
Orakeinui 23–4, 31–2, 42
Ōrari 65
Ormond, Jack, *see* Omana, Tiaki
Oroua 21
Otago Harbour 65
Otaiwi 63
Otamatea 62, 120

Paetahi, Mete Kingi Te Rangi 85
Pai, Rongoa, *see* Bolitho, Hector
Paihia 14
Paikea, Paraire 120, 132, 136–7, 147–8, 151, 154, 160, 186, 188–91, 207, 214–21
Paikea, Tapihana 214, 217, 223
Pakipaki 146, 168, 171
Pākiri 62–3

Palace de Nation 97
Palmerston North 24, 136–7, 192
Pamapuria 125
Paora, Otene (Otene Paul) 63, 105
Paora, Hori Tirau 78
Parea 170
Parewanui 21, 25–7, 29, 121
Parihaka 21, 65, 80, 166, 244, 251
Parnell 70
Paroa 61
Patea 24–6, 28, 35
Paterson, John 85
Peacock, A. 90
Pehimana, Ngawakataurua 35
Pene, Kereama 30, 90, 117, 120, 132, 239, 241
Pennsylvania 116
Pepene, Eketone 91
Perepe, Morehu A. 100, 106
Petane 19
Picton 65
Piki Te Kaha (hall) 67, 196
Piki Te Ora church 46, 48, 71, 113, 209
Pineaha, Whiuwhiu 106
Piri Wiri Tua (son of Iriaka Te Rio) 118
Piri Wiri Tua (title of T. W. Ratana) 89, 124, 136, 138, 165, 181, 193, 197–8, 236, 244
Pito, Mrs 34
Piupiu Te Wherowhero, Princess 156–7, 166–7, 176
Pomare, Sir Maui 13, 18, 75, 80, 86, 107, 121, 147–8, 153, 235
Porirua 241
Port Chalmers 65
Port Levy 50
Potatau, King 23, 29, 172, 175
Preston, S. S. 223
Puketohe, Pango 190

Raglan 230
Ranganui 62
Rangimārie (hall) 67, 196
Rangitāne iwi 20–1, 106
Ranston, Reverend Dr Harry 110
Rapaki Hall 64
Raroa, Tawake 190
Rarotonga 115
Rata, Matiu 220, 222, 229, 238
Ratana Ngahina, Te Pakaru 21–4, 26–8, 35, 111, 168, 187

Ratana Pā 38–9, 45–6, 48–56, 63–6, 70–1, 99, 100, 107–8, 110–1, 113–4, 120–1, 136–8, 140–2, 154–7, 166–8, 171–3
Ratana Temple 78, 105, 119, 122, 124, 126–34, 157, 180, 181–2, 210, 230
Ratana, Haami Tokouru 25, 29, 75, 94–7, 99, 106–7, 118, 147–8, 153–4, 160, 184–5, 188, 189, 191, 204, 207, 213–4
Ratana, Hamuera (Samuel) 141, 179–83
Ratana, Iriaka 215–6, 220–1, 223, 225, 227, 238
Ratana, Maata Tawhirimatea (Te Reo Hura) 25, 27, 30, 34, 36–7, 79, 91, 93, 102, 201, 203–4, 210, 237–8, 240–2
Ratana, Matiu 27, 29, 79, 210, 214–5, 216, 217, 221
Ratana, Piki Te Ora 25, 27, 34, 64, 79, 91, 93, 106, 210
Ratana, Puhi o Aotea 27, 204, 216, 221, 227, 230, 240
Ratana, Raniera 210
Ratana, Rawinia 25, 27, 34
Ratana, Reipa 155
Ratana, Ripeka 106
Ratana, Tahupotiki Wiremu (Bill) 12–4, 22–75, 77–81, 84–5, 87–110, 112–23, 126–33, 135–53, 155–9, 161–91, 193–207, 211–5, 230–2, 234–8, 240–6
Ratana, Te Arepa (Tommy) 27–8, 32, 35, 37, 64–5, 79, 85, 106, 117, 155–6, 163, 179–82, 194, 197, 199, 204
Ratana, Te Omeka (Joe Mick) 29, 32–4, 36–8, 64–5, 79, 85, 106, 112, 117, 161–3, 170, 179–82, 192, 194, 197, 204
Ratana, Te Omeka (twin of Te Arepa) 27–8
Ratana, Te Raupo 28, 237
Ratana, Te Urumanao 25, 27, 29, 32, 34, 36, 38, 64, 79, 91–2, 106, 112, 118, 124, 134, 210
Ratana, Winnie (Rawinia) 210
Rennie, Jack 55
Reremoana, Taani (Dan) 85, 106, 116
Restaurant Dumon 99
Rewiti 62
Rewiti, Paraone (Brown) 222
Ria Hamuera 24–5, 251
Rikiriki, Mere (religious leader) 21–2, 25–9, 39, 40, 50, 121, 139, 207, 244, 246
Rikiriki, Mere (religious leader's mother) 21
Ringapoto 22

Ropiha, Atareta Mere Rikiriki, *see* Rikiriki, Mere (religious leader)
Ropiha, Kawana 21
Ropiha, Rikiriki Tamati 21
Rotorua 61, 94, 107
Ruahine range 61
Ruatea 23
Ruatoki 61
Ruawharo 169–70
Russell, Frederick Nene 85

Salt Lake City 116–7
Samoa 87, 106
Samuel, Ria, *see* Ria Hamuera
San Francisco 117
San Francisco *Examiner* 116
Sankey, Ira 132
Savage, Michael Joseph 177, 184–7, 207, 214–5, 218, 231, 244–5, 252
Scotland 95
Seamer, Reverend A. J. 46, 74, 105, 109–10, 120, 150, 198, 207, 209
Seddon, Richard 86, 187
Sedgwick, Bishop 112, 122
Seward, Jackie 248
Sharples, Pita 246
Singapore 105
Solomon, Abel Abraham (Horomona) 50–1
Solomon, Hana 51
Solomon, Miria 50–1
Solomon, Rangi Wawahia 50–1, 64
Solomon, Tommy (Tame Horomona Rehe) 48
Solomon, Wharetutu 51
South Africa 88, 251
Sprott, Bishop 112
St Georges Hall 95
St James Palace 94
Stavenhagen, Rodolfo 244–5
Stewart Island 47
Sydney 87
Sydney Sun 87

Tahiti 115
Tahiwi, Kingi 110
Taiaroa, Naka 203
Taiaroa, Tete 190
Tainui 121, 197, 221
Tainui, Mihara Huiarei (Bess) 51
Taisho, Emperor 103
Taiwhanga, Hirini 85
Takitimu waka 168–9, 197
Tamaiparea, Homai 204
Tamaiparea, Iwiora 27, 111, 204
Tamati, Clement 190
Tamati o Raupo, Hone 23
Tamau, Peina Werahiko 106
Tamihana, Manakore 171
Tamihana, Wiremu 85
Tamou, Bill 190
Tamou, 'Sonny' Manuao Te Kohamutunga 249
Tamumu, Ngapae Aropeta 106
Tamumu, Te Akau 106
Tana, Hori 173
Tangoio 168
Taonui, Aperahama (Tautoro) 16, 76–7
Tararua range 61
Tasman, Abel 197
Taupiri Mountain 167
Tauranga 61, 158, 222
Tawhiao, King 21, 25, 29, 48, 75, 85, 90, 92, 99, 156, 160, 172–5, 180, 212
Tawhiao, Haunui 75, 166, 174–5
Tawhiao, Te Kore Mahuta 173
Tawhiao, Te Wherowhero 156
Taylor, Reverend Richard 21
Te Angina, Hamuera Uru 106
Te Ao Hou (newspaper) 17, 124
Te Arawa 106, 166, 197
Te Aroha (building at Ratana Pā) 67
Te Aroha (town) 58
Te Atahikoia, Mohi 146, 168
Te Atairangikāhu, Queen 233, 238
Te Āti Haunui-ā-Pāpārangi 106
Te Atiawa 173
Te Awarau, Hori 171
Te Awe Awe, Mihiterina 106
Te Awe Awe, Tariuha M. 106
Te Hāhi o te Wairua Tapu 21
Te Hauke Marae 238
Te Hekeua, Paikea 120
Te Ihipera 24
Te Kahu, Eruera (Edward Sutherland) 20
Te Kahu, Mere 106
Te Kahupukoro 20, 29, 39
Te Kaitekateka 141
Te Kao 125
Te Kauangaroa 19, 20
Te Kawau 24

Te Kere 139, 141
Te Kiri 62
Te Kooti Rikirangi 12, 16, 18–20, 22, 39, 40, 42, 47–8, 65, 83, 145, 171
Te Kumi 70
Te Maiharoa, Hipa 16, 64–5, 83, 179
Te Māramatanga Marae 233
Te Mete, Nikora (Nick Smith) 190, 194
Te Moananui, Tareha 85
Te Niho Tangata 180
Te Omeka Pā 194–5, 238
Te Oreore Marae 83, 139, 141
Te Piwa 170
Te Poi 123, 194
Te Potangaroa, Paora 20, 29, 139, 141–2, 144
Te Puea Herangi, Princess 75, 121–2, 166, 175–6, 186, 215, 221
Te Rangi Hiroa, *see* Buck, Sir Peter
Te Rata, King 29, 48–9, 75, 78, 86, 90, 121–2, 147, 150, 156–7, 165–8, 173–6, 221
Te Ratana, *see* Ratana Nghahina
Te Rauparaha (chief) 84
Te Rauparaha, Tamihana 84
Te Rere o Kapuni (Victoria Falls) 80–1, 146, 200, 202
Te Rio, Iriaka 106, 118, 178–9
Te Rito, Patu 169–71, 173
Te Tai, Ihaka 119
Te Tama 243
Te Temepara Tapu o Ihoa, *see* Ratana Temple
Te Tii 76–7, 232
Te Tikanga 20
Te Tokanganui-a-Noho 145
Te Tomo, Taite 140, 153, 156–7, 176, 185
Te Urewera 123
Te Uruangina, Hamiora Hamuera 180
Te Utupoto, Karitua 106
Te Waharoa, Tarapipipi Taingakawa Tamehana 29
Te Waharoa, Tupu Taingakawa, *see* Tupu Taingakawa
Te Whaea Iti, *see* Te Rio, Iriaka
Te Whaea o Te Katoa, *see* Ratana, Te Urumanao
Te Whare Mārama 67
Te Whena, Reweti 23, 75, 79, 94, 198, 211, 213
Te Wherowhero, King 29

Te Whetu Marama o Te Kotahitanga (newspaper) 79, 107, 119, 134, 142, 190, 196, 200, 204, 238, 241, 243, 247
Te Whiti o Rongomai 19, 21, 46, 80, 99
Temuka 16, 179
Tenetahi, Te Heru 63
Terrington, Lord 93, 95
Texas 116
Thomas, Lord 95
Thomas, Mr 95
Thomas, Sir Godfrey 94
Tikao, Te One Taare 51, 64, 155
Tikaraina 22
Tirikatene, Eruera Tihema 51–2, 131, 136, 147–9, 151, 154–5, 160–2, 173, 177–9, 184–6, 188–91, 202, 212–20, 223–5, 236–7
Tirikatene, Nukuroa 51
Tirikatene, Te One 64
Tirikatene, Te Rino 51, 233, 239, 241–2
Tirikatene-Sullivan, Whetu 51, 202, 210–1, 216, 222, 232, 238
Titokowaru, Riwha 29, 39, 80, 200
Tohu Kakahi 19, 21, 29, 38, 80–1, 172, 175, 200
Toka, Henare 62, 100, 105–6, 116
Toka, Huhana 106
Tokomaru 197
Tokugawa 101, 103
Topia, Kingi 190
Tregerthen, John Driver 179
Tuahiwi 179
Tuheitia Paki, King 233, 247
Tūhoe 20, 168
Tuhurua 180
Tupe, Patema 190
Tupu Taingakawa 29, 39, 49, 50, 75, 78–9, 86, 90, 94, 96, 98, 194, 198
Turakina 23, 31, 33, 48, 123
Turia, Tariana 243, 245
Tutanekai 166
Tuwha, Boggie 190
Tuwhakaririka 174–5

United Kingdom 79, 91, 96
United Nations Declaration of the Rights of Indigenous People (UNDRIP) 245, 246, 247
United States 79, 115, 117, 246
Uri-o-Hau 120
Uri Whakatupuranga (New Generation) Trust 14, 19, 243

Urukohai, *see* Wiremu Kowhai
Utah 116

Veitch, William 149–50, 152–3
Victoria, Queen 84–5, 90, 94, 170, 179

Waahi Pā 75
Waiapu 112, 122
Waihirere 170–1
Waikato 18–9, 46, 56, 74, 121, 156–8, 166–7, 172–6, 195, 204, 215, 218
Waimana 61
Waimārama 168
Waipapa Māori Hostel 62, 70
Waipu 23, 25, 33
Wairarapa 20, 86, 141–2, 166, 168
Wairau Pā 65
Wairoa 16, 168
Waitaha 16
Waitai, Bill 190
Waitangi 76–7, 232
Waitangi Tribunal 230
Waitara 166
Waitematā Harbour 104
Waitere, Erina 23
Waitoa 61
Wall Street 115, 117
Walthamston Guardian 96
Wanganui Chronicle 40
Wanganui Herald 40
Waranui, Tuarau 174
Ward, Sir Joseph 35, 149–50, 152
Waretini, Father Peehi 22
Warsaw 209–10

Watene, Puti Tipene (Steve) 220
Weeks, Dr G. E. 60
Wellington 42, 58, 69, 71, 87, 110–2, 151, 154, 160, 175, 239, 241
Wembley 92
Westminster Bridge 92
Westra, Ans 17, 83, 124, 245
Wetere, Koro 222
Whakarongo 22
Whakatāne 61
Whangaehu 19, 20, 30–1, 33, 40, 42, 132, 221, 246
Whanganui 107, 141, 246
Whangārei 18, 63, 228
Whare Herehere 83
Whare Mauri 82
Wharite 171
Whenuaroa, Huia (Boyce) 102, 106
Whenuaroa, Kimiora 106
Whenuaroa, Maata Te Reo, *see* Ratana, Maata
Whenuaroa, Mikaera 106
Whenuaroa, Te Okeroa 106
Wheriko (Parewanui church building) 21
Whitikau 23
Williams, Canon A. 109
Williams, Arthur F. 66
Williams, Venerable H. W. 71
Williams, Reverend W. G. 66, 109
Williams, Canon Wilfred 71
Williams, Archdeacon William 85
Wilson, Ormond 220
Winter, Christina 61
Wiremu Kowhai 24
Wyoming 116

ABOUT THE AUTHOR

Keith Newman is a writer with 50 years' experience across mainstream, trade, business and music media. He began his research into the life of T. W. Ratana in 1986; two decades later his first book, *Ratana Revisited*, was published. He has since published three other New Zealand history titles: the original *Ratana the Prophet* (2009), *Bible & Treaty* (2010) and *Beyond Betrayal* (2013). Keith has won several awards for his journalism, including the Qantas Media Award for Best Magazine Feature Writer (2004) and Best Produced Music Feature in the New Zealand Radio Awards (2007) for *The Blerta Years* documentary on Radio New Zealand National. Keith has two children, Miles and Olivia, and six grandchildren.

He is married to Paula and they live in Haumoana, Hawke's Bay.